# BEYOND A BOUNDARY

# BEYOND A BOUNDARY

BY

## C. L. R. JAMES

With an Introduction by Robert Lipsyte

PANTHEON BOOKS, NEW YORK

Introduction copyright © 1983 by Robert Lipsyte
Copyright © 1963 by C. L. R. James

All rights reserved under International and Pan-American
Copyright Conventions. Published in the
United States by Pantheon Books, a division of Random
House, Inc., New York, and simultaneously
in Canada by Random House of Canada Limited, Toronto.
Originally published in Great Britain by
Stanley Paul & Co. Ltd.

Library of Congress Cataloging in Publication Data

James, C. L. R. (Cyril Lionel Robert), 1901—
Beyond a boundary

Originally published: London: Stanley Paul & Co., 1963
Includes index.
1. Cricket—West Indies. 2. Sports and state—
West Indies. 3. West Indies—Social conditions.
I. Title.
GV928.W47J35    1984        796.35′8′09729        83–43148
ISBN 0–394–53568–5
ISBN 0–394–72283–3 (pbk.)

Manufactured in the United States of America
First American Edition

To

*Learie Constantine*

and

*W. G. Grace*

for both of whom this book hopes to right grave
wrongs, and, in so doing, extend our too limited
conceptions of history and of the fine arts.
To these two names I add that of

*Frank Worrell,*

who has made ideas and aspirations
into reality.

# CONTENTS

# Contents

# ACKNOWLEDGEMENTS

The author is grateful for the use of passages from the following books. *Don Bradman* by Philip Lindsay (Phoenix House), *Maurice Tate* by John Arlott (Phoenix House) and *The Island Cricketers* by Clyde Walcott (Hodder and Stoughton Ltd.).

# INTRODUCTION TO
# THE AMERICAN EDITION

I N A CRANNY of SportsWorld stands the black Tunapuna Cricket Club, racist, classist memento and victim of British imperialism. Impeccably attired, stiffly contained, the Saturday heroes strut on a stage that is also their cage; the Tunapuna C. C. seems at first an easy metaphor for oppression in sports.

Yet the matches held on this pitch, and the anticipation, gossip, and analysis that swirl around them, are also the joy of Tunapuna, a small town eight miles from Trinidad's capital, Port of Spain. Cricket heroes are not only entertainers here, they seem to offer promise and possibility. The metaphor becomes cloudy. There is liberation, too.

Sportswriters and academics have examined sport as trap and safety valve and escape hatch, usually in the context of an extraordinary hyperevent, such as a Super Bowl or the Olympics, or in the progress of an individual from ghetto to glory, and sometimes back. This book is very different. Originally published twenty years ago in Great Britain, where the author is a well-known radical historian and commentator, *Beyond a Boundary* is at the same time an idiosyncratic antique and a dazzling guide to all our contemporary games.

Drop the Tunapuna C. C. onto a dusty baseball diamond in Puerto Rico or a high school football field in western Pennsylvania, a boxing gym in Korea or a concrete basketball court in Harlem—any outpost of colonialism where a young man's only capital is his body. The exploitation is obvious, as is the hope. And, realistically, often the sheer lack of alternative opportunity.

Historically, the Negro Baseball Leagues provided many Americans with a similar experience; a small group of talented men expanded their own horizons as they became symbols of competence and achievement and survival for all blacks. Stylish and proud, they were beloved performers, role models, and, eventually, social pioneers—they created the player and fan pool that made integration possible beyond Jackie Robinson. The Negro Leaguers were never as bitter about their exclusion from mainstream baseball as one might imagine; they lived better than most black men of their time, and the only difference between them and their heroes, the white major leaguers, was degree. They had thrilling games, money, an adoring public, and ladies in the lobby.

The Tunapuna C. C. was Lord's, only smaller and darker; Grambling College in another country for another sport; any blood-soaked fight club in Mexico City. The universality of the experience makes this book so much more than the fan's notes of an elderly black Marxist scholar.

C. L. R. James gets to the root of the exhilarating liberation from class and race and future that exists during the transcendent moments of play; but he never forgets that this liberation exists only within the boundaries of the game, and then only for the gamers.

Lurking beyond the boundaries of every game are the controlling interests, the forces of oppression: the economics of the owners, the politics of the government, even the passions of the fans.

Sport is no sanctuary from the real world because sport is part of the real world, and the liberation and the oppression are inextricably bound.

James has been an athlete, a fan, and a sporting journalist, sometimes all three at once. He has no doubt, he writes, that the "clash of race, caste and class did not retard but stimulated West Indian cricket." Each club represented an economic level, a skin hue, a social stratum. The rivalries were so intense that cricket became an unending allegory. Leading players were symbols of a drama that would have become literally murderous had it been played out beyond the boundary.

James was born in 1901, in Tunapuna. Cricket was the only game in town, and the James house was located behind the wicket. James's father was an ambitious, disciplined schoolmaster; his mother, an avid, undisciplined reader. Throughout his youth, James seemed always to be re-reading *Vanity Fair* and clipping the cricket scores from the sports pages. "Two people lived in me," writes James, "one, the rebel against all family and school discipline and order; the other, a Puritan who would have cut off a finger sooner than do anything contrary to the ethics of the game."

Young James lied without remorse to get to the cricket pitch. He was a good player, and he shamed his family by shirking his scholastic responsibilities. His was a respectable island family too fine for calypso, barely tolerant of sport. There was nearly a public scandal, and countless family meetings. All the teachers in the family feared for their own careers if young James came a cropper.

They should not have worried. Between Thackeray and cricket, he was gaining an attitude as well as an education. When the great wicketkeeper Piggott was not included on an all-island team in favor of a lesser player who was white, James came to understand that even cricket was not always cricket.

Perhaps even more telling was the lesson of the frail white bowler he caught for. They were battery-mates in the cricket wars, classmates howling together over Dickens. The white boy went to Europe to study; afterward, there was only embarrassment and guilt when they met. Beyond the boundaries, learned James, the only real links are family and class.

The brotherhood of the game is only of the game.

James writes so dispassionately, almost distantly at times, that one must infer how cruelly personal this lesson was and, ultimately, how political.

It seemed like a classic ploy by the conquerors: games, particularly so restrained and ritualistic a game as cricket, could be imposed upon the colonies to tame them, to herd them into psychic boundaries where they would learn the values and ethics of the colonist.

But once given the opportunity to play the master's game, to excel at it, the colonials gained a self-esteem that would eventually free them.

C. L. R. James writes: "The British tradition soaked deep into me was that when you entered the sporting arena you left behind you the sordid compromises of everyday existence. Yet for us to do that we would have had to divest ourselves of our skins."

James brought this schizophrenia to the United States in 1938. He enjoyed the techniques of baseball, the game between the white lines, but not the heckling of the crowd, the disputes, what he perceived as poor sportsmanship. He introduced make-shift cricket to some friends and was bemused by the noisy, helter-skelter game they created; he attributed it to "differences of national character and outlook" and was not concerned. He prided himself on being superior to "so many otherwise intelligent Europeans" who failed to realize that the United States was, after all, a former colonial empire that couldn't be judged by European standards.

And then, in 1950, James's condescension gave way to shock, albeit ingenuous, but nonetheless curiously touching.

Nearing fifty, he was deeply moved by the revelations of a national basketball scandal. College players, in league with bookies, had thrown games or arranged the final score to create betting coups. He expressed revulsion. How could these young men betray their universities?

James's American colleagues and friends shrugged. Why should the athletes have put the school above what they wanted? The discussion continued long after James left America. He eventually concluded that "these young people had no loyalties to school because they had no loyalties to anything."

That James could not accept automatically that these athletes were the greedy spawn of an exploitative system is the positive proof of his own liberation and oppression through sports. He was ennobled and crippled by cricket; he reached beyond his boundary but would always have a blind spot.

Here were teen-aged athletes, often black and poor, being used to increase the wealth and prestige of universities. In return, they were given sub-minimum wages ironically called scholarships that would leave many of them helpless in the job market if they didn't become professional athletes.

And yet this sophisticated idealist could not make the complete connection. He could understand why they did what they did, but considered it treachery. He still thought that the school tie was a binding social contract.

James is a man of his times, but his sensibilities and the lessons of the Tunapuna C. C. may clarify our own. The roads from all the dusty pitches of the world now converge on a satellite feed. The thrill of victory and the agony of defeat is measured in audience share and dollars.

Yet at the heart of it all is the true glory of sport, the individual daring to be better. How society can nurture the dream without cynically exploiting it may be the true sports challenge of the century.

The answers are not in this book, but some of the questions are. Read it and keep a straight bat. Beyond *Beyond a Boundary* are wet, uncertain wickets for us all.

ROBERT LIPSYTE
Closter, New Jersey
September 1983

# A NOTE ON CRICKET

THE THEMES of this book reach, as its title suggests, far beyond the boundaries of the cricket field, and no detailed knowledge of the game is needed to appreciate their implications. However, an introduction to the terminology and rudimentary outlines of play may prove useful.

Two teams of eleven players each contend on a huge grassy oval, often as large as a football field, in the center of which lies the cricket *pitch*—a closely cropped area (occasionally covered by a mat) 22 feet by 5 feet, at either end of which stands a *wicket*—three vertical stumps connected at the top by two horizontal pieces called *bails*. The *batsman* and *bowler* face each other from opposite ends of the pitch, standing in front of the wickets in areas demarcated by lines called *creases (popping creases, bowling creases,* and *return creases)*. The distance between them is about the same as that between a baseball pitcher and batter. Rules specify where each must stand while throwing or batting, and which parts of the body may extend beyond the creases when. The *boundary* is the line that encircles the perimeter of the entire playing field, and across the field are strewn—in designated positions—members of the fielding (bowling) team.

*Point, cover point, silly point, long-stop, extra cover, mid-off, silly mid-off, short leg,* and *long leg* all refer to specific fielding positions (there are over thirty, including the bowler and the *wicketkeeper,* who functions much like a baseball catcher, with an equally critical and subtle, yet oft unheralded, role).

Orientation on the field and corresponding directions are taken laterally from the batsman's stance, which is perpendicular to the bowler (as batter to pitcher in baseball). The *off* side is that facing the batsman; the *leg* or *on* side is behind him as he stands to receive the hurled ball. The bowler must throw with his elbows straight, delivering the ball with an overarm, catapulting motion, much like a jai-alai player's, and less like that of a baseball pitcher, who makes more use of the gyroscopic capacities of wrist and elbow when "firing" at the plate. The *off-break, leg break,* and much dreaded (by James's companions) *dead shooter* describe different pitches, which can vary widely and dramatically according to the speed, spin, and swerve with which the ball is delivered. The *googly,* for example, which W.G. Grace meets "late in life and was said to be troubled by," is a kind of cricket screwball that turns in a way designed to catch the batsman by surprise—a powerful tool in a game that revolves to a great degree around the effort to catch the batsman unawares and make him "pop up" by hitting the ball with the edge, rather than the flat part, of the bat.

The bowler hurls the ball alternately from each wicket in sets called *overs*—six to eight balls per over (varying from country to country). When the requisite number of balls has been bowled, a new over is begun by a different bowler. The captain of the fielding team may allow any of his players to bowl, so long as no one bowls two successive overs. When James recounts, at an early moment in the book, that he has bowled three *maiden overs,* he's completed three overs in which no runs have been scored from the bat (that is, runs involving balls actually struck)—a feat of no small dexterity that can be duly appreciated by any pitcher who's attempted to carve out a no-hitter.

The condition of the pitch itself is critical to the game. Since the bowler essentially delivers a short-hop ball to the batsman, his effectiveness can be greatly changed (for the better or the worse) by the surface the ball hits—hence the attention to a wet, uneven, or matted pitch.

The bat is wooden, slightly over three feet long, and flat like a paddle with a slight wedge in it. The ball is made of red leather and weighs slightly more than a baseball; it is about nine inches in circumference. Players bat in pairs—one member of the batting team standing at each wicket. Their task is to keep the thrown ball from hitting the wicket by batting it away (here they function much like hockey goalies, but with the added benefit of being able to score points depending on how and where they hit the ball); in addition they attempt to score points by

running across the pitch to the opposite wicket, in effect exchanging places with each other. The batsman, therefore, tries to hit the ball in a way that gives him enough time to run to the other end of the pitch (while his non-batting partner runs to *his* end) before any fieldsman retrieves the ball and throws it back to one of the wickets. The key for the batsman, therefore, is not necessarily to hit the ball as hard as possible, but to hit it where there are no fieldsmen, which can even mean hitting it backwards, or behind himself. The fielding team, in anticipation or response, is constantly shifting positions, trying to get the batsman to make a mistake. Because of the many psychological calculations being made by batsmen, bowlers, and fieldsmen throughout the game, each trying to wear the other down, matches may seem to take a relatively long time to complete.

A run is scored each time the two batsmen cross on the pitch and successfully reach the opposite end before the fielding team can dislodge a bail in either wicket. They may exchange places up to six times per stroke (or hit). If the ball reaches the boundary of the field before being stopped, a total of four runs is scored automatically; if it reaches the boundary *full pitch* (on the fly, without hitting the ground—a cricket "homer"), six are scored. *Extras,* or additional runs, may also be scored for the batting team if the ball is bowled wide or high in a specific way or if the umpire calls a *no-ball* because the bowler has used an illegal hurling motion or stepped across the crease illegally (similar to a balk). In some instances, when the ball is bowled in this fashion, the batsmen may still run across the pitch to score even more additional points, much as a baserunner may advance on a wild pitch. A player achieves a *century* when he scores 100 runs in a single innings before being dismissed.

A batsman can be dismissed, or eliminated, in a number of ways: if the bowler can dislodge a bail in the wicket with the hurled ball or the batsman does the same accidentally with his bat or body; if a fieldsman catches the batted ball before it touches the ground or dislodges a bail while the batsmen are running; if the bowler is *lbw (leg before wicket)*— a kind of illegal interference, where he keeps the ball from hitting the wicket by stopping it with something other than his bat, batting hand, or glove; if he illegally moves beyond the crease while receiving the ball (steps out of the batter's box, so to speak), handles the ball illegally, or deliberately obstructs the field.

Each team bats in turn, completing an innings when ten of its eleven members have been dismissed. One-day matches usually consist of one innings per side, won by the team accumulating the most runs in their single innings. Test or international matches can go for thirty playing hours—lasting up to six days—with the winner determined by the aggregate score of two or more innings.

# PREFACE

This book is neither cricket reminiscences nor autobiography. It poses the question *What do they know of cricket who only cricket know?* To answer involves ideas as well as facts.

The autobiographical framework shows the ideas more or less in the sequence that they developed in relation to the events, the facts and the personalities which prompted them. If the ideas originated in the West Indies it was only in England and in English life and history that I was able to track them down and test them. To establish his own identity, Caliban, after three centuries, must himself pioneer into regions Caesar never knew.

C. L. R. JAMES

*London*

# BEYOND A BOUNDARY

# PART ONE

# A WINDOW TO THE WORLD

---

## I

## *The Window*

Tunapuna at the beginning of this century was a small town of about 3,000 inhabitants, situated eight miles along the road from Port of Spain, the capital city of Trinidad. Like all towns and villages on the island, it possessed a recreation ground. Recreation meant cricket, for in those days, except for infrequent athletic sports meetings, cricket was the only game. Our house was superbly situated, exactly behind the wicket. A huge tree on one side and another house on the other limited the view of the ground, but an umpire could have stood at the bedroom window. By standing on a chair a small boy of six could watch practice every afternoon and matches on Saturdays—with matting one pitch could and often did serve for both practice and matches. From the chair also he could mount on to the window-sill and so stretch a groping hand for the books on the top of the wardrobe. Thus early the pattern of my life was set. The traffic on the road was heavy, there was no fence between the front yard and the street. I was an adventurous little boy and so my grandmother and my two aunts, with whom I lived for half the year, the rainy season, preferred me in the backyard or in the house where they could keep an eye on me. When I tired of playing in the yard I perched myself on the chair by the window. I doubt if for some years I knew what I was looking at in detail. But this watching from the window shaped one of my strongest early impressions of personality in society. His name was Matthew Bondman and he lived next door to us.

13

He was a young man already when I first remember him, medium height and size, and an awful character. He was generally dirty. He would not work. His eyes were fierce, his language was violent and his voice was loud. His lips curled back naturally and he intensified it by an almost perpetual snarl. My grandmother and my aunts detested him. He would often without shame walk up the main street barefooted, 'with his planks on the ground', as my grandmother would report. He did it often and my grandmother must have seen it hundreds of times, but she never failed to report it, as if she had suddenly seen the parson walking down the street barefooted. The whole Bondman family, except for the father, was unsatisfactory. It was from his mother that Matthew had inherited or absorbed his flair for language and invective. His sister Marie was quiet but bad, and despite all the circumlocutions, or perhaps because of them, which my aunts employed, I knew it had something to do with 'men'. But the two families were linked. They rented from us, they had lived there for a long time, and their irregularity of life exercised its fascination for my puritanical aunts. But that is not why I remember Matthew. For ne'er-do-well, in fact vicious character, as he was, Matthew had one saving grace—Matthew could bat. More than that, Matthew, so crude and vulgar in every aspect of his life, with a bat in his hand was all grace and style. When he practised on an afternoon with the local club people stayed to watch and walked away when he was finished. He had one particular stroke that he played by going down low on one knee. It may have been a slash through the covers or a sweep to leg. But, whatever it was, whenever Matthew sank down and made it, a long, low 'Ah!' came from many a spectator, and my own little soul thrilled with recognition and delight.

Matthew's career did not last long. He would not practise regularly, he would not pay his subscription to the club. They persevered with him, helping him out with flannels and white shoes for matches. I remember Razac, the Indian, watching him practise one day and shaking his head with deep regret: how could a man who could bat like that so waste his talent? Matthew dropped out early. But he was my first acquaintance with that *genus Britannicus*, a fine batsman, and the impact that he makes on all around him, non-cricketers and cricketers alike. The contrast between Matthew's pitiable existence as an individual and the attitude people had towards him filled my growing mind and has occupied me to this day. I came into personal contact with Matthew. His brother was my playmate and when we got in Matthew's way he glared and shouted at us in a most terrifying manner. My aunts were uncompromising in their judgments of him and yet my grandmother's oft-repeated verdict: 'Good for nothing except to play cricket,' did not seem right to me. How could an ability to play cricket atone in any sense for Matthew's abominable way of life? Particularly as my grandmother and my aunts were not in any way supporters or followers of the game.

My second landmark was not a person but a stroke, and the maker of it was Arthur Jones. He was a brownish Negro, a medium-sized man, who walked with quick steps and active shoulders. He had a pair of restless, aggressive eyes, talked quickly and even stammered a little. He wore a white cloth hat when batting, and he used to cut. How he used to cut! I have watched county cricket for weeks on end and seen whole Test matches without seeing one cut such as Jones used to make, and for years whenever I saw one I murmured to myself, 'Arthur Jones!' The crowd was waiting for it, I at my window was waiting, and as soon as I began to play seriously I learnt that Arthur was waiting for it too. When the ball hit down outside the off-stump (and now, I think, even when it was straight) Jones lifted himself to his height, up went his bat and he brought it down across the ball as a woodsman puts his axe to a tree. I don't remember his raising the ball, most times it flew past point or between point and third slip, the crowd burst out in another shout and Jones's white cap sped between the wickets.

The years passed. I was in my teens at school, playing cricket, reading cricket, idolizing Thackeray, Burke and Shelley, when one day I came across the following about a great cricketer of the eighteenth century:

'It was a study for Phidias to see Beldham rise to strike; the grandeur of the attitude, the settled composure of the look, the piercing lightning of the eye, the rapid glances of the bat, were electrical. Men's hearts throbbed within them, their cheeks turned pale and red. Michael Angelo should have painted him.'

This was thrilling enough. I began to tingle.

'Beldham was great in every hit, but his peculiar glory was the cut. Here he stood, with no man beside him, the laurel was all his own; it seemed like the cut of a racket. His wrist seemed to turn on springs of the finest steel. He took the ball, as Burke did the House of Commons, between wind and water—not a moment too soon or late. Beldham still survives. . . .'

By that time I had seen many fine cutters, one of them, W. St. Hill, never to this day surpassed. But the passage brought back Jones and childhood memories to my mind and anchored him there for good and all. Phidias, Michelangelo, Burke. Greek history had already introduced me to Phidias and the Parthenon; from engravings and reproductions I had already begun a life-long worship of Michelangelo; and Burke, begun as a school chore, had rapidly become for me the most exciting master of prose in English—I knew already long passages of him by heart. There in the very centre of all this was William Beldham and his cut. I passed over the fact which I noted instantly that the phrase, 'He hit the House just between wind and water', had been used by Burke himself, about Charles Townshend in the speech on American taxation.

The matter was far from finished. Some time later I read a complicated description of the mechanism and timing of the cut by C. B. Fry, his warning that it was a most difficult stroke to master and that even in the hands of its greatest exponents there were periods when it would not work, 'intermittent in its service', as he phrased it. But, he added, with some batsmen it was an absolutely natural stroke, and one saw beautiful cutting by batsmen who otherwise could hardly be called batsmen at all. When I read this I felt an overwhelming sense of justification. Child though I was, I had not been wrong about Jones. Batsman or not, he *was* one of those beautiful natural cutters. However, I said earlier that the second landmark in my cricketing life was a stroke—and I meant just that—one single stroke.

On an awful rainy day I was confined to my window, Tunapuna C. C. was batting and Jones was in his best form, that is to say, in nearly every over he was getting up on his toes and cutting away. But the wicket was wet and the visitors were canny. The off-side boundary at one end was only forty yards away, a barbed-wire fence which separated the ground from the police station. Down came a short ball, up went Jones and lashed at it, there was the usual shout, a sudden silence and another shout, not so loud this time. Then from my window I saw Jones walking out and people began to walk away. He had been caught by point standing with his back to the barbed wire. I could not see it from my window and I

16

asked and asked until I was told what had happened. I knew that something out of the ordinary had happened to us who were watching. We had been lifted to the heights and cast down into the depths in much less than a fraction of a second. Countless as are the times that this experience has been repeated, most often in the company of tens of thousands of people, I have never lost the zest of wondering at it and pondering over it.

It is only within very recent years that Matthew Bondman and the cutting of Arthur Jones ceased to be merely isolated memories and fell into place as starting points of a connected pattern. They only appear as starting points. In reality they were the end, the last stones put into place, of a pyramid whose base constantly widened, until it embraced those aspects of social relations, politics and art laid bare when the veil of the temple has been rent in twain as ours has been. Hegel says somewhere that the old man repeats the prayers he repeated as a child, but now with the experience of a lifetime. Here briefly are some of the experiences of a lifetime which have placed Matthew Bondman and Arthur Jones within a frame of reference that stretches east and west into the receding distance, back into the past and forward into the future.

My inheritance (you have already seen two, Puritanism and cricket) came from both sides of the family and a good case could be made out for predestination, including the position of the house in front of the re-creation ground and the window exactly behind the wicket.

My father's father was an emigrant from one of the smaller islands, and probably landed with nothing. But he made his way, and as a mature man worked as a pan-boiler on a sugar estate, a responsible job involving the critical transition of the boiling cane-juice from liquid into sugar. It was a post in those days usually held by white men. This meant that my grandfather had raised himself above the mass of poverty, dirt, ignorance and vice which in those far-off days surrounded the islands of black lower middle-class respectability like a sea ever threatening to engulf them. I believe I understand pretty much how the average sixteenth-century Puritan in England felt amidst the decay which followed the dissolution of the monasteries, particularly in the small towns. The need for distance which my aunts felt for Matthew Bondman and his sister was compounded of self-defence and fear. My grandfather went to church every Sunday morning at eleven o'clock wearing in the broiling sun a frock-coat, striped trousers and top-hat, with his walking-stick in hand, surrounded by his family, the underwear of the women crackling with starch. Respectability was not an ideal, it was an armour. He fell grievously ill, the family fortunes declined and the children grew up in unending struggle not to sink below the level of the Sunday-morning top-hat and frock-coat.

My father took the obvious way out—teaching. He did well and gained a place as a student in the Government Training College, his course comprising history, literature, geometry, algebra and education. Yet Cousin Nancy, who lived a few yards away, told many stories of her early days as a house-slave. She must have been in her twenties when slavery was abolished in 1834. My father got his diploma, but he soon married. My two aunts did sewing and needlework, not much to go by, which made them primmer and sharper than ever, and it was with them that I spent many years of my childhood and youth.

Two doors down the street was Cousin Cudjoe, and a mighty man was he. He was a blacksmith, and very early in life I was allowed to go and watch him do his fascinating business, while he regaled me with stories of his past prowess at cricket and critical observations on Matthew, Jones and the Tunapuna C.C. He was quite black, with a professional chest and shoulders that were usually scantily covered as he worked his bellows or beat the iron on the forge. Cudjoe told me of his unusual career as a cricketer. He had been the only black man in a team of white men. Wherever these white men went to play he went with them. He was their wicketkeeper and their hitter—a term he used as one would say a fast bowler or an opening bat. When he was keeping he stood close to the wicket and his side needed no long-stop for either fast bowling or slow, which must have been quite an achievement in his day and time. But it was as a hitter that he fascinated me. Once Cudjoe played against a team with a famous fast bowler, and it seemed that one centre of interest in the match, if not the great centre, was what would happen when the great fast bowler met the great hitter. Before the fast bowler began his run he held the ball up and shook it at Cudjoe, and Cudjoe in turn held up his bat and shook it at the bowler. The fast bowler ran up and bowled and Cudjoe hit his first ball out of the world. It didn't seem to matter how many he made after that. The challenge and the hit which followed were enough. It was primitive, but as the battle between Hector and Achilles is primitive, and it should not be forgotten that American baseball is founded on the same principle.

At the time I did not understand the significance of Cudjoe, the black blacksmith, being the only coloured man in a white team, that is to say, plantation owners and business or professional men or high government officials. 'They took me everywhere they went—everywhere,' he used to repeat. They probably had to pay for him and also to sponsor his presence when they played matches with other white men. Later I wondered what skill it was, or charm of manner, or both, which gave him that unique position. He was no sycophant. His eyes looked straight into yours, and an ironical smile played upon his lips as he talked, a handsome head on his splendid body. He was a gay lad, Cudjoe, but somehow my aunts did not disapprove of him as they did of Bondman. He was a blood relation, he smiled at them and made jokes and they laughed. But my enduring memory of Cudjoe is of an exciting and charming man in whose life cricket had played a great part.

My father too had been a cricketer in his time, playing on the same ground at which I looked from my window. He gave me a bat and ball on my fourth birthday and never afterwards was I without them both for long. But as I lived a great deal with my aunts away from home, and they did not play, it was to Cudjoe I went to bowl to me, or to sit in his blacksmith's shop holding my bat and ball and listening to his stories. When I did spend time with my parents my father told me about cricket and his own prowess. But now I was older and my interest became tinged with scepticism, chiefly because my mother often interrupted to say that whenever she went to see him play he was always caught in the long field for very little. What made matters worse, one day when I went to see him play he had a great hit and was caught at long-on for seven. I remembered the stroke and knew afterwards that he had lifted his head. Joe Small, the West Indian Test player, was one of the bowlers on the opposite side. However, I was to learn of my father's good cricket in a curious way. When I was about sixteen my school team went to Tunapuna to play a match on that same ground against some of the very men I used to watch as a boy, though by this time Arthur Jones had dropped out. I took wickets and played a good defensive innings. Mr. Warner, the warden, a brother of Sir Pelham's, sent for me to congratulate me on my bowling, and some spectators made quite a fuss over me for I was one of them and they had known me as a child wandering around the ground and asking questions.

Two or three of the older ones came up and said, 'Your father used to hit the ball constantly into that dam over there,' and they pointed to an old closed-up well behind the railway line. I was taken by surprise, for the dam was in the direction of extra-cover somewhat nearer to mid-off, and a batsman who hit the ball there constantly was no mean stroke-player. But as my father always said, the cares of a wife and family on a small income cut short his cricketing life, as it cut short the career of many a fine player who was quite up to intercolonial standard. I have known intercolonial cricketers who left the West Indies to go to the United States to better their position. Weekes, the left-hander who hit that daring century in the Oval Test in 1939, is one of a sizable list. And George Headley was only saved for cricket because, born in Panama and living in Jamaica, there was some confusion and delay about his papers when his parents in the United States sent for him. While the difficulties were being sorted out, an English team arrived in Jamaica and Headley batted so successfully that he gave up the idea of going to the United States to study a profession.

West Indian cricket has arrived at maturity because of two factors: the rise in the financial position of the coloured middle class and the high fees paid to players by the English leagues. Of this, the economic basis of West Indian cricket—big cricket, so to speak—I was constantly aware, and from early on. One afternoon I was, as usual, watching the Tunapuna C.C. practise when a man in a black suit walked by on his way to the railway station. He asked for a knock and, surprisingly, pads were handed to him, the batsman withdrew and the stranger went in. Up to that time I had never seen such batting. Though he had taken off his coat, he still wore his high collar, but he hit practically every ball, all over the place. Fast and slow, wherever they came, he had a stroke, and when he stopped and rushed off to catch his train he left a buzz of talk and admiration behind him. I went up to ask who he was and I was told his name was MacDonald Bailey, an old intercolonial player. Later my father told me that Bailey was a friend of his, a teacher, an intercolonial cricketer and a great all-round sportsman. But, as usual, a wife and family and a small income compelled him to give up the game. He is the father of the famous Olympic sprinter. Mr. Bailey at times visited my father and I observed him carefully, looking him up and down and all over so as to discover the secret of his athletic skill, a childish habit I have retained to this day.

Perhaps it was all because the family cottage was opposite to the recreation ground, or because we were in a British colony and, being active people, gravitated naturally towards sport. My brother never played any games to speak of, but as a young man he gave some clerical assistance to the secretary of the local Football Association. In time he became the secretary. He took Trinidad football teams all over the West Indies and he was invited to England by the Football Association to study football organization. I met him in the United States trying to arrange for an American soccer team to visit Trinidad. In 1954 he brought the first team from the West Indies to play football in England, and before he left arranged for an English team to visit the West Indies. He has at last succeeded in organizing a West Indies Football Association, of which he is the first secretary.

Even Uncle Cuffie, my father's elder brother, who, like the old man from Bengal, never played cricket at all, was the hero of a family yarn. One day he travelled with an excursion to the other end of the island. Among the excursionists was the Tunapuna C.C., to play a match with Siparia C.C., while the rest of the visitors explored Siparia. Tunapuna was a man short and my father persuaded—nay, begged—Cuffie to fill the gap, and Cuffie reluctantly agreed. Siparia made forty-odd, not a bad score in those days, and Cuffie asked to have his innings first so that he could get out and go and enjoy himself away from the cricket field. Still wearing his braces and his high collar, he went in first, hit at every ball and by making some thirty runs not out won the match for his side by nine wickets. He quite ruined the game for the others. He had never even practised with the team before and never did afterwards.

The story of my elder aunt, Judith, ends this branch of my childhood days. She was the English Puritan incarnate, a tall, angular woman. She looked upon Matthew Bondman as a child of the devil. But if Matthew had been stricken with a loathsome disease she would have prayed for him and nursed him to the end, because it was her duty. She lost her husband early, but brought up her three children, pulled down the old cottage, replaced it with a modern one and whenever I went to see her fed me with that sumptuousness which the Trinidad Negroes have inherited from the old extravagant plantation owners. Her son grew to manhood, and though no active sportsman himself, once a year invited his friends from everywhere to Tunpuna where they played a festive cricket match. This, however, was merely a preliminary to a great spread which Judith always prepared. One year Judith worked as usual from early morning in preparation for the day, doing everything that was needed. The friends came, the match was played and then all trooped in to eat, hungry, noisy and happy. Judith was serving when suddenly she sat down, saying, 'I am not feeling so well.' She leaned her head on the table. When they bent over her to find out what was wrong she was dead. I would guess that she had been 'not feeling so well' for days, but she was not one to let that turn her aside from doing what she had to do.

I heard the story of her death thousands of miles away. I know that it was the fitting crown to her life, that it signified something to me, above all people, and, curiously enough, I thought it appropriate that her death should be so closely associated with a cricket match. Yet she had never taken any particular interest. She or my grandmother or my other aunt would come in from the street and say, 'Matthew made 55,' or 'Arthur Jones is still batting,' but that was all. Periodically I pondered over it.

My grandfather on my mother's side, Josh Rudder, was also an immigrant, from Barbados, and also Protestant. I knew him well. He used to claim that he was the first coloured man to become an engine-driver on the Trinidad Government Railway. That was some seventy years ago. Before that the engineers were all white men, that is to say, men from England, and coloured men could rise no higher than fireman. But Josh had had a severe training. He came from Barbados at the age of sixteen, which must have been somewhere around 1868. He began as an apprentice in the shed where the new locomotives were assembled and the old ones repaired, and he learnt the business from the ground up. Then he would go out on odd jobs and later he became regular fireman on the engines between San Fernando and Princes Town. This proved to be a stroke of luck. His run was over a very difficult piece of track and when the white engine-driver retired, or more probably died suddenly, there arose the question of getting someone who understood its special difficulties. That was the type of circumstance in those days which gave the local coloured man his first opportunity, and Josh was appointed. He took his job seriously and, unless something had actually broken, whenever his engine stopped he refused to have it towed into the shed but went under and fixed it himself.

Josh was a card. In 1932 I went to say good-bye before I left for England. He was nearing eighty and we had lunch surrounded by the results of his latest marriage, some six or seven children ranging from sixteen years to about six. After lunch he put me through my paces. I had been writing cricket journalism in the newspapers for some years and had expressed some casual opinions, I believe, on the probable composition of the West Indies team to visit England in 1933. Josh expressed disagreement with my views and I took him lightly at first. But although in all probability he hadn't seen a cricket match for some thirty years, it soon turned out that he had read practically every article I had written and remembered them; and as he had read the other newspapers and also remembered those, I soon had to get down to it, as if I were at a selection-committee meeting. Apart from half a century, the only difference between us that afternoon was that in his place I would have had the quoted papers to hand, all marked up in pencil.

I had never seen nor heard of any racial or national consciousness in Josh. He was a great favourite with everybody, particularly with the white men, managers, engineers and other magnates of the sugar estates. They often travelled between San Fernando and Princes Town on his train and always came up to talk to him. In fact, whenever one of them was talking to Josh, and my mother was anywhere near, Josh was very insistent on her coming up to be introduced, to her own considerable embarrassment and probably to theirs as well. Josh, after all, was a man of inferior status and fifty years ago you did that sort of thing only when you couldn't avoid it. Josh, however, here as elsewhere, was acting with his usual exuberance. And yet there was more to Josh than met the eye.

One Sunday afternoon near the end of the century he was sitting in the gallery of his house in Princes Town when he noticed, from certain peculiarities in the whistles and the smoke from the chimney, that the engines of one of the big sugar-estate factories had failed. Whenever this took place it caused a general crisis. During the season the factories ground cane often twenty hours a day. The cane was cut sometimes miles away and piled on to little open trucks which ran on rails to the factory and emptied on to the moving belt which took it to the grinders. Once the cane was cut, if it was not ground within a certain time, the quality of the juice deteriorated. So that if the big engines stopped and were not repaired pretty quickly the whole process was thrown out of gear, and if the break continued the cutters for miles around had to be signalled to stop cutting, and they sat around and waited for hours. I have worked on a sugar estate and the engineers, usually Scotsmen, walked around doing nothing for days; but as soon as there was the slightest sign of anything wrong the tension was immediately acute. The manager himself, if not an engineer, was usually a man who understood something about engines. There were always one or two coloured foremen who had no degrees and learnt empirically, but who knew their particular engines inside out. All these worked frantically, like men on a wrecked ship. And if the engine stayed dead too long engineers from other factories around all came hurrying up in order to help. Whenever she (as they called the machinery) came to a stop, and the stop lasted for any length of time, the news spread to all the people in the neighbourhood, and it was a matter of universal excitement and gossip until she started off again.

Well, this afternoon Josh sat in his gallery, knowing pretty well what was going on, when suddenly an open carriage-and-pair drew up in front of the house. He recognized it, for it belonged to the manager of the factory who used to drive it to and from the railway station. The groom jumped down and came in and Josh knew what he wanted before he spoke.

'Mr. —— has asked you to come round at once,' said the groom. 'He has sent his carriage for you.'

'All right,' said Josh, 'I'll come.'

He drove over the few miles to the factory, and there they were, the usual assembly of engineers, foremen and visitors, by this time baffled and exhausted, while the factory workers sat around in the yard doing nothing, and in the centre the distracted manager. When Josh drove in everyone turned to him as if he were the last hope, though few could have believed that Josh would be able to get her going.

Now, on his way to the factory Josh may have dug up from his tenacious memory some half-forgotten incident of an engine which would not go, or he may have come to the conclusion that if all of these highly trained and practised engineers were unable to discover what was wrong the probability was that they were overlooking some very simple matter that was under their very noses. Whatever it was, Josh knew what he was about. When the manager invited him to enter the engine-room and, naturally, was coming in with him (with all the others crowding behind) Josh stopped and, turning to all of them, said very firmly, 'I would like to go in alone.' The manager looked at him in surprise, but, probably thinking that Josh was one of those who didn't like people around when he was working, and anxious to do anything which might get the engines going again, he agreed. He turned round, told the others to stand back and Josh entered the engine-room alone. No one will ever know exactly what Josh did in there, but within two minutes he was out again and he said to the astonished manager, 'I can guarantee anything, sir, but try and see if she will go now.' The foreman rushed inside, and after a few tense minutes the big wheels started to revolve again.

An enthusiastic crowd, headed by the manager, surrounded Josh, asking him what it was that had performed the miracle. But the always exuberant Josh grew silent for once and refused to say. He never told them. He never told anybody. The obstinate old man wouldn't even tell me. But when I asked him that day, 'Why did you do it?' he said what I had never heard before. 'They were white men with all their M.I.C.E. and R.I.C.E. and all their big degrees, and it was their business to fix it. I had to fix it for them. Why should I tell them?'

In my bag already packed was the manuscript of what the next year was published as *The Case for West Indian Self-Government*. I recognized then that Josh was not only my physical but also my spiritual grandfather. The family strains persist. I continue to write about cricket and self-government. Some time ago I saw in a West Indian newspaper that the very week that final decisions were being taken about West Indian Federation in Jamaica, my younger brother was also in Jamaica, putting finishing touches to the West Indian Football Association. A few years ago he was appointed the chief accountant of Josh's Trinidad Government Railway—as far as I know, the first coloured man to hold that post.[1]

Josh was no Puritan, but when his first wife died early it was noteworthy that he sent my mother to live with some maiden ladies, Wesleyans, who kept a small establishment which they called a convent. Convent it was. As far as I could gather, she was not taught much scholastically, but she gained or deve oped two things there. We were Anglicans, but from these Wesleyans my mother learnt a moral nonconformism of a depth and rigidity which at times far exceeded Judith's. She was a tall handsome woman of elegant carriage and beautiful clothes, but her principles were such that she forbade my playing any sort of game on Sundays, or even going to hear the band play. I was fascinated by the calypso singers and the sometimes ribald ditties they sang in their tents during carnival time. But, like many of the black middle class, to my

[1] Recently appointed general manager.

mother a calypso was a matter for ne'er-do-wells and at best the common
people. I was made to understand that the road to the calypso tent was
the road to hell, and there were always plenty of examples of hell's
inhabitants to whom she could point. She was not unkind, and before I
grew up I understood her attitude better when some neighbours of ours
defied the elementary conventions to such a degree that she and my
father had to pack my young sister off to stay with our aunts until the
temperature cooled down somewhat.

There was, however, another side to my mother which she brought
from her convent. She was a reader, one of the most tireless I have ever
known. Usually it was novels, any novel. Scott, Thackeray, Dickens,
Hall Caine, Stevenson, Mrs. Henry Wood, Charlotte Brontë, Charlotte
Braeme, Shakespeare (she had her own copy which I read to pieces),
Balzac, Nathaniel Hawthorne, a woman called Mrs. E. D. E. N. South-
worth, Fenimore Cooper, Nat Gould, Charles Garvice, anything and
everything, and as she put them down I picked them up. I remember
her warning me not to read books by one Victoria Cross, but I found the
books hidden in one of her dressers and read them just the same.

My mother's taste in novels was indiscriminate, but I learnt discrimination from my father. He was no reader, except for books connected with his teaching, but as a man of some education he knew who,
if not what, the classics were. Our bookseller was an itinerant who came
once a fortnight carrying a huge pack on his shoulders. He heaved it off
and spread his wares, the *Review of Reviews, Tit-Bits, Comic Cuts, The
Strand Magazine, Pearson's Magazine*, sixpenny copies of the classics.
'*The Pickwick Papers*,' my father would say, taking up the book. 'By
Charles Dickens. A great book, my boy. Read it.' And he would buy it.
If he took me to a department store he would do the same. And so I began
to have my own collection of books as well as my own bat and balls.
But in those magazines, particularly *Pearson's*, appeared, periodically,
cricketing stories. There would be also articles on the great cricketers of
the day, W. G. Grace, Ranjitsinhji, Victor Trumper, C. B. Fry. My
father held forth on W. G. Grace and Ranjitsinhji, but he knew little
of the others. I found out for myself. I knew about them before I knew
the great cricketers of the island. I read about them from paper to paper,
from magazine to magazine. When we moved into Port of Spain, the
capital, I read two daily papers and on Sundays the green *Sporting Chronicle*
and the red *Sporting Opinion*. I made clippings and filed them. It served

no purpose whatever, I had never seen nor heard of anyone doing the like. I spoke to no one about it and no one spoke to me.

Side by side with this obsession was another—Thackeray's *Vanity Fair*. My mother had an old copy with a red cover. I had read it when I was about eight, and of all the books that passed through that house this one became my Homer and my bible. I read it through from the first page to the last, then started again, read to the end and started again. Whenever I finished a new book I turned to my *Vanity Fair*. For years I had no notion that it was a classical novel. I read it because I wanted to.

So there I was, way out in the West Indies, before I was ten, playing games and running races like other little boys, but almost in secret devoting my immense energies to the accumulation of facts and statistics about Grace and Ranjitsinhji, and reading *Vanity Fair* on the average once every three months. What drew me to it? I don't know, a phrase which will appear often in this book. As I dig into my memory I recall that the earliest books I could reach from the window-sill when I had nothing to do, or rain stopped the cricket or there was no cricket, were biblical. There was a series of large brightly coloured religious pamphlets telling the story of Jacob and the Ladder, Ruth and Naomi and so forth. There was a large book called *The Throne of the House of David*. One day somebody must have told me, or I may have discovered it from listening to the lessons being read in church, that these stories could be found in the many bibles that lay about the house, including the large one with the family births and deaths. Detective-like, I tracked down the originals and must have warmed the souls of my aunts and grandmother as they saw me poring over the Bible. That, I had heard often enough, was a good book. It fascinated me. When the parson read the lessons I strove to remember the names and numbers, second chapter of the Second Book of Kings, the Gospel according to St. Matthew, and so on, every Sunday morning. Rev. Allen had a fine voice and was a beautiful reader. I would go home and search and read half aloud to myself. (In school I was still fooling about with Standards 1 or 2: 'Johnny's father had a gun and went shooting in the forest.') Somewhere along the way I must have caught the basic rhythms of English prose. My reading was chiefly in the Old Testament and I may have caught, too, some of the stern attitude to life which was all around me, tempered, but only tempered, by family kindness.

I must have found the same rhythms and the same moralism when I came to *Vanity Fair*. Certainly of the lords and ladies and much of the life described, as a West Indian boy of eight, I hadn't the slightest idea. When I later told people how and when I had read the book some were sceptical and even derisive. It was not to me an ordinary book. It was a refuge into which I withdrew. By the time I was fourteen I must have read the book over twenty times and I used to confound boys at school by telling them to open it anywhere, read a few words and I would finish the passage, if not in the exact words at least close enough. I can still do it, though not as consistently and accurately as before.

Me and my clippings and magazines on W. G. Grace, Victor Trumper and Ranjitsinhji, and my *Vanity Fair* and my puritanical view of the world. I look back at the little eccentric and would like to have listened to him, nod affirmatively and pat him on the shoulder. A British intellectual long before I was ten, already an alien in my own environment among my own people, even my own family. Somehow from around me I had selected and fastened on to the things that made a whole. As will soon appear, to that little boy I owe a debt of gratitude.

I find it strange, and the more I think of it the stranger I find it. If the reader does not find it strange then let him consider what has happened since.

When I was ten I went to the Government secondary school, the Queen's Royal College, where opportunities for playing cricket and reading books were thrown wide open to me. When I was fifteen, the editor of the school magazine, a master, asked me to write something for it. Such was my fanaticism that I could find nothing better to write about than an account of an Oxford and Cambridge cricket match played nearly half a century before, the match in which Cobden for Cambridge dismissed three Oxford men in one over to win the match by two runs.

I retold it in my own words as if it were an experience of my own, which indeed it was. The choice was more logical than my next juvenile publication. At the end of term, during the English composition examination, I was very sleepy, probably from reading till the small hours the night before. I looked at the list of subjects, the usual stuff, 'A Day in the Country', etc., etc., including, however, 'The Novel as an Instrument of Reform'. Through the thorough grounding in grammar given me by my father and my incessant reading, I could write a good school composition on anything, and from the time I was about eight my English composition papers usually had full marks, with once every three or four weeks a trifling mistake. I sat looking at the list, not knowing which to choose. Bored with the whole business, I finally wrote each subject on a piece of paper, rolled them, shook them together and picked out one. It was 'The Novel as an Instrument of Reform'. For me it seemed just a subject like any other. But perhaps I was wrong. Literature? Reform? I may have been stimulated. But I drew on my knowledge and my long-ingrained respect for truth and justice, and I must have done very well, for at the beginning of the following term the English master called me and surprised me by telling me that he proposed to print the 'very fine' essay in the school magazine. Still more to my astonishment, when the magazine appeared I was constantly stopped in the street by old boys and the local literati, who congratulated me on what they called 'this remarkable essay'. I prudently kept the circumstances of its origin to myself.

As I say, those were the first two printed articles. Nearly forty years have passed, and very active and varied years they have been. In the course of them I have written a study of the French Revolution in San Domingo and a history of the Communist International. I went to the United States in 1938, stayed there for fifteen years and never saw a cricket match, though I used to read the results of Tests and county matches which the *New York Times* publishes every day during the season. In 1940 came a crisis in my political life. I rejected the Trotskyist version of Marxism and set about to re-examine and reorganize my view of the world, which was (and remains) essentially a political one. It took more than ten years, but by 1952 I once more felt my feet on solid ground, and in consequence I planned a series of books. The first was published in 1953, a critical study of the writings of Herman Melville as a mirror of our age, and the second is this book on cricket. The first two themes. 'The Novel as an Instrument of Reform' and 'Cobden's Match', have reappeared in the same close connection after forty years. Only after I had chosen my themes did I recognize that I had completed a circle. I discovered that I had not arbitrarily or by accident worshipped at the shrine of John Bunyan and Aunt Judith, of W. G. Grace and Matthew Bondman, of *The Throne of the House of David* and *Vanity Fair*. They were a trinity, three in one and one in three, the Gospel according to St. Matthew, Matthew being the son of Thomas, otherwise called Arnold of Rugby.

## 2

# *Against the Current*

WE KNOW nothing, nothing at all, of the results of what we do to children. My father had given me a bat and ball, I had learnt to play and at eighteen was a good cricketer. What a fiction! In reality my life up to ten had laid the powder for a war that lasted without respite for eight years, and intermittently for some time afterwards—a war between English Puritanism, English literature and cricket, and the realism of West Indian life. On one side was my father, my mother (no mean pair), my two aunts and my grandmother, my uncle and his wife, all the family friends (which included a number of headmasters from all over the island), some eight or nine Englishmen who taught at the Queen's Royal College, all graduates of Oxford or Cambridge, the Director of Education and the Board of Education, which directed the educational system of the whole island. On the other side was me, just ten years old when it began.

They had on their side parental, scholastic, governmental and many other kinds of authority and, less tangible but perhaps more powerful, the prevailing sentiment that, in as much as the coloured people on the island, and in fact all over the world, had such limited opportunities, it was my duty, my moral and religious duty, to make the best use of the opportunities which all these good people and the Trinidad Government had provided for me. I had nothing to start with but my pile of clippings about W. G. Grace and Ranjitsinhji, my *Vanity Fair* and my Puritan instincts, though as yet these were undeveloped. I fought and won. This was the battleground. The Trinidad Government offered yearly free exhibitions from the elementary schools of the island to either of the two secondary schools, the Government Queen's Royal College and the Catholic college, St. Mary's. The number today is over four hundred, but in those days it was only four. Through this narrow gate boys, poor but bright, could get a secondary education and in the end a Cambridge Senior Certificate, a useful passport to a good job. There were even more glittering prizes. Every year the two schools competed for three island scholarships worth £600 each. With one of these a boy could study law or medicine and return to the island with a profession and therefore independence. There were at that time few other roads to independence for a black man who started without means. The higher posts in the Government, in engineering and other scientific professions were monopolized by white people, and, as practically all big business was also in their hands, the coloured people were, as a rule, limited to the lower posts. Thus law and medicine were the only ways out. Lawyers and doctors made large fees and enjoyed great social prestige. The final achievement was when the Governor nominated one of these coloured men to the Legislative Council to represent the people. To what degree he represented them should not distract us here. We must keep our eye on the course: exhibition, scholarship, profession, wealth, Legislative Council and the title of Honourable. Whenever someone brought it off the local people were very proud of him.

That was the course marked out for me. The elementary-school masters all over the island sought bright boys to train for this examination, and to train a boy for this and win with him was one of the marks of a good teacher. My father was one of the best, and now fortune conspired to give him in his own son one whom he considered the brightest student he had ever had or known. The age limit for the examination was twelve and when I was eight I stopped going to my aunt's for half the year and my father gave me a little extra coaching. On the day of the examination a hundred boys were brought from all parts of the island by their teachers, like so many fighting cocks. That day I looked at the favourites and their trainers with wide-open eyes, for I was a country bumpkin. My father when asked about me always dismissed the enquiry with the remark, 'I only brought him along to get him accustomed to the atmosphere.' This was true, for he had great confidence in himself and in me and the most we ever did that year was half an hour extra in the morning and the same in the afternoon. I was only eight and he would not press me. But some weeks afterwards, when the daily paper arrived, I heard him shout to my mother: 'Bessie! Come and look at this!'

I had not won a place, but was among the ten or a dozen boys who gained special mention and had been placed seventh.

'If I had taught you seriously, boy, you would have won,' my father said to me.[1] The next year, though I had still two other chances, I ran away with the examination, came first and at that time was the youngest boy ever to have won a place. Congratulations poured in from all over the island and particularly from the teaching fraternity.

Being Protestant, I naturally went to the Government College. The masters here, too, welcomed me with interest, for these highly trained winners of Government exhibitions formed the best material for defeating the rival college in the annual race for island scholarships, and I was coming in with a reputation second to none. Very soon I attracted public attention again. The British Empire Society or the British Empire League or some such patriotic organization publicized extensively an island-wide essay competition on the British Empire. I sent in my piece and, though there were competitors sixteen and seventeen years of age, I won second prize. (I was given two volumes of Kipling's stories. I could not read or understand them at all for four years. One vacation I picked them up and for two years they supplanted *Vanity Fair* as my perpetual companions. Then I went back to *Vanity Fair*. But that was to come.) The winning of that prize so soon after my brilliant performance in the exhibitioners' examination set the seal on me as a future candidate for the Legislative Council.

It is only now as I write that I fully realize what a catastrophe I was for all—and there were many—who were so interested in me. How were they to know that when I put my foot on the steps of the college building in January 1911 I carried within me the seeds of revolt against all it formally stood for and all that I was supposed to do in it? My scholastic career was one long nightmare to me, my teachers and my family. My scholastic shortcomings were accompanied by breaches of discipline which I blush to think of even today. But at the same time, almost entirely by

[1] On my return to the West Indies I heard a legend that I had really won a place but that I was so young and so certain to win again in my remaining three chances that another student having his last chance was gi·en the place. It is, of course, impossible to know if this is true. I hope it is.

my own efforts, I mastered thoroughly the principles of cricket and of English literature, and attained a mastery over my own character which would have done credit to my mother and Aunt Judith if only they could have understood it. I could not explain it to their often tear-stained faces for I did not understand it myself. I look back at that little boy with amazement, and, as I have said, with a gratitude that grows every day. But for his unshakable defiance of the whole world around him, and his determination to stick to his own ideas, nothing could have saved me from winning a scholarship, becoming an Honourable Member of the Legislative Council and ruining my whole life.

The first temptation was cricket and I succumbed without a struggle. On the first day of the term you were invited, if you wanted to play, to write your name on a paper pinned to the school notice-board. I wrote down mine. The next day the names appeared divided up into five elevens. The college had its own ground in the rear of the building and with a little crowding there was room for five elevens. That afternoon the elevens met and elected their captains. Later, as I grew older and won my place in the cricket and soccer elevens, I took my part in the elections of the captains, the secretaries and the committees. A master presided, but that was all he did. We managed our own affairs from the fifth eleven to the first. When I became the secretary I kept a check on the implements used in all the elevens, wrote down what was wanted on a sheet of paper, had it signed by a master and went off to buy them myself for over two hundred boys. We chose our own teams, awarded colours ourselves, obeyed our captains implicitly. For me it was life and education.

I began to study Latin and French, then Greek, and much else. But particularly we learnt, I learnt and obeyed and taught a code, the English public-school code. Britain and her colonies and the colonial peoples. What do the British people know of what they have done there? Precious little. The colonial peoples, particularly West Indians, scarcely know themselves as yet. It has taken me a long time to begin to understand.

One afternoon in 1956, being at that time deep in this book, I sat in a hall in Manchester, listening to Mr. Aneurin Bevan. Mr. Bevan had been under much criticism for 'not playing with the team', and he answered his critics. He devastated them and brought his audience to a pitch of high receptivity and continuous laughter by turning inside out and ripping holes in such concepts as 'playing with the team', 'keeping a stiff upper lip', 'playing with a straight bat' and the rest of them. I too

33

had had my fun with them on the public platform often enough, but by 1956 I was engaged in a more respectful re-examination and I believe I was the solitary person among those many hundreds who was not going all the way with Mr. Bevan. Perhaps there was one other. When Mr. Bevan had had enough of it he tossed the ball lightly to his fellow speaker, Mr. Michael Foot. 'Michael is an old public-school boy and he knows more about these things than I.' Mr. Foot smiled, but if I am not mistaken the smile was cryptic.

I smiled too, but not whole-heartedly. In the midst of his fireworks Mr. Bevan had dropped a single sentence that tolled like a bell. 'I did not join the Labour Party, I was brought up in it.' And I had been brought up in the public-school code.

It came doctrinally from the masters, who for two generations, from the foundation of the school, had been Oxford and Cambridge men. The striking thing was that inside the classrooms the code had little success. Sneaking was taboo, but we lied and cheated without any sense of shame. I know I did. By common understanding the boys sitting for the valuable scholarships did not cheat. Otherwise we submitted, or did not submit, to moral discipline, according to upbringing and temperament.

But as soon as we stepped on to the cricket or football field, more particularly the cricket field, all was changed. We were a motley crew. The children of some white officials and white business men, middle-class blacks and mulattos, Chinese boys, some of whose parents still spoke broken English, Indian boys, some of whose parents could speak no English at all, and some poor black boys who had won exhibitions or whose parents had starved and toiled on plots of agricultural land and were spending their hard-earned money on giving the eldest boy an education. Yet rapidly we learned to obey the umpire's decision without question, however irrational it was. We learned to play with the team, which meant subordinating your personal inclinations, and even interests, to the good of the whole. We kept a stiff upper lip in that we did not complain about ill-fortune. We did not denounce failures, but 'Well tried' or 'Hard luck' came easily to our lips. We were generous to opponents and congratulated them on victories, even when we knew they did not deserve it. We lived in two worlds. Inside the classrooms the heterogeneous jumble of Trinidad was battered and jostled and shaken down into some sort of order. On the playing field we did what ought to be done. Every individual did not observe every rule. But the majority of the boys did. The best and most-respected boys were precisely the ones who always kept them. When a boy broke them he knew what he had done and, with the cruelty and intolerance of youth, from all sides our denunciations poured in on him. Eton or Harrow had nothing on us.

Another source of this fierce, self-imposed discipline were the magazines and books that passed among us from hand to hand. *The Boy's Own Paper*, a magazine called *The Captain*, annuals of which I remember the name of only one: *Young England*, the Mike stories by P. G. Wodehouse and scores of similar books and magazines. These we understood, these we lived by; the principles they taught we absorbed through the pores and practised instinctively. The books we read in class meant little to most of us.

To all this I took as a young duck to water. The organizing of boys into elevens, the selection of teams, the keeping of scores, all that I had been doing at second-hand with Grace and Ranjitsinhji and Trumper I now practised in real life with real people. I read the boys' books and magazines, twice as many as any other boy. I knew what was done and what was not done. One day when I bowled three maiden overs in succession and a boy fresh from England said to me, 'James, you must take yourself off now, three maiden overs,' I was disturbed. I had not heard that one before, this boy was from England and so he probably knew.

Before very long I acquired a discipline for which the only name is Puritan. I never cheated, I never appealed for a decision unless I thought the batsman was out, I never argued with the umpire, I never jeered at a defeated opponent, I never gave to a friend a vote or a place which by any stretch of imagination could be seen as belonging to an enemy or to a stranger. My defeats and disappointments I took as stoically as I could. If I caught myself complaining or making excuses I pulled up. If afterwards I remembered doing it I took an inward decision to try not to do it again. From the eight years of school life this code became the moral framework of my existence. It has never left me. I learnt it as a boy, I have obeyed it as a man and now I can no longer laugh at it. I failed to live up to it at times, but when I did I knew and that is what matters. I had a clue and I cared, I couldn't care more. For many years I was a cricket correspondent in the West Indies, having to write about myself, my own club, my intimate friends and people who hated me. Mistakes in judgment I made often enough, but I was as righteous as the Angel

Gabriel, and no one ever challenged my integrity. Thus it was that I could not join wholeheartedly in the laughter at Mr. Bevan's witticisms. Particularly so because in order to acquire this code I was driven to evasions, disobedience, open rebelliousness, continuous lies and even stealing.

My business at school was to do my lessons, win prizes and ultimately win the scholarship. Nobody ever doubted that if I wanted to I could. The masters wrote regularly in my reports 'Bad' or 'Good', as the case might be, but usually added, 'Could do much better if he tried.'

I did not try. Without any difficulty I could keep up in school, but an exhibition winner was being paid for by Government money and had to maintain a certain standard. I fell below it. My distracted father lectured me, punished me, flogged me. I would make good resolutions, do well for one term and fall from grace again. Then came a resounding scandal. I was reported to the Board of Education and threatened with the loss of my exhibition. It appeared in the public Press and all the teaching fraternity, who always read the reports of the meetings of the Board, read it, and thus learned what was happening to the prospective scholarship winner and Honourable Member of the Legislative Council. There were family meetings, the whole family, to talk to me and make me see the error of my ways. I was not only ruining my own chances. My godfather was a teacher, Judith's husband was a teacher, my sister's godfather was a teacher. The James clan had a proud status in the teaching profession, my father was an acknowledged star in that firmament and here was I bringing public disgrace upon him and all of them.

I was given orders to stop playing and get home by a certain train. I just couldn't do it. I would calculate that it would take me twenty-five minutes to catch the train. Then I would think I could do it in twenty, then just one last over and then it was too late to try anyway. I invented beforehand excuses which would allow me to stay and play and take the late train. When I got into the eleven there were matches on Saturdays. I devised Saturday duties which the masters had asked me to perform, I forged letters, I borrowed flannels, I borrowed money to pay my fare, I borrowed bicycles to ride to the matches and borrowed money to repair them when I smashed them. I was finally entangled in such a web of lies, forged letters, borrowed clothes and borrowed money that it was no wonder that the family looked on me as a sort of trial from heaven sent to test them as Job was tested. There were periods when my father

relented and I lived normally. But then bad reports would come, the prohibitions would be re-imposed and I would plan to evade them. I was not a vicious boy. All I wanted was to play cricket and soccer, not merely to play but to live the life, and nothing could stop me. When all my tricks and plans and evasions failed I just went and played and said to hell with the consequences.

Two people lived in me: one, the rebel against all family and school discipline and order; the other, a Puritan who would have cut off a finger sooner than do anything contrary to the ethics of the game.

To complicate my troubled life with my distracted family the Queen's Royal College fed the other of my two obsessions, English literature. When I entered the school at ten I was already primed for it, and the opportunities it offered completed my ruin for what the school and my father considered to be my duty. I spent eight years in its classrooms. I studied Latin with Virgil, Caesar and Horace, and wrote Latin verses. I studied Greek with Euripides and Thucydides. I did elementary and applied mathematics, French and French literature, English and English literature, English history, ancient and modern European history. I took certain examinations which were useful for getting jobs. I was fortunate enough to go back to the same school for some years as a teacher and so saw the system from within. As schools go, it was a very good school, though it would have been more suitable to Portsmouth than to Port of Spain.

What did all this matter to me when I discovered in the college library that besides *Vanity Fair* Thackeray had written thirty-six other volumes, most of them with pictures by himself? I read them through straight, two volumes at a time, and read them for twenty years after. (I stopped only when I came to England in 1932 and read him only sporadically. Recently I have started again.) After Thackeray there was Dickens, George Eliot and the whole bunch of English novelists. Followed the poets in Matthew Arnold's selections, Shelley, Keats and Byron; Milton and Spenser. But in the public library in town there was everything, Fielding, Byron, with all of *Don Juan*. I discovered criticism: Hazlitt, Lamb and Coleridge, Saintsbury and Gosse, *The Encyclopaedia Britannica*, *Chambers' Encyclopaedia*. Burke led me to the speeches: Canning, Lord Brougham, John Bright. I cannot possibly remember all that I read then, and every now and then I still look up an essay or a passage and find that I had read it before I was eighteen. And all the time I read

the boys' books, *Eric, or Little by Little, St. Winifred's* or *The World of School, The Hill* by H. A. Vachell, Kipling's *Stalky and Co.*, an incredible number of books by G. A. Henty—there is no need to go through them all—and at the same time I kept up with (and now supplemented) my mother's ever-expanding list. The literature of cricket was easier. There were not many around, so those I could put my hands on I had to read over and over again. *The Jubilee Book of Cricket* by Ranjitsinhji was large, with many words on the page—I treasured it.

But this school was in a colony ruled autocratically by Englishmen. What then about the National Question? It did not exist for me. Our principal, Mr. W. Burslem, M.A., formerly, if I remember rightly, of Clare College, Cambridge, part Pickwick, part Dr. Johnson, part Samuel Smiles, was an Englishman of the nineteenth century, and if it were not outside the scope of what I am doing I could spend many pages recalling his quirks. But no more devoted, conscientious and self-sacrificing official ever worked in the colonies. He was immensely kind to me and often after telling me at the end of a term that he hoped he would never see my face again (implying that he would report me a second time to the Board of Education—which meant the guillotine) he would write mitigating words in my report, call me to do some personal task for him (a way of showing favour) and in the course of it try to show me the error of my ways. He did it constantly with me and other waywards. He was a man with a belief in the rod which he combined with a choleric and autocratic disposition. But he was beloved by generations of boys and was held in respectful admiration throughout the colony. To such a degree that when he died a journalist who had never been one of his pupils was moved to a piece of obituary prose which had all the old boys reading to one another for days. How not to look up to the England of Shakespeare and Milton, of Thackeray and Dickens, of Hobbs and Rhodes, in the daily presence of such an Englishman and in the absence of any nationalist agitation outside? In the nationalist temper of today Mr. Burslem would be an anachronism, his bristling Britishness a perpetual reminder not of what he was doing but of what he represented. I write of him as he was, and today, forty years after, despite all that I have learnt between, what I think of him now is not very different from what I thought then.

It was only long years after that I understood the limitation on spirit, vision and self-respect which was imposed on us by the fact that our masters, our curriculum, our code of morals, *everything* began from the

basis that Britain was the source of all light and leading, and our business was to admire, wonder, imitate, learn; our criterion of success was to have succeeded in approaching that distant ideal—to attain it was, of course, impossible. Both masters and boys accepted it as in the very nature of things. The masters could not be offensive about it because they thought it was their function to do this, if they thought about it at all; and, as for me, it was the beacon that beckoned me on.

The race question did not have to be agitated. It was there. But in our little Eden it never troubled us. If the masters were so successful in instilling and maintaining their British principles as the ideal and norm (however much individuals might fall away) it was because within the school, and particularly on the playing field, they practised them themselves. Here and there, as we grew older and more perceptive, you could discern that in our elections, granting of colours, etc., a master might let slip a personal preference for a white boy who was a member of a distinguished local family or a mulatto boy who was the same. But that was human nature. They were correct in the letter and in the spirit. When I went back to the college to teach (I acted as a master for years) they welcomed me in the masters' common-room and the then principal, a Mr. A. M. Low, a man of pronounced Tory, not to say chauvinist, ideas, amazed me by the interest he took in me. Once in an expansive moment, when discussing work prospects, he muttered a phrase, 'We do our work and in time you people will take over.' I hadn't had the faintest idea that he thought about such things—I certainly hadn't. That must have been about 1924 and it was the first and only time in some fifteen years that I heard a word in that school from a master or from anyone else about the national or racial question.

So soothing were our waters that I could be struck hard blows in the outside world and be cured as soon as I returned.

Nineteen-eighteen was my last year, and it was also the last year of the war. I was under age, but I got it into my head that I would like to see the world, and the best way would be to go to the war. We had been deluged with propaganda, but I don't think that had much to do with it. There were two ways by which one could go: the public contingent, recruited by the local Government from among the masses of people, and the Merchants' Contingent, young men of the upper middle classes sent direct to England to join English regiments and financed by the local merchants. The rumour was, and the facts seemed to show, that the merchants selected only white or brown people. But though I was dark, I was widely known as a coming cricketer and I kept goal for the college team in the first-class football league. I was tall and very fit. So on a morning when I should have been at school I went down to the office where one of the big merchants, perhaps the biggest of all, examined the would-be warriors. Young man after young man went in, and I was not obviously inferior to any of them in anything. The merchant talked to each, asked for references and arranged for further examination as the case might be. When my turn came I walked to his desk. He took one look at me, saw my dark skin and, shaking his head vigorously, motioned me violently away.

What matters is that I was not unduly disturbed. I remember that the English sergeant, instructor of the cadet corps, was quite angry when I told him about it. 'Here,' he said, 'they say they want men and when they have a likely lad they won't take him.' White boys from the school joined the public contingent as commissioned officers and came back to the college to see us with chests out and smart uniforms and shining buttons. When the masters heard what had happened to me some of them were angry, one or two ashamed, all were on my side. It didn't hurt for long because for so many years these crude intrusions from the world which surrounded us had been excluded. I had not even been wounded, for no scar was left.

Yet before I left I was to receive one sharp reminder of what was waiting for me. For years among my closest friends were three white boys, and the fathers of two of them were heads of departments and, as such, official members of the Legislative Council. I had other friends, coloured, and these were the friends I invited to my house to spend time during the holidays. But these white boys were in my own class and for years we were inseparable. Year after year whichever arrived first at the beginning of term chose a seat, strategic in relation to the master's desk, sprawled over the two seats next to it and fought off all comers until the other two arrived. One of them and I read through the whole of the *Pickwick Papers* on afternoons between two and three o'clock and whenever we exploded the third would ask what it was and we would tell him.

My great friend was U——. He was a rather frail boy and somewhat lacking in physical confidence, but he was a left-hander. I took him under my wing. I fielded second slip to him to feeble batsmen and took catches

that I never afterwards equalled. I went out to extra-cover for hitting
batsmen. Caught James, bowled U—— was a regular feature of the
score-sheet in our school matches. That can be a close bond, and we spent
countless hours together. But there came a day when U—— left, while
I remained behind. Faithful to his promise, he came back to the school
to see me. He came before six o'clock to see me playing on the field and
then to walk with me the mile and a half to the railway station. He told
me about his new life, and I gave him some news of the school. But after
the first effusion there was an awkwardness between us. The conversation
would stop and we would have to search to begin it again. He came
another day to see me to the station and this time it was worse. We had
nothing to say to each other, our social circles were too different, and he
never came again. He went to Europe to study medicine and years
afterwards, when we were grown men, I met him once or twice. We
greeted each other warmly, but I was always embarrassed and I think
he was too. There was a guilty feeling that something had gone wrong
with us. Something had. The school-tie can be transplanted, but except
on annual sporting occasions the old school-tie cannot be. It is a bond of
school only on the surface. The link is between family and friends,
between members of the class or caste.

When I left school I was an educated person, but I had educated
myself into a member of the British middle class with literary gifts and
I had done it in defiance of all authority. The last year had seen an end
to all my lies and deceptions and borrowings, for after a fearful row with
my father, during which I left home and swore I would never go back, he
decided to accept me as I was and I became a respectable and self-respect-
ing member of society and have remained so to this day. In the course of
duty and for my own information I have read the classics of educational
theory and taken an interest in systems of education. Each suited its time,
but I have a permanent affinity with only one, the ancient Greek. When
I read that the Greeks educated their young people on poetry, gymnastics
and music I feel that I know what that means, and I constantly read (and
profit by) the writings of most learned professors of Greek culture, who
I am sure don't know what they are talking about. Let the reader judge
for himself. I did not merely play cricket. I studied it. I analysed strokes,
I studied types, I read its history, its beginnings, how and when it changed
from period to period, I read about it in Australia and in South Africa.
I read and compared statistics, I made clippings, I talked to all cricketers,

particularly the intercolonial cricketers and those who had gone abroad. I compared what they told me with what I read in old copies of *Wisden*. I looked up the play of the men who had done well or badly against the West Indies. I read and appreciated the phraseology of laws. It was in that way, I am confident, that the Greeks educated themselves on games with their records and traditions orally transmitted from generation to generation. Amateur though I am, I see signs of it in Greek literature, but you must have gone through the thing yourself to understand them.

I am the more certain of the Greek education because it was only after I left school that I began to distinguish between the study of cricket and the study of literature, or rather, I should say, the pursuit of cricket and the pursuit of literature. I did with the one exactly what I did with the other. I paid no attention to the curriculum. At the beginning of the school year we would be given, for example, Virgil Book II or a book of Thucydides. The class went painfully from twenty lines to twenty new lines twice a week, as it might be. I was always very busy that first week. As each new author was introduced to us I rushed off to the public library looking for translations. There were extracts from critics in the introductions. I pursued the originals. There were old numbers of the *Cornhill*, *Blackwood's* and other magazines in the library. I would be looking for an article by Walter Pater and find one on county cricket, or vice versa.

All this had nothing to do with education in school. I remember one brilliant boy, and ultimately a scholarship winner, who studied *The Merchant of Venice* three or four pages at a time twice a week as the master took us through. At the end of the term we had reached only Act III and I discovered, quite by chance, that he didn't know how the play ended. At the end of the school year I would see boys who had made good marks giving away their Shelleys and their Burkes, swearing that they had finished with them for ever, and when I met them in later years they appeared to have kept their promises well. What was even more tragic was that boys who after six years had acquired a remarkable competence in Latin and Greek treated them ever afterwards as dead languages. All that did not encourage me to change my ways.

I was not a swan among geese. There were other boys who read hard, and with more discrimination than I did, for I read everything. But none pursued criticism to any degree and not one read cricket literature except in the most casual way. (One curious fact: I read one book on soccer and never read another.) But for cricket and English literature I fed an inexhaustible passion. I had had it from the earliest days that I remember. The boys in ancient Greece must have had the same. If for them games and poetry were ennobled by their roots in religion, my sense of conduct and morals came from my two, or rather my twin, preoccupations, and I suspect that it was not too different with a Greek boy. But he went out into a world for which his training had prepared him. There was no world for which I was fitted, least of all the one I was now to enter.

At any rate when I left school in 1918 I had penetrated deep into English literature and into cricket. Of literature I have written elsewhere. It is the second with which I am here chiefly concerned. Cricket is a game of high and difficult technique. If it were not it could not carry the load of social response and implications which it carries. I played for years, but from the start that was secondary.

By the time I left school at the age of eighteen I was a good defensive bat and could have held my own in any English public-school side. I could bowl fast-medium with a high action, swing the ball late from leg and break it with shoulder-and-finger action from the off. I was looked upon as one of the coming players in the island, and the captain of the island team, Nelson Betancourt, had gone so far as to say that I was a born bowler. So I was, but only in my head. I have read many books on bowling, and one of the latest, by Ray Lindwall, gave me a lot of pleasant amusement. Lindwall teaches that you bowl one kind of ball from the edge of the crease, you bowl the same from the centre, then from near the wicket; you vary the pitch and the pace, and so on and so forth. I smile because I knew all that and was practising it since I was fifteen. I have at various times dismissed for small scores St. Hill, Small, Constantine, Wiles and other Test players and in my best days I would have opened the bowling cheerfully against any batsman I have ever seen, including Bradman—in a one-day match, of course. But while bowling and batting are often written about by great cricketers, most of them say little of value (when you talk to them, if you know how, that's a different matter altogether), and quite early I had definite views which I have very rarely seen written down.

A great bowler has physical power, determination, co-ordination and some special gift, usually pace from the pitch, which makes him dangerous to begin with. But if you give those same qualities to another man, one would be a great bowler and another would not be. The ultimate greatness of a bowler is in his head. He has a series of methods of attack at his command, but where he pitches any ball and the ball following, where he delivers one and from where he delivers another, where he quickens the pace and where he slows it down, this is the result of a psychological sensitivity and response to a particular batsman at a particular time on a particular wicket at a particular stage in the game. To watch cricket critically you have to be in good form, you must have had a lot of practice, you must have played it. There were times in our club cricket at home, or when I went round English cricket grounds reporting the matches of the Lancashire team, or when I watched all the Test matches through the season of 1938, these were times when I could sense the course of an over from the way the batsman stood waiting between balls. If you knew him well you could see when he was bothered. When Jim Laker writes that he bowled Bradman an over and knew that he had beaten him with every ball he is talking about bowling at its highest. In the rout of the Australians in 1956 the decisive factor was not Laker's off-spin. It was that he had them on the run and kept them there. I have watched Sidney Barnes in his old age and McDonald long after he had retired from first-class cricket, bowling at Constantine, whose batting I knew intimately. The interplay was as subtle as that of men playing bridge or poker. Somehow I was aware of this from the time I entered my teens. From as far back as I can remember I have captained the fielding side of every match I have seen and many in which I was batting.

I had bowling gifts and they could have been developed, but the pace, the length, the command, the stamina, the concentration, I did not have and never had. Now and then even I could bring it off for an over or two. The great gain was that it taught me how to watch. It is no more necessary to look at cricket this way than it is to study counterpoint in order to listen to Bach. Quite often it is harmful. But that is how it was with me.

Batting was the same. I was reading cricket and looking at it critically so early that casual experiences which would have passed unnoticed stayed with me and I worked at them as if on some historical problem. Before we reached the second eleven we played on dirt pitches, and there was always the problem of the dead shooter. Some of us learned to play it. As soon as, playing back, you lost sight of the ball on the rise, you dug your bat deep down behind where you stood so that it sloped towards the bowler. More than that, you could see the shooting off-break and calculate where to dig down. But to play this stroke, which we had to play twice every three overs or so, you could not take the right foot across the wicket. If you did you could not possibly get the bat down in time, you would hit your own foot more often than not. I am convinced that it was the right foot stationary or taken straight back which allowed W. G. Grace to play the four shooters in succession for which the crowd rose at him at Lord's in the days of treacherous wickets. We got to take these shooters in our stride. Two years later, after playing on the carefully prepared matting wickets of the first eleven, if a ball kept unusually low and hit the feet in front we felt that the gods had conspired against us. Much of the answer to the perpetual comparison between great players of different periods is contained in that experience.

Quite early I learnt that, far more than with bowling, a batsman's innings is played more in his head than on the pitch. I have believed this from the days of Wallen until George Headley told me with passion that the ball he feared most in a Test match was the loose ball which came after he had been tied down for two or three overs. 'You went at it greedily and made a stupid stroke,' he said over and over again. Nor is it the response of any individual. There is a *zeitgeist* of cricket. A particular generation of cricketers thinks in a certain way and only a change in society, not legislation, will change the prevailing style. More of that to come. First to Wallen.

Wallen was a slow left-hander who came into the first eleven one year, opened the bowling and had an incredible series of analyses, six for 11, eight for 17 and figures of the kind. When we talked about cricket to the girls at the High School even they would tell us: 'Cricket! Wallen is the man.' But to the rest of us in the first eleven Wallen was a push-over. We had hit him all over the place for years and we continued to hit him. Our nets were open and at practice the earnest Wallen would place his field and we would drive him through the covers and as soon as he pitched short hook him round. We would go out to him and hit him from the off-stump to square-leg. The more wickets he took in competition matches, the more we hit him. Wallen complained that, contrary to practice, in matches he had a new ball, and undoubtedly he did dip in a bit while the shine was on. I was the secretary and manœuvred to take a new ball out for practice and saw that Wallen had it just as I went in to bat. I hit him harder than ever. The climax came in the house match when

Chinasing (Chinese, not Indian) and I put on 100 for the first wicket against the demon bowler, and that is a lot of runs on a matting wicket. I was a little more cautious (I didn't want him to get me out because I lived at the time in the same town with him, Arima, and we were good friends). But Chinasing drove him continuously. Came Saturday and, sure as day, Chinasing and I stood in the slips and saw Wallen mow down the opposite side.

A great military authority of the eighteenth century stood on a height one day watching his master Napoleon carry out one of his audacious manœuvres and was heard to say that he wished he had charge of the opposing army for but one half-hour. But if he had he would not have had the nerve to guess what Napoleon was doing and take the steps that seemed so easy. So it is with batting. Over and over again in every class of cricket one sees someone walking out with 'What a colossal ass I have been!' written all over him. I haven't the slightest doubt that if an unknown Wallen had played for any of the outside teams he would have got us out and taken his seven for 15 as usual. David Buchanan, one of the destructive slow bowlers of his day, coached at Rugby and held no terrors for the boys there, who hit him about fearlessly. A great deal of cricket, and big cricket too, is wrapped up in that parcel. Sir Brian de Bois Guilbert, you remember, was slain not by the lance of Ivanhoe but by the 'violence of his own contending passions'.

We fought out at school in 1917 and 1918 the battle which is still being fought today—when in doubt push out for play back? Our wicket was coconut-matting on hard clay on which the ball always turned and quickly. Following my master, C. B. Fry, experience and observation, I fought for back-play. Chinasing and others brought out some ancient manuals and argued for the forward defensive push. I routed them, with the proviso that to slow bowling you left the crease when you did not play back. I enjoyed a serene mind on this vital question until 1938. I came back to cricket in 1953 to find that battle being fought all over again, with Sir Leonard Hutton at the head of cohorts far more formidable than my schoolday opponents. But I am far more confident of the ultimate result now than when I fought that battle so many, many years ago. And before this book is ended I hope to reinforce or convince many of its readers (not excluding Sir Leonard), though my weapons this time will be majestic and, I hope, imposing: the history of modern Britain and scientific method.

# 3

## Old School-tie

WHAT was it that so linked my Aunt Judith with cricket as I, a colonial, experienced it? The answer is in one word: Puritanism; more specifically, restraint, and restraint in a personal sense. But that restraint, did we learn it only on the cricket field, in *The Captain* and the *Boy's Own Paper*, in the pervading influence of the university men who taught me, as I once believed? I don't think so. I absorbed it from Judith and from my mother—it was in essence the same code—and I was learning it very early from my *Vanity Fair*. In recent years, as I have re-read Thackeray, I see the things which I did not note in the early days. I took them for granted and they were therefore all the more effective. I used to read and re-read and repeat the famous passage on Waterloo which ended: 'No more firing was heard at Brussels—the pursuit rolled miles away. Darkness came down on the field and city: and Amelia was praying for George, who was lying on his face, dead, with a bullet through his heart.'

I can remember the violent shock which that gave me. To my child-hood imaginings George Osborne was the hero, here he was killed and the book I could see had still much more than half to go. I laughed without satiety at Thackeray's constant jokes and sneers and gibes at the aristocracy and at people in high places. Thackeray, not Marx, bears the heaviest responsibility for me.

But the things I did not notice and took for granted were more enduring: the British reticence, the British self-discipline, the stiff lips, upper and lower. When Major Dobbin returns from India, and he and Amelia greet each other, Thackeray asks: Why did Dobbin not speak? Not only Dobbin, it is Thackeray who does not speak. He shies away from the big scene when Rawdon Crawley returns and finds Becky entertaining Lord Steyne. George Osborne writes a cold, stiff letter to his estranged father before going into battle, but he places a kiss on the envelope which Thackeray notes that his father did not see. Rawdon Crawley (whom I have always liked) chokes when he tries to tell Lady Jane how grateful he is for her kindness, he chokes when he discusses with Macmurdo the arrangements for the duel. Rawdon is a semi-illiterate and Jos Sedley is little better. But how much different is the erudite Major Dobbin? His life is one long repression of speech except when he speaks for others.

In *Pendennis* it is the same. George Warrington returns from Europe and he and Arthur exchange the most casual of greetings. Two Frenchmen, Thackeray says, would have embraced and kissed. George's mind is full of the great things he has seen, he will talk of them at odd times later. When Warrington is grinding out the story of his disastrous early marriage Laura begins to stretch out her hand to him, but restrains herself and manages it later only by a great effort. Henry Esmond, that supreme embodiment of the stiff upper lip, finally unlooses his tongue only when a kingdom has been lost by the lasciviousness of the young King. 'I lay this at your feet and stamp upon it: I draw this sword, and break it and deny you: and had you completed the wrong you had designed us, by heaven I would have driven it through your heart, and no more pardoned you than your father pardoned Monmouth. Frank will do the same, won't you, cousin?'

The last sentence takes us immediately back to normal. This is not the aristocracy of the early eighteenth century. It is the solid British middle class, Puritanism incarnate, of the middle of the nineteenth. If Judith had been a literary person that is the way she would have spoken. The West Indian masses did not care a damn about this. They shouted and stamped and yelled and expressed themselves fully in anger and joy then, as they do to this day, whether they are in Bridgetown or Birmingham. But they knew the code as it applied to sport, they expected us, the educated, the college boys, to maintain it; and if any English touring team or any member of it fell short they were merciless in their condemnation and shook their heads over it for years afterwards. Not only the English masters, but Englishmen in their relation to games in the colonies held tightly to the code as example and as a mark of differentiation.

I was an actor on a stage in which the parts were set in advance. I not only took it to an extreme, I seemed to have been made by nature for nothing else. There were others around me who did not go as far and as completely as I did. There was another cultural current in the island, French and Spanish, which shaped other characters. I have heard from acute observers that in Barbados, an island which has known no other strain but British, the code was unadulterated and even more severe. In his book *Cricket Punch* Frank Worrell tells that his being suspected of conceit as a youthful cricket prodigy made his life so miserable that he ran away from Barbados as soon as he could. When Worrell played for Barbados as a schoolboy he had to go to school every morning of the match and leave only an hour before play. We were not quite as extreme in Trinidad, but that was the atmosphere in which I grew and made my choices. Read the books of Worrell and Walcott, middle-class boys of secondary education, and see how native to them is the code. In an article welcoming the West Indies team of 1957 E. W. Swanton has written in the *Daily Telegraph* that in the West Indies the cricket ethic has shaped not only the cricketers but social life as a whole. It is an understatement. There is a whole generation of us, and perhaps two generations, who have been formed by it not only in social attitudes but in our most intimate personal lives, in fact there more than anywhere else. The social attitudes we could to some degree alter if we wished. For the inner self the die was cast. But that is not my theme except incidentally. The coming West Indies novelists will show the clash between the native temperament and environment, and this doctrine from a sterner clime.

The depth psychologists may demur. I can help them. Long before I had begun my immersion into *Vanity Fair*, when I was so small that I had to be taken to school, I would refuse to leave the school grounds with the older child who brought me in the morning. I would fight and resist in order to watch the big boys playing cricket, and I would do this until my grandmother came for me and dragged me home protesting. I was once knocked down by a hard on-drive, my ear bled for a day or two and I carefully hid it by exemplary and voluntary washings. Later, when reading elementary English history books, I became resentful of the fact that the English always won all, or nearly all, of the battles and read every new history book I could find, searching out and noting the battles they had lost. I would not deny that early influences I could know nothing about had cast me in a certain mould or even that I was born with certain characteristics. That could be. What interests me, and is, I think, of general interest, is that as far back as I can trace my consciousness the original found itself and came to maturity within a system that was the result of centuries of development in another land, was transplanted as a hot-house flower is transplanted and bore some strange fruit.

Along with restraint, not so much externally as in internal inhibitions, we learnt loyalty. It is good to be loyal to what you believe in—that, however, may be tautology. Loyalty to what is wrong, outmoded, reactionary is mischievous. To that in general all will agree, even the reactionary. The most profound loyalty can co-exist with a jealously critical attitude. Should loyalty be taught? Can it be taught? Or must it be learned? I don't know the answers to these questions, and perhaps they are too abstract. I am not asking them as a syllogistic exercise. The national characteristics of great nations are involved. Here are the concrete facts.

At the school we learnt not only to play with the team. We were taught and learnt loyalty in the form of loyalty to the school. As with everything else in those days, I took it for granted. It was only long afterwards, after gruesome experience in another country, that I saw it for the specifically British thing that it was.

Our loyalty revolved around rivalry with St. Mary's College and its active centre was sport. We sat for the same examinations and on the results of these the island scholarships were awarded. When the results came by cable there was much rejoicing if we had won two out of the three places, or the first place, or all three, as sometimes we did or they did. Periodically one of our island boys would be placed third in mathematics or eleventh in Latin among the thousands who took the Cambridge examinations all over the world, and there was applause and satisfaction that, backward colonials though we were, we could produce scholars as good as any.

But the victories that really mattered were those in the yearly games when the two teams met in the open cricket or football competitions. Old boys who had never seen a game all the season turned out to see the old school play. Gloom followed defeat. Victory was joy, and decisive victory meant a thrill of achievement which lasted for weeks and could be revived at any time until the next encounter, and even after. How to forget when George Rochford led Q.R.C. in a massacre of St. Mary's, 16—0?

Mr. Burslem, the principal, fought a losing battle against boys who refused to wear either a college cap or a straw hat with the college hatband. He could not get that plant to grow in the colonial soil, among other reasons because a felt hat was more economical—one shower of tropical rain could ruin a straw hat. But more college hatbands were worn for an inter-school game than on any other day during the year. The old school-tie came into its own. One year we gave St. Mary's a terrific beating at soccer, six goals to one or something of the kind. Next morning boys stood in groups around the ground and cheered each member of the team as he came in, and, as we walked about the town for days afterwards, unknown old boys came up to us, shook our hands and spoke of old times.

Perhaps the loyalty plant that flourished most miraculously in the thinnest of soils was our house matches. We had only one house, Boarding House, attached to the living quarters of the principal, which were situated on the college grounds. The rest of us were day-boys. But some inventive English master had divided us into City, Suburbs and Savannah. Savannah incorporated those who lived around the huge Queen's Park. Suburbs included boys who travelled in daily from the provinces. One attractive aspect was that in a school of about 200 boys four house teams of necessity had to include some quite junior boys, who thus got a chance to play with first-eleven boys and masters. But in the heads of many of us was the idea of the house matches we read so much about in stories and magazines of English public-school life.

In 1938 I went to the United States. At that time, especially after the debunking autobiographies of the twenties by Robert Graves, Siegfried Sassoon and others, and, later, Labour politics in England, my attitude to the code was not merely critical. It was, if anything, contemptuous. I had said good-bye to all that. I didn't know how deeply the early attitudes had been ingrained in me and how foreign they were to other peoples until I sat at baseball matches with friends, some of them university men, and saw and heard the howls of anger and rage and denunciation which they hurled at the players as a matter of course. I could not understand them and they could not understand me either—they asked anxiously if I were enjoying the game. I was enjoying the game; it was they who were disturbing me. And not only they. Managers and players protested against adverse decisions as a matter of course, and sometimes, after bitter quarrels, were ordered off the field, fined and punished in other ways. When I played in some friendly games, from the start the players shouted and yelled at one another, even at their own side. One day I explained cricket to friends at a camp and at their request organized a little game with bats hacked from pieces of wood, and a rubber ball. As soon as the fielders took position, they burst out with hue and cry, and when a ball was hit towards a fieldsman his own side seemed to pursue him like the hounds of heaven until he had gathered the ball and thrown it in.

All this seemed natural to them. It was very strange to me. However, I ignored it as differences of national character and outlook. If they played that way that was their way.

Then in 1950 came a series of events which I could not ignore. Day after day there appeared in the Press authenticated reports that university basketball teams had sold out games or played for results arranged beforehand, in return for money from bookmakers. The reports continued until an astounding number of teams from the best schools in the United States had been found guilty of these crimes. One case which particularly struck me was that of a boy who had taken the money, had hidden it in the basement of his house and left it there. When questioned, it appeared from his answers that he had had no idea of what to do with so large a sum and so had put it away and out of his mind. My usual restraint vanished and I expressed my horror to my friends with an unaccustomed freedom that astonished them. Unaccustomed, because from the first day of my stay in the United States to the last I never made the mistake that so many otherwise intelligent Europeans make of trying to fit that country into European standards. Perhaps for one reason, because of my colonial background, I always saw it for what it was and not for what I thought it ought to be. I took in my stride the cruelties and anomalies that shocked me and the immense vitality, generosity and audacity of these strange people. But this was too much—how could these young men behave in that way? Before I could choose my words I found myself saying that adults in Trinidad or in Britain, in the world of business or private life, could or would do anything, more or less. But in the adult world of sport, certainly in cricket, despite the tricks teams played upon one another, I had never heard of any such thing and did not believe it possible. That young men playing for school or university should behave in this way on such a scale was utterly shocking to me.

Shock succeeded shock. My friends and associates were chiefly political people. Some of them, young university graduates or students themselves, had demonstrated that they could not be shifted from their political and social principles by threats of gaol or promise of any material benefit. Some of them had rejected all the bribes offered by wealthy parents to return to the fold of Democrats or Republicans. But to my outburst they shrugged their shoulders and could not understand what I was talking about. The boys were wrong in being caught, that was all. The school? Why should they put 'the school' above what they wanted? Would one of them do such a thing? After some brief thought the answer was always: 'No. I am not interested in that sort of business. I don't want to get money from a bookie or to help him with money from another bookie or from the public. But if the bookie wants to and the players want to, I couldn't care less.'

As one of the older ones, I was among those responsible for the general education of these young people. I didn't press the matter, but it would not let me rest. I found, too, that the unusual definiteness of my views, my instinctive repulsion, had made some impression upon some of them. They felt for the first time that something was wrong with their own attitude, though what it was they could not say.

Periodically we returned to it. Older ones and I exchanged the practices, events and ideas of our early days. I left the United States, but the discussion continued, and we have arrived at some conclusions. These young people had no loyalties to school because they had no loyalties to anything. They had a universal distrust of their elders and preceptors, which had begun with distrust of their teachers. Each had had to work out his own individual code. Too many of them have assured me of this as true, not only of themselves but of their friends, for it to be the quirk of a few egotistic individuals. In 1956 Hollywood, as Hollywood will today, stated the case in that revealing film *Rebel Without a Cause*: though, as Hollywood does, it dodged any serious attempt to investigate either causes or conclusions. So do I. This is not the place for it. I merely record the immensity of the gulf that suddenly opened between me and people to whom I was so closely bound, speaking the same language, reading the same books and both of us ready when we had nothing better to do to make our jokes at the old school-tie.

When the discussions began they had looked at me a little strangely. I, a colonial born and bred, a Marxist, declared enemy of British imperialism and all its ways and works, was the last person they had expected that sort of thing from. By the time we had discussed for some little while I was looking at myself a little strangely. At the age of fifty I was questioning what from the time I had met it forty years before I had accepted and never questioned. I could be ribald about the old school-tie but the school itself had done me no harm. I hadn't allowed it to. I had read the stories of boys who had been unhappy at school. My Puritan soul had not been too sympathetic to them. But that there were people of my own way of thinking in the important things of my life who were utterly indifferent as to whether the boys in their old school or any other school sold games for money or not, that had never crossed my provincial mind. Where, I asked myself, would they want to send their own children to school? Where indeed? Not only they had to answer it. I too had to give some answer.

# PART TWO

# ALL THE WORLD'S A STAGE

—————

# 4

# *The Light and the Dark*

I LEFT school and had my year of cricketing glory. I headed the second-class averages with over seventy per innings. I never approached the same form again, and woefully disappointed all my friends. In over ten years I was once chosen for the North against the South. That is my score and biography, the frame in which all references to my own performances are to be seen.

That year I played for a new club called Old Collegians. We were a composite of the motley racial crew who attended the colleges, with one significant exception: only one white man joined our team, and he was a Portuguese of local birth, which did not count exactly as white (unless very wealthy). We swept through the second division, but at the end of the season the team broke up. With my excellent batting record, good bowling and fielding, admittedly wide knowledge and fanatical keenness, it was clear that I would play for one of the first-class clubs. The question was: which one? This, apparently simple, plunged me into a social and moral crisis which had a profound effect on my whole future life.

The various first-class clubs represented the different social strata in the island within clearly defined bounds. Top of the list was the Queen's Park Club. It was the boss of the island's cricket relations with other islands and visiting international teams. All big matches were played on their private ground, the Queen's Park Oval. They were for the most part white and often wealthy. There were a few coloured men among them, chiefly members of the old well-established mulatto families. A black man in the Queen's Park was rare and usually anonymous: by the time he had acquired status or made enough money to be accepted he was much too old to play.

The second club (in prestige) was Shamrock, the club of the old Catholic families. It was at that time almost exclusively white. At one time there had been a political upheaval and a bloody riot in the island. As part of the pacification, the British Government appointed a local coloured lawyer as Attorney-General. His sons were members of Shamrock.

I would have been more easily elected to the M.C.C. than to either. Constabulary, the cricket detachment of the local police force, was also out. I would have had to become a policeman, I did not want to become a policeman, and, in any case, in those days people with secondary education did not become policemen. The inspectorate was reserved exclusively for whites. Even the Constabulary team, all black, was captained by a white inspector.

Also excluded for the me of those days was Stingo. They were plebeians: the butcher, the tailor, the candlestick maker, the casual labourer, with a sprinkling of unemployed. Totally black and no social status whatever. Some of their finest players had begun by bowling at the nets. Queen's Park and Shamrock were too high and Stingo was too low. I accepted this as easily in the one case as I did in the other. No problem there. Two more clubs remained and here the trouble began.

One of these clubs was Maple, the club of the brown-skinned middle class. Class did not matter so much to them as colour. They had founded themselves on the principle that they didn't want any dark people in their club. A lawyer or a doctor with a distinctly dark skin would have been blackballed, though light-skinned department-store clerks of uncertain income and still more uncertain lineage were admitted as a matter of course.

The other club was Shannon, the club of the black lower-middle class: the teacher, the law clerk, the worker in the printing office and here and there a clerk in a department store. This was the club of Ben Sealey the teacher, of Learie Constantine the law clerk and W. St. Hill the clerk in a department store. Their captain was Learie's father, an overseer on an estate. He enjoyed such immense prestige that it didn't matter what work he was doing. This did not, however, apply to his children.

None of these lines was absolute. One of the founders of the Maple Club was Kenneth Gibson, a soccer forward who in my eyes remained unexceeded in natural gifts until I saw Stanley Matthews. Kenneth had a lifelong friend, old Q.R.C., a charming boy, well connected, a splendid player—but dark. Maple on principle didn't want him. Kenneth refused to play if his friend was not accepted. So in the end the very first Maple eleven that took the field included Kenneth's outsider. Genius is wayward. In later years Kenneth had a row with Maple and left them to play for another club, Sporting Club, whose foundation members ranged themselves between the lighter members of Maple and the dark Portuguese.

The reader is here invited to make up his mind. If for him all this is 'not cricket', then he should take friendly warning and go in peace (or in wrath). These are no random reminiscences. This is the game as I have known it and this is the game I am going to write about. How could it be otherwise? A dozen years after, just before I left Trinidad, I wrote the following as part of a political study of the West Indies.

'The Negroid population of the West Indies is composed of a large percentage of actually black people and about fifteen or twenty per cent of people who are a varying combination of white and black. From the days of slavery these have always claimed superiority to the ordinary black, and a substantial majority of them still do so (though resenting as bitterly as the black assumptions of white superiority). With emancipation in 1834 the blacks themselves established a middle class. But between the brown-skinned middle class and the black there is a continual rivalry, distrust and ill-feeling, which, skilfully played upon by the European peoples, poisons the life of the community. Where so many crosses and colours meet and mingle the shades are naturally difficult to determine and the resulting confusion is immense. There are the nearly white hanging on tooth and nail to the fringes of white society, and these, as is easy to understand, hate contact with the darker skin far more than some of the broader-minded whites. Then there are the browns, intermediates, who cannot by any stretch of imagination pass as white, but who will not go one inch towards mixing with people darker than themselves. And so on, and on, and on. Associations are formed of brown people who will not admit into their number those too much darker than themselves, and there have been heated arguments in committee as to whether such and such a person's skin was fair enough to allow him or her to be admitted without lowering the tone of the institution. Clubs have been known to accept the daughter who was fair and refuse the father who was black; the dark-skinned brother in a fair-skinned family is sometimes the subject of jeers and insults and open intimations that his presence is not required at the family social functions. Fair-skinned girls who marry dark men are often ostracized by their families and given up as lost. There have been cases of fair women who have been content to live with black men but would not marry them. Should the darker man, however, have money or position of some kind, he may aspire, and it is not too much to say that in a West Indian colony the surest sign of a man having arrived is the fact that he keeps company with people lighter in complexion than himself. Remember, finally, that the people most affected by this are people of the middle class who, lacking the hard contact with realities of the masses and unable to attain to the freedoms of a leisured class, are more than all types of people given to trivial divisions and subdivisions of social rank and precedence.'

I had gone to school for years with many of the Maple players. But I was dark. Left to myself I would never have applied for membership to the Maple Club. Some of them wanted me, not all subscribed to the declaration of independence of the Founding Fathers. The Maple cricket captain, concerned only with getting good men for his team, declared that he had no patience with all that foolishness and he was ready to have James in the club; also his brother was married to my mother's sister. He approached me in a roundabout manner: 'Well, I hear you want to join us,' he said with a big smile.

Other faces also wore smiles. When I was scoring heavily W. St. Hill had made it his business to come and watch me at the nets. He had told his friends that James could bat and was a coming man. Already whenever he and I met we used to talk. Similarly with Constantine Jnr. Though St. Hill and Learie said nothing to me, Shannon wanted me to join them and let me know it. My social and political instincts, nursed on Dickens and Thackeray, were beginning to clarify themselves. As powerful a pull as any was the brilliant cricket Shannon played. Pride also, perhaps, impelled me to join them. In social life I was not bothered by my dark skin and had friends everywhere. It was the principle on which the Maple Club was founded which stuck in my throat.

Interested paragraphs began to appear in the Press that I was joining this one or the other. Finally I decided to do what even then I very rarely did—I decided to ask advice. I spoke to Mr. Roach, Clifford Roach's father, a close friend, himself a brown man, but one openly contemptuous of these colour lines. He listened gravely and told me to let him think it over, he would talk to me in a day or two. (Clifford, as tens of thousands of English people know, was as dark as I am, but his hair was not curly and both his parents were brown.)

When Mr. Roach was ready he said: 'I understand exactly how you feel about all this God-damned nonsense. But many of the Maple boys are your friends and mine. These are the people whom you are going to meet in life. Join them; it will be better in the end.'

Not altogether convinced, but reassured, I joined Maple and played cricket and football for them for years. I made fast friends, I became a member of the committee and vice-captain of the cricket club. The original colour exclusiveness of the Maple Club has gradually faded out, but it mattered very much then, in fact it was my first serious personal problem. For that I did not want to be a lawyer and make a lot of money and be nominated to the Legislative Council by the Governor, that I preferred to read what I wanted rather than study statics and dynamics, those were never problems to me. They involved me in conflict with others. They cost me no inner stress. This did. If Mr. Roach had told me to join Shannon I would have done so without hesitation. But the social milieu in which I had been brought up was working on me. I was teaching, I was known as a man cultivated in literature, I was giving lectures to literary societies on Wordsworth and Longfellow. Already I was writing. I moved easily in any society in which I found myself. So it was that I became one of those dark men whose 'surest sign of . . . having arrived is the fact that he keeps company with people lighter in complexion than himself'.

My decision cost me a great deal. For one thing it prevented me from ever becoming really intimate with W. St. Hill, and kept Learie Constantine and myself apart for a long time. Faced with the fundamental divisions in the island, I had gone to the right and, by cutting myself off from the popular side, delayed my political development for years. But no one could see that then, least of all me.

The foregoing makes it easy to misunderstand the atmosphere in which we played. We never quarrelled. When we played scratch matches or went to the country on Sundays for a holiday game, Shannon, Maple and Stingo members mixed easily on the same side. They sent or came to find me for such games; I went or sent to find them. Where the antagonisms and differences appeared was in the actual cricket, the strokes, the length and the catches.

To begin with we all played on the same field. Except for the Queen's Park Club with its Oval, we all had pitches on the Queen's Park Savannah, one of the finest open grounds in the world, where thirty full-size matches can be played without crowding. The grounds of Maple, Shannon, Stingo and Constabulary were so close that you could stand on one spot and watch them all at practice. The wickets were coconut matting on hard clay. They were much the same for all four innings and on a well-prepared wicket the rise of the ball was fairly regular. But they took all the spin you put on the ball and there was always some lift. On the whole, against bowlers who could use it, the matting was difficult. No visitor ever made a century on it against Trinidad bowlers until 1930. In the Savannah, where the wickets were not so well prepared as at the Oval, there might be a canvas patch just where a good-length ball dropped; a strong breeze blew intermittently from the Dry River. Batting was a problem and fifty runs a triumph. Especially against Shannon, and most especially for a Maple batsman against Shannon. For the Shannon Club played with a spirit and relentlessness, they were supported by the crowd with a jealous enthusiasm which even then showed the social passions which were using cricket as a medium of expression.

Shannon opened their bowling with Constantine and Edwin St. Hill, both Test players. In time I opened the Maple batting with Clifford Roach, and I have looked with real envy on English batsmen who opened the England innings against Waite and McCabe of Australia on the monstrous billiard tables of the thirties. First change was Victor Pascall, for long years the best slow left-hander in the West Indies, who had visited England in 1923. Then might follow Cyl St. Hill, well over six feet, fast left-hand, his arm as straight as a post. When he dropped the ball on the off-stump it might straighten, to take the outside edge of the bat, or continue to the inside of your ribs. Cyril Fraser, genuine leg-spinner, sound bat and a brilliant field anywhere, would be welcome in most English counties today (though not in the thirties). I exaggerate? I do no such thing.

Take Ben Sealey. Ben made 1,000 runs with three centuries in England in 1933. He was fourth or fifth change for Shannon and took only fifteen wickets in England. On the matting wicket he took three steps, dropped the ball on the leg-wicket at medium pace and could hit the top of the off-stump three times in an over. The English team came in 1930. Ben had Hendren, Haig and Calthorpe in the first match for fifteen runs and, in the second, Sandham, G. T. S. Stevens, Townsend and Astill for thirteen in fifteen overs, nine of which were maidens. In the second innings he bowled nine overs, of which six were maidens, for one wicket. This was at the Queen's Park Oval where the wicket was of a better quality than in the Savannah. I stood next to the sightscreen and enjoyed the sight of these famous batsmen in the same mess as myself with Ben's leg-break. At their best, under their own conditions in the Queen's Park Savannah, the Shannon bowling and fielding would have made a shambles of most English counties then or now. In 1929 the bowling of the Trinidad eleven which won the intercolonial cup consisted of the six Shannon bowlers.

It was not mere skill. They played as if they knew that their club represented the great mass of black people in the island. The crowd did not look at Stingo in the same way. Stingo did not have status enough. Stingo did not show that pride and impersonal ambition which distinguished Shannon. As clearly as if it was written across the sky, their play said: Here, on the cricket field if nowhere else, all men in the island are equal, and we are the best men in the island. They had sting without the venom. No Australian team could teach them anything in relentless concentration. They missed few catches, and looked upon one of their number who committed such a crime as a potential Fifth Columnist. Wilton St. Hill chased a ball from slip to third-man as if he were saving the match and not a possible single. Except for the Constantine family, the patriarch, Old Cons, the always genial Learie and his benign uncle, Pascall, Shannon were not given to smiling on the field, and he was an utter nincompoop who was deceived into believing that the Constantine clan was not of the true Shannon toughness. They were not tough with you; they were tough with one another. I have seen Fraser signal for a glove and run to meet Ben Sealey who ran out with one. They met half-way, threw the gloves at ten yards distance, each catching with one hand; and almost before Ben was off the field Fraser was at the wicket ready to bat, while the ground rippled with applause. The crowd expected it from them, and if they lapsed let them know. Queen's Park were the big shots . . . and the great batsmen? They would bowl them out, and show them some batting too. As for Maple, with our insolent rejection of black men, they would show us. They usually did.

Sharp as were the tensions underlying a Maple-Shannon match, their sportsmanship was clean and good fellowship kept breaking in on the field of play. After all, Ben Sealey's family and friends were very close to mine. Sealey, Fraser and I went from sports ground to sports ground competing in athletics. I didn't run as they did, but I used to jump and for years beat them every time—no Shannon superiority there. Clifford Roach was an untalkative but cheerful soul. Whenever he, opening international batsman, and Constantine, opening international bowler, faced each other they had rare fun. I played two high-rising balls from Edwin St. Hill down in front of me. At the end of the over, without turning his head, the grim-faced Wilton St. Hill murmured as he passed, 'What you think you will get by playing at those!' Next over I dropped my bat out of the way of a similar ball and was weak enough to steal a glance at him. I was met by a stony stare. Later in the week, however, when we met casually, he gave me a long disquisition on the technique of playing such balls, illustrated with reminiscences of Challenor and other players. Challenor might leave one alone. If you bowled him another he got over it and cut through the slips.

Constantine, a privileged person, especially with me, between overs would discuss my play freely. 'You played back to that one?' 'What should I have done?' 'Jumped at it, of course. That's the second time Ben has been on since you are in.' 'Suits you.'

From a fast-rising ball he made one of his incredible back-strokes over mid-on's head. Mid-on, a very tall man, jumped and threw up his hand. The ball touched the very tip of a finger, giving the illusion of a chance. At the end of the over Constantine came over to me in a great wrath. 'That damned Hamid spoilt my stroke,' he complained. 'What did he interfere with it for?'

These were but moments. They were out to beat us, to humble us, to put us in our place. We fought back of course, but in ten years we beat them only once. In another game they had eighty to make, reached 70 for three and won by only one wicket. That day you would have thought they were the last of the Three Hundred at Thermopylae. Constantine had fallen seriously ill after the three-Saturday match had begun. He was looking on and when the eighth wicket fell crawled in to bat in ordinary shoes and clothes. He moved into the wicket to play back, but hadn't the strength to bring his bat down in time and I had him lbw first ball. David, the last man, a slow left-hand bowler, was so frightened that the next ball was in the wicketkeeper's hand before he had finished raising his bat. I have never forgiven myself for not bowling him neck and crop with a plain, straight, pitched-up ball.

Shannon! It is another of their credits that they bore me no ill-will for not joining them. Keen and devoted, they appreciated the same in me. Constantine told me one day, in the only reference he ever made to it: 'If you had joined us we would have made you play cricket.' He meant as an international player. The remark was a tribute to Shannon, not to me. Years afterwards, in a quite insignificant friendly match in Lancashire, I was standing at short-leg when some batsman played an uppish stroke in my direction. Not one county cricketer in three could possibly have got to it, and in any case friendly is friendly. So I thought, until I heard a savage shout from Constantine who had bowled the ball. 'Get to it!' I recognized the note. It was one Shannon player calling to another.

Shannon in the field was the best the island could show. Batting on the whole was not nearly so good. C. A. Wiles and André Cipriani batted finely for Queen's Park. There were players like W. St. Hill, Roach of Maple and Small of Stingo, whose play is sufficiently known. But no club had a line of batsmen like the line of Shannon bowlers. In all the clubs knowledge of the finer points of the game and of the latest developments abroad was pretty widespread, and in general the all-round standard, seen in perspective, was surprisingly good. Apart from intercolonial games, our players visited England in 1923 and 1928. The M.C.C. came in 1926 and 1930. We visited Australia in 1931–2. We could learn and compare.

The old Shannon Club of those days is a foundation pillar of this book. A man's unstated assumptions, those he is often not aware of, are usually the mainspring of his thought. All of Constantine's fierce and sustained attacks against the way West Indian cricket is managed stem from his Shannon experience. He believes that the real West Indies team should be a team that would play with the spirit and the fire, the spontaneous self-discipline and cohesion, of Shannon. With such a West

Indian side as he has always visualized he would throw down the gauntlet without fear to a world eleven of Graces, Bradmans, Ranjitsinhjis, Spofforths and O'Reillys. Between the wars he never ceased to argue with me that after Austin in 1923, the West Indies team being what it was, the captain should be a black man. I opposed him with the idea that the captain should be the best man. He was not concerned about the colour or social status of any individual. He was confident that such a team as he had in mind would make all types play the cricket he wanted, as confident as he was that Shannon could have made me into a good cricketer. The view of that great master of batting, George Headley, is not very different. Who would guess that George's ideal captain, the man he would have liked to play under, is Jardine? In the 1957 West Indies team there were players of a standard far above ours in 1919–32. I saw only one Shannon player and that for only one day—Gilchrist bowling and fielding on the first day of the Test match at Edgbaston. There is more in West Indies cricket than is dreamt of in contemporary cricket philosophy. No one could appear to play more gaily, more spontaneously, more attractively, than Constantine. In reality he was a cricketer of concentrated passion, irked during all his big cricket life by the absence of what he found only when he played with Shannon.

Shannonism symbolized the dynamic forces of the West Indies yesterday. I ask the question Gibbon first asked and so many historians have followed, and my answer is this: If by some unimaginable catastrophe cricket had been wiped away from the face of the earth the Shannon Club would have preserved cricket's accumulated skills, its historical traditions and its virtues,[1] uncontaminated by any vice and endowed with a sufficient vitality to ensure reconquest of the world. But there was racialism! So what? I am the one to complain. I don't. 'But racialism! In cricket!' Those exquisites remind me of ribaldry about Kant's Categorical Imperative: there was racialism in cricket, there is racialism in cricket, there will always be racialism in cricket. But there ought not to be.

I am, as I have said, quite convinced that the racialism I have described was in its time and place a natural response to local social

---

[1] It is so throughout the West Indies. George Headley who, behind his reserve, is a very human creature, likes a flutter. But as captain of a West Indian Test side, having to toss a coin against G. O. Allen, he found himself in a cold sweat of self-condemnation at spinning a coin on cricket. It took him some time to realize that he was not committing a breach of what had become an integral part of his personality, the ethics of cricket.

conditions, did very little harm and sharpened up the game. If I had the power I wouldn't alter one selection, one over of it. Yet I may as well deal with the racialist critics here once and for all. They are of two kinds.

There are the people who, having enjoyed the profits and privileges of racialism for most of a lifetime, now that racialism is under fire and in retreat, profess a lofty scorn for it and are terribly pained when you so much as refer to it in any shape or form. Their means have changed, not their ends, which are the same as they always were, to exploit racialism for their own comfort and convenience. They are a dying race and they will not be missed. They are a source of discomfort to their children and embarrassment to their grandchildren.

There is a less obvious fraternity. They not only understand but sympathize. When you delve into your own history they see in it a search for catharsis! You are getting the poison out of your system. Unsubtle self-adulation. Here Mr. T. S. Eliot will help. In addition to what all poetry gives, he is of special value to me in that in him I find more often than elsewhere, and beautifully and precisely stated, things to which I am completely opposed.

In *Little Gidding* he says:

> 'This is the use of memory:
> For liberation—not less of love but expanding
> Of love beyond desire, and so liberation
> From the future as well as the past.'

That is exactly what I do not think about these memories. They do not liberate me in any sense except that once you have written down something your mind is ready to go further. I do not want to be liberated from them. I would consider liberation from them a grievous loss, irreparable. I am not recording tragedy. I do not wish to be liberated from that past and, above all, I do not wish to be liberated from its future. Not me. Most of this book had already been written when it so happened that I revisited the West Indies after twenty-six years' absence and stayed there for over four years. Greedily I relived the past, every inch of it that I could find, I took part in the present (particularly a grand and glorious and victorious campaign to make a black man, Frank Worrell, captain of the West Indies team to Australia) and I speculated and planned and schemed for the future; among other plans, how to lay racialism flat and keep stamping on it whenever it raises its head, and at the same time not to lose a sense of proportion—not at all easy. I do not deny that there are memories, and West Indian ones, that I may wish to be liberated from.

> 'The conscious impotence of rage
> At human folly, and the laceration
> Of laughter at what ceases to amuse.
> At last, the rending pain of re-enactment
> Of all that you have done, and been; the shame
> Of motives late revealed, and the awareness
> Of things ill done and done to others' harm
> Which once you took for exercise of virtue.'

Eliot again. (Somewhat too much of Anguish and Anxiety and the other bathing beaches of contemporary philosophy—wash and be dirty.) Yet there were such and precisely because of the self-imposed limits of this book it would be a mistake not to remind occasionally of the spaces and depths it does not touch. But there are no retrospective agonies around the yellow sticks and the green grass and the shining sun, the heaving toil and passion which in the end did so little harm to anyone. Racialists, *au revoir*. We shall meet again.

Such were our first-class competition matches. There was a similar competition for the second-class clubs. Both were run democratically by committees with equal representation from all the clubs. The South ran a competition of its own. When intercolonial or M.C.C. games were due the Queen's Park Club invited about twenty-five players to practise at the Oval on afternoons and play trial games on weekends. George John, who was head groundsman at the Oval, would organize a trial game for any reason or none. There were games to welcome teams going out to play and games to welcome them back.

There was a Sunday competition and some who could not get away on Saturday afternoons would play in this. Many an old first-class club cricketer would come back to the game in these less-exacting Sunday matches. There were competitions in the country that were played on Sundays and some of our first-class players who lived in the country would play regularly in these. In addition, teams from Port of Spain were always going to the country to play. On the whole, we must have played about eight months in the year.

A scratch game was always played out with deadly seriousness until perhaps the end was in sight. The atmosphere associated with village cricket in England was quite foreign to us. I have seen a young player in a country scratch match hook Constantine four times to the boundary in a single over, while his father, a big, heavy man, stood swelling with such pride that I would not have been surprised if he had fallen in an apoplectic fit. Every little village in Trinidad comprising fifty houses had its recreation ground. They practised on afternoons and played their match on a Sunday. Often they would travel miles to play. It was always serious.

All this cricket was not enough for some of us. On a Sunday morning or Sunday afternoon, when the season was coming to an end or just beginning, we would wander up to the Savannah looking for a game. We would push ourselves into some scratch match or make up one ourselves. I ran into Constantine on an afternoon and we played a four-a-side match which turned out to be historic. By some accident of rain and sun and our empirical preparation, the matting wicket which we appropriated rolled out firm and absolutely true—the only one I have ever seen or heard of. We were playing single wicket and Constantine began by taking two steps and bowling slow leg-breaks. He increased to medium pace with half a dozen steps. He ended by running almost his full run and sending them down fast enough. No use. We made 167 for three. I was keeping wicket to help out (the fielders were only three), and I had a good view of a memorable innings. The batsman was a Chinese boy, Nathaniel, who studied medicine and became well known in the North of England where he practised. He was not a batsman at all but a wicket-keeper. This afternoon, however, he stuck out his foot, played at the pitch, and ball after ball hit the centre of the bat half-stump high. Nathaniel never got out at all and we had in the end to take pity on the great Constantine and his unfortunate pals and give them a chance. The real excitement, however, was to have experienced the perfect wicket we had heard so much about.

That is what made all this haphazard cricket so exciting. International and Test players were always in and out of it, the island being so small.

My own history in this respect is probably unique, but in those days not unusual. When I was about seven or eight my father took me to see him play in a match in Princes Town, and Joe Small played on the opposite side. My mother had close friends in St. Joseph, two miles from Tunapuna, and from the time I was fifteen they were always talking of one Ben who sang in the choir, played the organ, taught in Sunday School, starred in athletics and was a model citizen. This turned out to be Ben Sealey. In the vacation my Greek was polished up by our clergyman, the Rev. F. L. Merry, a Yorkshireman who lent me some yearbooks of the Yorkshire County Club. Cyril Merry is his younger son and Mr. Merry used to watch us playing and give a word or two of advice. I gave private lessons to Clifford Roach and even coached him at cricket a little, though he was rapidly able to coach me. On a Friday afternoon I might wander up to the Savannah early and run into Joe Small up from the South to play in the first-class competition the next day. We would decide to have ten minutes each before the others came. International cricketers are not as ordinary men. There might be only two boys fielding, but if you bowled Joe a half-volley outside the off-stump he hit it with all his force, though he would have to wait until the ball came back from 150 yards away. Then he would bowl at me for ten minutes. By this time it would be 4.20, the others would start to come, Joe would practise with Stingo, I with Maple, and the next day, Saturday, we might be opposed to each other. Achong, Roach and I played for Maple, practised together and played many a Sunday match. The two Grants, West Indies captains in 1933 and 1939, were both boys in my classes at school when I taught at the college and we played a lot of cricket together. When I taught at the Teachers' Training College Ben Sealey was at the Model School attached to it. I played for Training College against him playing for the school. I even touched the generation that came to maturity after I left. Victor Stollmeyer, brother of Jeffrey, was in one of the last classes I taught. He was a little boy of ten, handsome, very witty, lively yet well behaved, with an almost professional skill in persuading me to come and umpire or referee a lower-school match on afternoons when I had other plans. A boy in the class asked what were the names of the Three Wise Men from the East. Victor held up his hand and said he knew—their names were Gold, Frankincense and Myrrh. I never found out whether he was serious or not.

So it went. All of us knew our West Indian cricketers, so to speak, from birth, when they made their first century, when they became engaged, if they drank whisky instead of rum. A Test player with all his gifts was not a personage remote, to be read about in papers and wor-shipped from afar. They were all over the place, ready to play in any match, ready to talk. There was never a net at which you could not bowl to them if you could keep a length. If you couldn't you could always stand behind. It was one of our greatest strengths, why we have been able to do so much with so little.

There was a group of us, players and non-players, who saw every-thing, knew everything, talked about everything. We discussed with all the players, but I especially with Constantine. I played enough cricket to be able to argue technical points. I knew what had happened. I could quote books, papers and what other players had said. Constantine was always ready to argue and never (except once) used the argument that he had been there and we were only spectators. The only sign of petulance he ever gave was in a scratch match after some very heated arguments. Cecil Bain and I, his two chief controversialists, were on one side, he was on the other. He bowled us out first ball with as fast and as vicious inswingers as I have ever seen. We heard later that he had said, 'I abso-lutely have to bowl out those two for ducks.' It didn't help him one bit. We argued with him as much as ever. He must have got something out of it, for he was always game. Me it brought very close to the actual tech-nique of players in big matches. With our other international players it was the same.

As I look back, all sorts of incidents, episodes and characters stand out with a vividness that does not surprise me: they were too intensely lived. What is surprising is the altered emphasis which they now assume. A Chinese would land in the island from China unable to speak a word of English. He would begin as a clerk in a grocery store in some remote country district. He and others like him would pool their monthly salaries and turn by turn set up a small business in some strategic spot, usually in the midst of some village populated by Negro agriculturalists. These Negroes worked on contract. They were given a piece of land which they cleaned and cultivated. After five years they got so much for every mature cocoa tree, and then handed back the land to the owner. Naturally such a cultivator would be very hard up for cash, and very often by the time his five years were up he had pledged most of it to the Chinese shopkeeper. He, on the other hand, lived at the back of his shop, saved his money and in time sold not only foodstuffs but shoes and clothes and gadgets of all sorts. This often made for bad blood between the Chinese and his creditors. But this man, after about fifteen years, would be seized with a passion for cricket. He did not play himself but he sponsored the local village team. He would buy a matting for them and supply them with bats and balls. On the Sunday when the match was to be played he provided a feast. He helped out players who could not afford cricket gear. He godfathered very poor boys who could play. On the day of the match you could see him surrounded by the locals, following every ball with a passionate intensity that he gave only to his business. All night and half the day his shop was filled with people arguing about the match that was past or the match that was to come. When the team had to travel he supplied transport. The usual taciturnity of the local Chinese remained with him, except in cricket, where he would be as excited and as voluble as the rest. You could find people like him scattered all over the island. I didn't find it strange then. Today he and such as he are as intriguing as any of my cricket memories. I don't believe that, apart from his business and his family life, he had any contact whatever with the life around him except his sponsorship of the local cricket club.

Yet if you had asked me then, or for many years afterwards, where cricket stood in my activities as a whole, I would have without hesitation placed it at the bottom of the list, if I had listed it at all. I believe and hope to prove that cricket and football were the greatest cultural influences in nineteenth-century Britain, leaving far behind Tennyson's poems, Beardsley's drawings and concerts of the Philharmonic Society. These filled space in print but not in minds. This is heresy but a heresy which for years was not so much a heresy to me as a nonentity. Cricket was entertainment. Its physical and moral value concerned me not at all. If I stuck rigidly to its code it was because I had learnt it that way. To my house on personal subscription came a mass of periodicals from abroad. I have to give the list. Not only *The Cricketer*, but the *Times Literary Supplement*, the *Times Educational Supplement*, the *Observer*, the *Sunday Times*, the *Criterion*, the *London Mercury*, the *Musical Review*, the *Gramophone*, the *Nouvelle Revue Française*, the *Mercure de France*, for some time the *Nation* and the *New Republic*, the editions of the *Evening Standard* when Arnold Bennett wrote in it, and the *Daily Telegraph* with Rebecca West. I read them, filed most of them, I read and even bought many of the books they discussed. I had a circle of friends (most of them white) with whom I exchanged ideas, books, records and manuscripts. We published local magazines and gave lectures or wrote articles on Wordsworth, the English Drama, and Poetry as a Criticism of Life. We lived according to the tenets of Matthew Arnold, spreading sweetness and light and the best that has been thought and said in the world. We met all visiting literary celebrities as a matter of course. Never losing sight of my plan to go abroad and write, I studied and practised assiduously the art of fiction: Dostoevsky, Tolstoy, Tchekov, Flaubert, Maupassant and the Goncourt brothers, their writings, their diaries and their correspondence; Percy Lubbock and Edwin Muir; I balanced the virtues of Thackeray, Dickens and Fielding against the vices of Hemingway, Faulkner and Lawrence. Intellectually I lived abroad, chiefly in England. What ultimately vitiated all this was that it involved me with the people around me only in the most abstract way. I spoke. My audience listened and thought it was fine and that I was a learned man. In politics I took little interest. I taught at schools, but there were no controversies on education. I taught the curriculum. I didn't think it was any good, but I didn't bother about it. What now stands out a mile is that I was publicly involved only in cricket and soccer. I played both of them, but the playing was only the frame. I was a sports journalist. The conflicts and rivalries which arose out of the conditions I have described gripped me. My Puritan soul burnt with indignation at injustice in the sphere of sport. I had to be careful: papers, even sporting papers, live by advertisements. Our community was small. I fought the good fight with all my might. I was in the toils of greater forces than I knew. Cricket had plunged me into politics long before I was aware of it. When I did turn to politics I did not have too much to learn.

# 5

## Patient Merit

I HAVEN'T the slightest doubt that the clash of race, caste and class did not retard but stimulated West Indian cricket. I am equally certain that in those years social and political passions, denied normal outlets, expressed themselves so fiercely in cricket (and other games) precisely because they were games. Here began my personal calvary. The British tradition soaked deep into me was that when you entered the sporting arena you left behind you the sordid compromises of everyday existence. Yet for us to do that we would have had to divest ourselves of our skins. From the moment I had to decide which club I would join the contrast between the ideal and the real fascinated me and tore at my insides. Nor could the local population see it otherwise. The class and racial rivalries were too intense. They could be fought out without violence or much lost except pride and honour. Thus the cricket field was a stage on which selected individuals played representative roles which were charged with social significance. I propose now to place on record some of the characters and as much as I can reproduce (I remember everything) of the social conflict. I have been warned that some of these characters are unknown and therefore unlikely to interest non-West Indian readers. I cannot think so. Theirs is the history of cricket and of the West Indies, a history so far unrecorded as so much village cricket in England and of cricketers unknown to headlines have been recorded, and read with delight even in the West Indies.

George John, the great fast bowler, indeed knight-errant of fast bowling (we shall come to him in a moment), had a squire. This squire was not short and fat and jovial. He was some six foot four inches tall and his name was Piggott. Where he came from, what he did in the week, I do not know and never asked. He came every Saturday to play and was a man of some idiosyncrasy: Piggott never or rarely wore a white shirt, but played usually in a shirt with coloured stripes without any collar attached. He did it purposely, for all his colleagues wore white shirts. His place in history is that he was John's wicketkeeper, and never was fast bowler better served. Piggott was one of the world's great wicketkeepers of the period between the wars. He always stood up to John, his hands one inch behind the stumps, and if you edged or drew your toe over the line you were through.

I wish some of our modern batsmen had had the experience of playing Lindwall or Miller with a wicketkeeper's hands an inch behind the wicket. Something startled where you thought you were safest. Your concentration on John was diluted. Everton Weekes says he pays no attention to short-legs. He plays as usual, keeping the ball down as usual, placing it as usual. Long may his method flourish! But, with Piggott so close behind, ordinary mortals felt as if they were being attacked from front and rear at the same time.

He had a peculiar trick that was characteristic of him. On the rare occasions that John bowled on the leg-side, Piggott jumped sideways with both feet and pushed his legs at the ball, hoping to bounce it on to the wicket and catch the batsman out of his crease. (He was also credited with being able to flick a bail if the ball was passing very close to the wicket and might miss. But I never saw him do it and never heard of any authentic instance. The legend, however, illustrates his uncanny skill.) He may not have been quite so good at slow bowling, but I am inclined to believe that it was the constant miracles he performed standing up to John which put his other keeping in the shade. He was no Evans. He didn't fall five feet to the right or hurl himself like a goalkeeper to the left and scoop up a leg-glance with the tip of his fingers. He had less need to, standing where he did. In his own way and in his own style he was unique. In addition Piggott was one of the few comic characters I have known in West Indies cricket. He walked with shoulders very much bent forward and with a kind of hop. When he was excited he gabbled rather than spoke. He was apt to get upset when things went wrong, usually a catch or sometimes two in an over missed in the slips off John. At the end of the over John would stamp off to his place in the slips glaring at the offender, while Piggott ambled up the pitch peering from side to side over his bent shoulders, gesticulating and muttering to himself.

He was without the slightest doubt the finest wicketkeeper we had ever seen, and to this day I have not seen or heard of any West Indian wicketkeeper who surpassed him. No one ever dared to say otherwise. The sight of him standing up to John and Francis in England in 1923 would have been one of the never-to-be-forgotten sights of modern cricket. Yet, to the astonishment of all Trinidadians, when the 1923 team was selected he was left out and Dewhurst taken instead. The only excuse current at the time was the following: 'You can't depend on a man like that. Who knows, when you are looking for him for some important match you will find him somewhere boozing.'

It was untrue. It was also stupid.

The real reason could be seen in a glance at the Trinidad contribution to the 1923 side. John and Small (Stingo), Constantine and Pascall (Shannon). Piggott would have meant three Stingo and two Shannon. All would have been absolutely black. Not only whites but the Queen's Park Club would have been left out altogether. Dewhurst was a fine wicketkeeper, and he was recognized as such and praised in England. But it was a guilty conscience that made so many people say to me: 'And, by the way, everywhere the team goes they comment on our stumper—they say he is very good.' I knew that as well as anybody else. I read more English papers than they.

Poor Piggott was a nobody. I felt the injustice deeply. So did others. He was a man you couldn't miss in a crowd and one day at the Queen's Park Oval during a big match I stood and talked with him. Dewhurst, now firmly established as the island and West Indian 'keeper, was doing his job excellently as he always did. But as the ordinary people came and went an astonishing number of them came up to tell Piggott, 'You should be out there, Piggie.' 'If you had his skin, Piggie, you would be behind today.' Most of them didn't know him except by sight. Piggott was very good-natured about it. What is most curious is that to this day I don't know whether this superb cricketer was a tailor, a casual labourer or a messenger. Socially he did not register.

There was another player in the Stingo team who was of a different type. Telemaque was not a plebeian. He was a genuine proletarian, a shipwright or waterfront worker of some kind. He made good money, and was a member of a very independent workers' organization, one of the few in the island at the time. In 1919 the waterfront workers had upset the island for days with a strike which they tried hard to turn into a general strike, and Telemaque may well have been one of them. That he was a different type of man from Piggott was apparent in every line of his body and every tone of his voice.

Of the Stingo players, George John on the field rarely relaxed his concentration to talk to anybody. Piggott was ignored except by his team-mates. Small talked to everybody and everybody talked to him: Joe radiated good nature and self-satisfaction. Telemaque could laugh heartily at a joke, but he never introduced it, and when it was finished he was finished too.

He was not a great player, but he was good. His bat, quite often a little crooked, made a lot of runs, in sad contrast to mine which was always impeccably straight but somehow unproductive. Telemaque was also a safe catch anywhere and a useful medium-paced off-break bowler. He could easily have played for the island but he never did. One year his form was so striking that it seemed impossible for the authorities to leave him out. All of us in the Savannah were looking eagerly to see him chosen. One afternoon Hutcheon, the Maple captain, came up late to the ground and walked over to me. Hutcheon loved cricket and he loved words. The day Hobbs and Sutcliffe replied to Australia's 600 by making 283 without being parted we all followed it breathlessly, admiration and wonder growing hour by hour. When the day was finally over with the pair still undefeated, I met Hutcheon. He raised his hand in the air, shook his finger oratorically and said one word: 'Homeric!' He was a man of spontaneous phrase but this time I knew that all afternoon he must have been working at something suitable to this high occasion. He and I often exchanged phrases and expectations, and usually about cricket. This afternoon I could see by his manner that he bore not news but tidings.

He said only, 'They left him out, you know.'

'For Christ's sake! They left him out again!'

'They left him out. And his wife—she weighs 200 pounds—is sitting on a chair out on the pavement, crying because her husband isn't going to Barbados with the Trinidad team, and all the neighbours are standing round consoling her and half of them are crying too.'

With Piggott I was merely angry. This one hurt. I knew how all these people felt, and though Telemaque and I rarely talked, I liked the man.

When I saw him some days later I said to him, 'These —— left you out.'

He gave one of his rare smiles, fleeting, and for that reason, in his reserved face, of a singular charm. He had a very deep voice.

'These things—you know—well . . .' he said, and threw it into space with a brief upward motion of his hand.

He was about thirty-five and his last chance had gone. The moral pretensions of our rulers looked very small beside the unruffled calm of this dignified man. His lip was not stiff. It was merely firm, as it always was.

The case of Telemaque was very different from that of Piggott. I heard later that of his fellow waterfront workers, an independent lot, several were all ready to pay their own way to Barbados to see him play, and no doubt to fraternize and rejoice with their fellow stevedores in Barbados at this great honour which one of their number had conferred upon the whole. No wonder men and women stood in the street and wept. Plato and Pythagoras, Socrates and Demosthenes would have understood that these public tears expressed no private grief.

How much actual cheating was there? At this distance of time I would say, on the whole, very little. You have to make allowances for genuine differences of opinion, inevitable mistakes and the predilection for those people you know best. The primary cause was the consciousness of a small minority being pressed by an ever-growing number of players from among the black masses. The immediate cause was almost always the captaincy. The authorities needed always to have one white player as captain, and one or two others in reserve in case of accidents and as future candidates. They believed (or pretended to, it does not matter) that cricket would fall into chaos and anarchy if a black man were appointed captain. (By the grim irony of history we shall see that it was their rejection of black men which brought the anarchy and chaos and very nearly worse.) Because they had to safeguard these positions they could appoint only dependable selection committees. These, however, had to have a coloured man or two who would give a democratic colour to the manœuvre. Wherefore a Solomon of a selector, who once said to me, *sotto voce*, 'Explain to me, James, which *exactly* is the outswinger and which the inswinger?' It had obviously been troubling him for a long time. It is easy to imagine my rage and scorn and fury at such a selector.

In such questions the actual or relative quantity of misdemeanour is quite irrelevant. It is the surrounding atmosphere which converts misdemeanour into felony. I could have made an excellent case against the inclusion of Telemaque. Instead, in my innocence I simply could not accept that the Queen's Park Club had not given Telemaque his chance —didn't they know how people felt? It would have taken the captain of the club half an hour to drive over to Telemaque's house, give him the news in person and shake his wife by the hand. And yet I am not at all sure that they were not wise in their own day and generation. I was in the press-box at Brighton when the news broke that Hutton might be replaced as England's captain by the Rev. Sheppard. I saw Bruce Harris of the *Evening Standard* scribbling furiously, then take up the telephone and dictate a blistering protest to the London office for immediate publication. We were not so very backward in the West Indies of those days. I had written many such.

I repeat: There was not much in actual fact. Yet it is this web of jealousy and suspicion which surrounds the greatest tragedy of West Indies cricket history—the failure in England in 1928 of Wilton St. Hill. It is all over now and St. Hill died in 1957, but in him all the subterranean aspirations of West Indies cricket met and crashed, as they were later to meet in Constantine and soar. But before St. Hill we must make the acquaintance of the great George John.

# 6

## *Three Generations*

O N JUNE 28TH, 1900, in a match against Gloucestershire on the Bristol cricket ground, a West Indian bowler went to his captain and asked permission to take off his boots. West Indies captain Aucher Warner, a brother of Sir Pelham, asked him why; he replied that he could bowl properly only when barefooted. Woods was making the best response he knew to a truly desperate situation. Gloucestershire had won the toss and batted. Three wickets fell rapidly. Then Wrathall, followed by C. L. Townsend, followed by G. L. Jessop, all made centuries. Jessop hit 157 in an hour. The bowling averages make curious reading. Burton took five wickets for 68 runs in 25 overs. On the figures he was not hit. If Mignon's 33·3 overs cost 162 runs he had the satisfaction of getting five wickets, including those of the three century-makers.[1] One Hinds bowled three overs which cost 72 runs and if these figures from *Wisden* are correct I would dearly like to know exactly how that happened. The men who really got it were Ollivierre with 137 runs for 23 overs, and Woods with 141 runs for 33 overs. Ollivierre, however, was a batsman who headed the batting averages for the tour. Woods was a bowler and nothing else, so that his emotion prompting

[1] I paid a call on Mignon in Grenada a year or two ago. He was a bit shaky but very much alive. I asked him if he remembered how he got those wickets. He chuckled and said quietly: 'Yes, I do. I kept a good length.' I got the impression that he had sized up the situation and while the others had been prompted into all sorts of experiments, he had come to the conclusion that only length could weather the storm and had stuck rigidly to his length.

a return to nature can be understood. Aucher Warner promptly refused his request. Woods returned to the bowling crease. Jessop despatched his fast balls over the boundary, out of the ground, on to roof-tops. Woods made a last attempt. 'Mr. Warner,' he pleaded, 'let me take off one—just one and I could get him—just one, sir.' 'Out of the question. You can't do that here, Woods.' Dragging his feet, Woods had to endure this martyrdom, to the end encumbered by full armour.

The story is true, though perhaps of that higher order of truth which good fiction is. To West Indians it recalls the origin of many a fine bowler of sixty years ago. He came to the nets, often without shoes. He picked up the ball and bowled. In his *Cricket in Many Climes* Pelham Warner relates that he and his fellow Englishmen practised to these boys at the nets and found some of them definitely difficult. The Warners, the Austins, the Goodmans and the Sprostons took over the best of them, shod them and clothed them, and brought them to England. Woods was one of these. His nickname was Float, after a local delicacy, as an Englishman might be called Chips from fish-and-chips. Woods was a very fine fast bowler, and it is to be hoped that he did not take his misadventure with Jessop too hard. Most of the greatest bowlers of the day were wrung through the same mill, not once but many times.

The next generation of black men bowling fast was more sure of itself. In actual fact it produced the greatest of them all, George John. World War I interrupted his international career as it interrupted George Challenor's. These two, the gentleman and the player, the white batsman and the black bowler, were the two finest cricketers the West Indies had produced up to this time, and the most characteristic. John was a man of the people, and an emigrant from one of the most backward of the smaller islands. It is only recent political events in the West Indies which taught me that John incarnated the plebs of his time, their complete independence from the values and aspirations that competed in the spheres above.

The English public who saw him in 1923 and those Englishmen who played against him in 1926 do not know the real John. In 1923 he was already thirty-eight (some say over forty) and, despite his magnificent physique, he was already past his best. His greatest years were, I would say, between 1914 and 1920. He could bowl finely for years afterwards, but three-day cricket was, by 1923, too much for him. I was on the field with him and played against him many times, and the difference between his early years and the later ones was marked.

He was just the right height, about five foot ten, with a chest, shoulders and legs on him all power and proportion. With his fine features he was as handsome a man as you would meet in a day's journey. He was one of those rare ones, a fast bowler who proposed to defeat you first of all by pace and sheer pace. He ran about fifteen yards, a quick step or two first, a long loping stride that increased until near the crease he leapt into the air and delivered, his arm high. Unlike Lindwall, for instance, who seemed to need his arm low to get his thunderbolts. Thunderbolts they were. Read or talk to anybody who knew John and the opinion is always the same: 'One of the most formidable fast bowlers who ever handled a ball.' Even of the 1923 John and Francis, Mr. Pelham Warner wrote that he wished England had them to bowl against Australia, and in those days there were great fast bowlers in the land. I believe England in 1923 saw him only once as his real self—in the Scarborough match when he and Francis reduced a powerful England XI to six for 19 on a good wicket and (it is the considered opinion of too many to be ignored) would have bowled them out for less than the thirty-one they had to make but for some atrocious umpiring. That was the John we knew: pace and body-action off-break, and many a poor batsman hit on the inside of the knee collapsed like a felled ox.

I played against him for the first time in a competition match some time around 1921. It was an experience. After the first ball whizzed past me, I, a confirmed advocate of back-play, played forward, right forward at the ball in the air, with faith in the straight bat and the genius who presides over the universe. I caught sight of one ball outside the off-stump and let loose a drive to mid-off—it flew to the boundary behind point. Next over (it was five minutes before the end of play) I danced down the pitch to a slow left-hander, pushed out at him and was stumped by feet. I was congratulated for having 'stood up' to John. And I certainly didn't flinch. But my head was in a whirl and that was why I made the stupid stroke at the slow bowler. Statham is a splendid bowler and Trueman is a very fine one. But a fast bowler in the sense that John was a fast bowler I have seen only one—Tyson in 1954—and that is the type I will plump for every time, especially against modern batsmen. How I revelled in the accounts of Tyson's doings in Australia in 1954-5! I don't say John was the best fast bowler I have ever seen; that would be silly. But when I read of Tyson hitting the wicket with balls that did not touch the ground I recognized my John. If

Spenser is the poet's poet, John was the fast bowler's bowler.

Bowler John had to be seen to be believed. The whole of a powerful physique and a still more powerful temperament had been educated and moulded by the discipline required to hurl a batsman out and the result was a rare if not unique human being. Other bowlers can be qualified as hostile. John was not hostile, he was hostility itself. If he had been an Italian of the Middle Ages he would have been called Furioso. He had an intimidating habit of following down after the delivery if the ball was played behind the wicket. When his blood was really up he would be waiting to receive it only a few yards from you. A more striking feature of his routine was his walk back to his starting point. At the end of the day he strode back like a man just beginning. Almost every ball he was rolling up his sleeves like a man about to commit some long-premeditated act of violence. He was not the captain of his side, but I never saw his captain take him off. John always took himself off. If two batsmen made a stand against him John bowled until he broke it. Then he would take a rest, never before. The only sign of pressure was his taking a few deep breaths as he walked to his place at the end of an over. In between he did not seem to need air. Like the whale doing its business in great waters, he came up to breathe periodically. In a North *v.* South match during the middle twenties he had been overbowled all one day and it had become obvious that the man to get out the South was young Ellis Achong. This was agreed upon before the second day's play began. When the team walked on to the field John went up to the umpire, took the ball and measured out his run. Though the North captain was a member of the Queen's Park Club, one of John's employers and a famous cricketer besides, neither he nor anyone else dared to say a word to John, who was bowling the match away. So can a strong man's dedication subdue all around him. He was head groundsman of the Queen's Park Oval and he ruled there like a dictator. Once they actually had to fire him. But I believe they took him back again. He belonged to the Oval and the Oval belonged to him.

In the 1923 tour he was for one reason or another left out of some matches, in his opinion unjustly. He went and sat in a remote corner of the pavilion, ostentatiously avoiding his fellow West Indians, gloomily resentful, like Achilles in his tent. After a day or two of this Austin sent one of the senior members of the team to him. 'John, you don't seem very pleased with things.' John (he told me this himself) replied: 'What you complainin' about? I haven't said nothin' to nobody.' 'Yes—but your face——' John cut him short. 'My face is my own and I'll do what I like with it.'

When John was routed everybody talked of it, as people must have talked of Napoleon's defeats. He got into an argument with another intercolonial fast bowler named Lucas, at that time a man who had not played cricket for ten years. John's only argument was that Lucas was a has-been. Lucas therefore challenged him to a single-wicket match. Money was staked and ten of us agreed to field. John won the toss and batted first. He was not a bad batsman, he could hit hard and straight and he could cut, but he batted only because otherwise he would not have been able to bowl. This day the creaking Lucas bowled him a medium-paced off-break. John played and missed, the ball hit his pads and cannoned into the wicket. John had been dismissed for a duck. He rolled up his sleeves and sent down a terrible ball at Lucas. Lucas pushed out blindly, edged it for a single and John was beaten. The whole thing took two minutes. At moments like this you looked at John in a sort of terror, as if he were going to do something dreadful. He never did. I have seen him scowl at umpires, and grumble to himself, never anything else. I have never known him to get into any fight either on or off the field. Strangest of all, in the whirligig of time I have never seen this fierce and formidable man bowl a short ball aimed at a batsman's head, now dignified by the euphemism of bumper. His mentality was organized around the wicket, not the player.

One afternoon at a scratch match Joe Small lifted his 2 lb. 10 oz. bat and drove a half-volley so hard at John's feet that he had to skip out of the way. John bowled a faster one and Small made him skip out of the way again. It was near the end of play and what did we do? As soon as play was over we hurried over to walk in with the players just to see John's face. It was a spectacle. He wasn't saying nothing to nobody and his face was his own. Long after Joe told me that he hit those balls purposely back at John's feet to make him skip: he knew it would get him mad.

Yet he had his inner discipline, and it had been hard-earned. He described to me how he had beaten a great batsman all over the place only to see an easy catch dropped in the slips.

'I suppose you were mad as hell, John.'

'Me!' he said solemnly: 'Not me! When that happen' to you, you have to say, "Don't mind that, old chap," and go on bowling as if nothing happened.'

It was as if he had quoted a line of Virgil to me. He must have sensed my surprise.

'No,' he continued, 'you have to forget it at once, for if you don't it will stay inside and upset your bowling for the rest of the day.'

He had arrived at it by a road different from mine, but he had learned it well. This discipline, however, he reserved strictly for great occasions. In club games he did not disguise his always tempestuous feelings.

For some reason or other he hated Cyl St. Hill, the tall left-hander, and, in any case, he was always panting to dismiss the whole Shannon crew for nothing. I do him an injustice. John was always ready to bowl out any side for nought, preferably taking all ten wickets himself. This day he was bowling like the avenging angel, and had routed the powerful Shannon side, nine for about 38 (all nine to John), when Cyl, last man in, walked to the wicket. Cyl was no batsman. He was, as I have said, a very tall and very strong man. He was also a very determined one, and in all cricket, big as well as small, a little determination goes a long way. Cyl too was the type to say exactly what he thought of John, preferably in John's hearing.

First ball Cyl lashed out, the ball spooned up forty feet over the wicket and John had had all ten Shannon wickets, except that the wicket-keeper dropped the catch. Then came twenty glorious minutes. Cyl drove John through the covers to the boundary, a low humming hit. It was breast-high, but if you can hit hard enough there is a lot of room between gully and cover. He drove high and he drove low. He drove John straight back. When John shortened he cut him over the slips, but so hard that third man didn't bother to move. He hit him for a towering six to long-on, not too wide either. One or two went where they were not intended, but Cyl made as many as all the rest put together and Shannon, the invincible Shannon, finally reached seventy or eighty. Worst of all, I don't think John got the last wicket. When it fell he unrolled his sleeve and walked away as if he would never stop walking until he walked into the sea. Don't think he was defeated. Not he. He would put that away in his mind, and if you knew him well, and were wise enough to go to see him playing Shannon the following year, you would probably see Cyl bowled first ball for a duck, or his wicket shaved with a ball that only the skill of his famous brother could deal with so early in an innings.

John was one cause why I forswore umpiring, which I loved for the close view it gave. In a trial match one afternoon he bowled a ball to Dewhurst, who played back to it. The ball hit the pad and John appealed. Before I could say anything Dewhurst's bat caught up with the ball, played it away to cover and the batsmen ran. John appealed again. I said, 'Not out.' He glared at me and at the end of the over remarked to whoever was near, 'Some people think they know a lot about cricket, but as soon as something out of the way happen' they can't see it!' 'You had to be sharp to see that one,' etc., etc. I paid no attention to him.

Then minutes afterwards he said to me: 'That one was too fast for you. He was out before he hit the ball.' This was John's idea of a peace-offering. I was having none of it. 'You mean the ball hit his foot before he played it,' I replied. 'But he was not out. The ball pitched outside the off-stump.' He looked daggers at me and wouldn't speak to me for the rest of the afternoon. I was on tenterhooks. Suppose there was another appeal. John would not protest nor do anything out of the way. I had never known him to do that. But he would be angry, angry without compromise, and a man who can get uncompromisingly angry is one of the most effective works of God. I just didn't wish to get in the way of John's cricketing anger. In any other sphere of life I would simply have ignored him, but his cricket drew me like a magnet and in his complete dedication and disregard of all consequences I saw something of the quality which made the tragic hero, except that in John there was no tragic flaw. He was flawlessly intent on getting the batsman out and when anything went wrong he was flawlessly angry. I decided not to umpire when he was bowling. A few days after, we met and talked cricket as usual. I was a little apprehensive until I saw that he had forgotten the incident.

He would show me how he had got Hendren out at Lord's, how Hobbs turned his bat inwards and so avoided outswingers that moved away almost as they touched the bat, how A. E. Relf had told him after the last match in British Guiana in 1912: 'I would like to take this team back to Barbados now'—in Barbados Relf and his fellows had been badly beaten. He was always ready to talk and I to listen. At odd times, if I was down at the Oval early, he would bowl to me for a quarter of an hour, and it was then that I saw fully what a master of the bowling business he was. He bowled a comfortable medium pace, changing from off-break to leg-break at will. He bowled the ordinary top-spinner, and an off-break which was as near a shooter as to make no difference. His length was impeccable and if he corrected a stroke he could always bowl what was wanted for me to try again.

One afternoon in a cup match I batted for two hours against him for twenty-five runs, and when he finally got me out I was as exhausted as if I had made 225. When he finished me off he gave me a wide-eyed look and a brief 'Well played'. I don't believe he thought much of me as a player. One day, however, I really surprised him. He was umpiring at my end. I bowled two inswingers which the batsmen tried to glance and missed, and then an outswinger from just off the leg-stump which he tried to glance again. It bowled him middle-stump. John looked at me rather startled, and I saw for the first and only time a genuine respect in his eyes.

'You move them both ways?' he said, almost as if he couldn't believe what he had seen.

'Yes,' I replied, and continued to demonstrate it.

Of all the fine cricketers of the day, John more than any made me acutely aware that I was outside the pale of big cricket. He said nothing about it, and he was never nasty or sarcastic. Simply he had high standards and knew who was good and who was not. I just was not good and he saw me accordingly. St. Hill talked to me as one man to another. He was always sympathetic and often gracious. John was quite unsentimental and whenever I pulled a boner about some technical detail, or played a stupid stroke, his face registered a resigned look which I found quite depressing. However, I wrote admiringly about John, I knew a lot. So wherever and whenever we saw each other, even in town far away from the cricket field, he and I stood or crossed the street to talk.

John was a formidable fast bowler. He was more than that. He was a formidable man. He was said to be jealous of Francis, and indeed of all other fast bowlers, and he could be furious about articles in the papers. Yet he had an absolutely independent judgment of cricketers and I always found him reasonable in his opinions. 'Francis can bowl,' he would say, shaking his head slowly. 'That feller can bowl.' He would say it a little slowly and a little sadly: he regretted that when he and Francis were bowling together he was not the man he had been ten years earlier. If at times he was contemptuous about laudatory articles on Constantine, at other times he would tell me that if Learie settled down to it he could be one of the greatest of fast bowlers. I believe I was one of his few friends. People did not love John as they loved Victor Pascall. He was not a national hero as was Constantine and his father before him. He did not evoke the enthusiasm and excitement that surrounded Wilton St. Hill. He was respected as a cricketer of tremendous force, a cricketer and nothing else. He in turn seemed to have respect for no one except in so far as that person could bat or bowl or field. All the heart-burning about who should be or should not be selected never affected John. No selection committee in the world would have dared to leave him out of anything, and he didn't worry about anyone else. If I sounded him out on some flagrant case like Piggott's he didn't hesitate to say, 'Mr. Dewhurst, he can never keep like Piggie.' Having said it, he dropped the matter. He had cleared for himself a good space and he was quite satisfied with it so long as no one threatened to trespass. He was not Shannon. A sense of injustice, the desire to prove, was not evident in John at all. He was above that or below it. Yet in his utter rejection of all standards and interests except his own I see his fast bowling as stoked by more dynamite than there was in all the Shannon eleven put together.

Mr. Neville Cardus circumscribes his vision of Lancashire and Yorkshire professionals within the muse of comedy. Their West Indian counterparts would crack any such limitations like egg-shells. Everything they were came into cricket with them. It is my view of them that is partial. I met men like St. Hill and John only as cricketers. I never once invited them to my house, nor did I ever go to theirs. Only in England did I learn to break through the inherited restraints of my environment and by that time it was too late. What was John like in private life? He may have been a very mild man. I would have liked to know, though I do not believe it would have altered much my view of him. Errol John, the actor and playwright, winner of the *Observer* drama prize for 1957, is the son of George John. Except that he is not trained to the ounce, he is the living image of his father. George, Errol's brother, is a journalist accredited to the best established of West Indian newspapers; a quiet man, competent, modest and even mild. One day in 1960, during the Second Test match in Port of Spain, a West Indian fast bowler demolished the wickets of an English batsman. Instantaneously, to the amazement of those who knew him, George leapt from his seat, stretched out his arms and shouted, 'That is ball fa'der,' an expression in the local lingo meaning that the ball was so distinguished that it was the parent of all balls. Where-upon the son of his father sat down, once again part of the dignity and propriety of his fellow middle-class West Indians. Errol John is known to all his many friends and acquaintances as a delightful, pleasant fellow. I follow Sainte-Beuve in always looking very carefully at the blood relations of any remarkable individual I am studying. Thus I am fore-warned. When Errol speaks of his early struggles, and particularly of his plans for the future of drama in England and the West Indies, I listen and expect much from him. Behind the graceful exterior and modulated tones of the professional public figure I see always the shadow of his formidable father, rolling up his sleeves.

# 7

## *The Most Unkindest Cut*

WILTON ST. HILL. In my gallery he is present with Bradman, Sobers, George Headley and the three Ws, Hutton and Compton, Peter May and a few others. To them he is a stranger. But when he takes his turn at the mythical nets they stop to look at him and then look at one another: they recognize that he belongs. That, however, is what I have to prove. I am playing a single-wicket match on a perfect wicket against a line of mighty batsmen. But great deeds have been done under similar conditions. This is my opportunity to make history. Here goes.

W. St. Hill was just about six feet or a little under, slim, wiry, with forearms like whipcord. His face was bony, with small sharp eyes and a thin, tight mouth. He was, I think the expression is, flat-footed and never gave the impression of being quick on his feet. His first, and I believe his greatest, strength was judging the ball early in the flight. When in form he could play back to anything, including George John at his fastest. He never got in front in advance, but almost as soon as the ball was out of the bowler's hand he had decided on his stroke and took position. No one I have seen, neither Bradman nor Sobers, saw the ball more quickly, nor made up his mind earlier. Time; he always had plenty of time. From firm feet he watched the ball until it was within easy reach and only then brought his bat to it with his wrists. He never appeared to be flurried, never caught in two minds. With most of his strokes the only sign of tension or effort was the head very slightly bent forward on the shoulders so as to assist the concentration of his eyes riveted on the ball. But you had to be near to see that. I do not remember any more frightening sight at cricket than John running, jumping and letting loose at his terrific pace, and St. Hill playing back as if he had known he would have to do so long before the ball was bowled and was somewhat bored by the whole business. You felt that he was giving the ferocious John legitimate reason to hurl the ball at him or take him by the shoulders and shake him. In all his strokes, even the most defensive, the ball always travelled. I have taken people who knew nothing at all about cricket to see him and as soon as they saw this easy, erect, rhythmic back-stroke to the fast bowler they burst into murmurs of admiration. His right toe was always towards point, left elbow high and left wrist as a fulcrum.

Playing so late, he preferred to score behind point and behind square-leg. His famous stroke was the leg-glance. It is a modern fetish that long-leg makes this stroke only decorative and I was glad to see Burke's leg-glance in 1956 repeatedly beat long-leg standing on the boundary. For wizardry Ranjitsinhji's leg-glance, when he crossed the left foot over towards point and flicked the ball to fine-leg, comes first. St. Hill's leg-glance was of the same unnatural stamp. To a ball a little over the good length on the middle or middle-and-leg he advanced the left leg a short distance straight at the ball, so that if he missed he was lbw for sure. With the leg almost straight and his body bending slightly over it from the waist, he took the ball as it rose from the matting and wristed it where he chose towards the leg-boundary. From accounts and photographs it can be seen that Ranjitsinhji had to make a sharp twist of the body as well as the wrist. St. Hill bent forward slightly from the waist and flicked his wrist—that was all. He never followed round with the right foot. He put the ball where he pleased and John, being the finest bowler, was, of course, the chief sufferer. Describing his play in 1928, *Wisden* of 1929 says in one place that he showed fine strokes on the off-side and in another that he was strong on the leg-side. When Wilton was 'on the go' that depended entirely on the bowler. My negative memory may be at fault here, but I do not remember ever seeing a batsman standing straight, waiting for the shortish rising ball and as it passed flicking it between the slips. He didn't cut these down. He merely touched them and then pulled the bat away. That seemed sufficient to send them flying to the boundary.

The short fast ball of ordinary height he could get back to for a slash behind point, but he preferred to cut late. The finest of all his cuts was the late-cut off the slow bowler, to beat first slip and yet give third-man no chance. To save that four on a fast ground third-man would have had to stand on the boundary behind second-slip which would have been both ridiculous and useless. All that it would have meant was his running like crazy back to the usual position. One afternoon at the Queen's Park Oval in 1926 Percy Holmes, fielding at deep third-man and on the boundary behind the bowler, gave a great exhibition. St. Hill had him running now thirty yards for the on-drive and then the other way for the off-drive. But it was the late-cuts to third-man that gave Holmes the most trouble. He couldn't anticipate the stroke. We had a wonderful time with Holmes, asking him if he had ever seen in his life strokes like those. The little Yorkshireman never relaxed for an instant and chased each ball like a hare, but he had time and strength to talk to us and admire this superlative batting. Each time St. Hill made a stroke we could see Holmes smile as he ducked his head to chase the ball.

I never had enough of talking to St. Hill about this late-cut. In so far as it was explicable, his secret was that he never timed the ball from the pitch, as I have seen great batsmen do and get out. He did not lie back and lash across, as George Cox used to do. He didn't hammer the bat into the ground as Frank Worrell does (one of the great strokes of our time). He took up position early, watched the ball well on its way and then launched his wrists into the stroke.

This modern theory that the leg-glance does not pay is a fetish, first because you can place the ball, and secondly if you can hook then the life of long-leg is one long frustration. St. Hill did not hook by preference to long-leg. (None of us used the modern theory of getting outside the ball first. We faced the ball square so that if you missed it hit you.) He seemed merely to step inwards and swish the blade across the flight so that when it hit the ball it was pointing at the bowler. The ball went past the square-leg umpire like a bullet. If the square-leg boundary was blocked he might move over and, leaning towards point, flick over his shoulder. But there was no catch to long-leg. The ball dropped twenty or thirty yards from his bat. He was completely master of the on-side. He played the back-glance as well as his own special. To bowlers experimenting around his leg-stump he sometimes upset all calculations by waiting until the ball was almost on him and making a late on-drive, almost all right wrist with practically no follow-through. The ball went between mid-on and the bowler to the boundary, making monkeys of all the fieldsmen on the leg-side.

So far he was all grace, all elegance, always there long in advance. But there was a primitive hidden in him. If a fast bowler blocked his leg-glance—it was no use putting short-legs for he kept the ball down, *always*—or sometimes for no visible reason, all this suavity disappeared. He stretched his left foot down the wicket and, with a sweep that seemed to begin from first-slip and encompassed the whole horizon, smashed the ball hard and low to square-leg. Sweep is not the correct word. It was a swing, begun when the ball was almost within reach, and carried out with a violence that seemed aimed at the ball personally, to hit it out of sight or break it into bits.

One afternoon I bowled the first ball of a match which swung from his leg-stump past the off. He played forward at it and missed. Full of eagerness and anticipation, I let loose the next as fast as I could, aiming outside the leg-stump to swing into him. Out came his left foot, right down the pitch. He seemed to be waiting for hours for the ball to reach, and then he smashed it to the square-leg boundary. Root could get the ball to swing in British Guiana, and in 1926 he was at the height of his form. St. Hill made seventy-five for the All West Indies XI and when the players came back they told us that when St. Hill was batting, Root's short-legs were an apprehensive crew. They were concerned with him, not he with them. I have seen a bunch of short-legs cower when a batsman shaped at a loose one, but kept my eye on Tony Lock and saw him bend at the waist a little and face it. Time enough to dodge when he had seen the stroke. You couldn't do that with St. Hill's stroke because no fieldsman could sight the ball off that ferocious swish.

His off-drive to a fast bowler was of the same ferocity. He used to tell me that on the fast Barbados turf wicket all you had to do was to push forward and the ball went for four. He would outline the stroke and even though we might be standing in the street under a street-light, his left elbow, and even the left shoulder, would automatically swing over and the right wrist jerk suddenly and check. His body would be curiously straight, but the head would be bent over the imaginary ball and his eyes would shine. On the matting, with its uncertain rise, he put the left foot well over, the toe usually pointing to cover, not to mid-off. He took the bat so far back, at the end of the back-lift it was parallel to the ground with the blade facing the sky. From there he swung with all he had and smashed the fast ball through the covers. A minute later he would be standing almost as if back on his heels (with his head, however, slightly forward) playing the ball back along the ground to the bowler, often as if he were not looking at it. In moments of impishness he would move his feet out of the way, drop the bat sideways on the leg-stump yorker and disdain even to look at the ball racing to the boundary. But this I have seen him do only in friendly games, though I have been told that in earlier days he would do it even in competition matches, and Constantine, who played with him in the Shannon side for years, writes of it as a habit of his. One of his regular phrases in talking about a batsman was 'on the go'. He would say 'When Challenor is on the go . . .' or 'When Hammond is on the go . . .' For him batting began only when a batsman was 'on the go'. All the rest was preliminary or fringe. I have seen no player whose style could give any idea of St. Hill's. The closest I have read of is the Australian boy, Jackson, and perhaps Kippax.

His play has come to mean much in my estimate of the future of cricket. One afternoon, some time in the twenties, Griffith, the Barbados fast bowler, was bowling to St. Hill from the pavilion end at the Queen's Park Oval in an intercolonial match. Griff was bowling fast, and this afternoon he was almost as fast as John. The ball hit on the matting, and then, s-h-h-h, it plumped into the hands of the wicketkeeper standing well back. All of us noted the unusual speed. Griff was as canny then as he was in England in 1928, and in fact there could never have been a fast bowler who so disliked being hit and took so much pains to avoid it. Griff would not bowl short to St. Hill on the matting wicket: he knew he would be mercilessly hooked. He kept the ball well up, swinging in late from outside the off-stump to middle-and-off or thereabouts. The field was well placed, mid-off fairly straight, short extra-cover to pick up the single, deep extra-cover, deep point for accidents, the leg-side well covered. Griffith had his field set and he bowled to it. That was his way. He was as strong as a horse, he always bowled well within himself, and he would wait on the batsman to give him an opening. He didn't know his St. Hill.

St. Hill watched him for an over or two while we shivered with excitement tinged with fear. We had never seen Wilton up against bowling like this before and he was surely going to do something. (One thing we knew he would not do, and that was in any way hit across the flight of a pitched-up ball.) Soon he countered. With his left shoulder well up, almost scooping up the ball, his body following through almost towards point, St. Hill lifted Griff high over mid-off's head for four. Griff moved away a bit and then came back again to be sent hurtling over mid-off's head once more. He dropped mid-off back. St. Hill cleared mid-off's head again. *I am pretty sure he had never had to make that stroke before in his life.* But he was 'on the go' and if to remain on the go required the invention of a stroke on the spot, invented it would be. There, for me, is where a future for big cricket lies.

How comes it, then, that all this style and all this fire came to so little? St. Hill's record is not negligible. He made his centuries in intercolonial matches, against the M.C.C. team in 1926 and again in 1930. Lord Harris, who knew of George Challenor's form in England in 1923 and saw him at his best in the West Indies in 1926, said of Wilton St. Hill that year that he was the finest batsman in the West Indies and certain to be a great success in England in 1928. In England he was a terrible, a disastrous, failure, so that even now it hurts to think of it, the solitary painful memory of those crowded cricket years.

W. St. Hill was a very curious man of strongly marked character of which the defects belonged more to his time than to himself. He was born in 1893, of the lower middle class. The family was brownish, but Wilton was the lightest of them. By 1912 he was a great batsman and a universal favourite. He got a job selling in a department store, and I believe he worked there for the rest of his life. But this St. Hill was, as I say, not only an exceptional cricketer. He was an unusual man. I got to know him about 1916 and ever afterwards we used to talk. Even in my youthful days I could not miss his reserve (with sudden bursts of excitement, rapidly repressed as if he had made a mistake), his ironical outlook on life, his tight mouth and, when an issue was over and done with, the slight smile at the corners of his lips that belied the unchanging gravity of his eyes. In all the talk about who should have been selected and who was left out and why, I do not ever remember him saying a word. He may have done so to his more intimate friends—we were never intimate, though if I had been a member of his club I am pretty certain we would have been.

Macartney once scouted the mere idea that he was as good as Victor Trumper. Nobody was ever good as Vic, he laughed, you only had to see him walk. St. Hill with a bat in his hand had a similar quality. His smoking of a cigarette while John fixed his field was not mere youthful bravado and baiting of John, who was a man born to be baited. He smoked his cigarette because until he had to play the ball he kept himself removed from all routine details. Even when he was declining and as likely to get out as to score, as soon as he started to stride to the wicket everyone stopped what he was doing and paid attention. As he took guard, all the Maple players or the scratch team used to watch him in a sort of thoughtful silence and none more so than the Maple captain, Hutcheon, a cultivated man with a taste for the sharper contours of life and character. Fires burned in St. Hill and you could always see the glow. Whatever his form, whether he was out of practice or not, end of the season or the beginning, he played his own game, letting loose his wrists at the off-side ball and getting caught in the slips, or missing his glance and going lbw.

He was reported to be partial to what the late Aga Khan has defined as 'the good things of life'. On the field he was a martinet. 'Pull your socks up. Pull your socks up,' he would say between overs when things were going badly. Constantine Snr. was captain of the Shannon side, but he no more captained W. St. Hill than the Stingo captain did John. That very day that he asked me why I was playing at the lifting ball, Constantine was, as often with him, carrying out one of his experiments. The wicket was slow, he bowled me a short ball and I hooked him for four. This was always the signal for a recurrent blow and counter-blow. Learie bowled short, you hooked him round in dignity bound. But he now aimed to efface the indignity by tempting you to hook again and getting you caught at short-leg. In the same over he bowled short again and I hooked him round again. Then he tried what I presumed was intended to be a fast yorker, but it turned out to be a high full pitch and I would have hit that for four too, but I was almost in position for another hook and only got three. God, how angry St. Hill got! He obviously believed that I could hit Constantine for eleven in an over only if Constantine were playing the fool. At such moments he simply took over the side. 'Pull your socks up! Pull your socks up!' he hissed, took the ball at the end of the over, changed the bowler, rearranged the field and did the same thing at Learie's end the next over. Old Cons merely stood silent and watched, and Learie strolled off to cover.

John I understood. St. Hill I could never quite make out. His eyes used to blaze when he was discussing a point with you; but even within his clipped sentences there were intervals when he seemed to be thinking of other things, far removed. As early as 1921 I had an intimation which I never fully grasped until many years later when I was helping Constantine with his autobiography and he told me some of his own private thoughts. That year there was an intercolonial tournament in Trinidad, the first since 1912. Pascall bowled splendidly and St. Hill was in glorious form, making a century. When the tournament was over I wrote some comic verses about the devastating bowling of Pascall. The thing amused everybody. Great cricketers came from everywhere in the West Indies, from England and Australia, to play Trinidad, but Pascall bowled and they were sent away humbled. The last verse went as follows:

> 'And when to England back they reach
> And tread the sands of Dover's beach,
> And people crowd around to know
> The reason for their wretched show,
> A tear will shine in Hendren's eye,
> Jack Hearne will heave a bitter sigh,
> And Hobbs will shake his head and cry,
> "Well, friends, we made a decent try,
> Armstrong and Bardsley, Hearne and I,
>     But—Pascall bowled." '

One night that week I was paid a visit by a St. Hill follower. I knew him as one of those who almost every afternoon religiously watched Shannon practise, and came to the match on Saturdays to see Wilton bat, as nationalist crowds go to hear their political leaders. There were quite a few such.

He didn't beat about the bush. The article on Pascall, he called it the article, was fine. But what about Wilton? Couldn't I do something on Wilton? The man was in dead earnest. I said that of course I would, and he left satisfied. I was in a quandary. He didn't want prose, obviously. Much prose, including my own, had been written on Wilton's batting. A celebrated professor of philosophy had long ago established that what was not prose was verse. Verse it therefore had to be. But my antipathy to writing verse was far deeper than my antipathy to umpiring. The one I had acquired, the other was almost instinctive: you just didn't play with poetry, and I knew that comic verse was out. By ancient tradition sporting prowess should be celebrated by an ode, but a sonnet at least was limited to fourteen lines, and so with much misgiving I sweated out a sonnet to W. St. Hill which duly appeared in the next issue of the paper. At the critical ninth line it ran:

> 'O Wilton St. Hill, Trinidadians' pride,
> A century and four came from your bat,
> And helped to win the victory for your side,
> But more than that you did, yea, more than that.'

It is just possible that I may have written yes instead of yea. But yea, yea, nay, nay, what did it matter then, much less now? The watchful guardian of St. Hill's interests who had commissioned it sought me out and told me it was 'good'. My clique of literary friends who had laughed at the Pascall squib as not beneath a literary man were polite enough to mention that they had read it and passed on. They must have believed that I was serious about it, and in a sense I was. I let them think what they pleased.

It was the earnestness of my visitor which remained with me. Why should it matter so much to him? I think I know now what was being prepared. Wilton St. Hill had decided to go to England with the next team (his place was sure) and to stay there and play cricket as a professional. He would leave behind this selling of yards of cloth and ever more yards of cloth over a counter. In those days, at least, it offered little scope. He would finish with it and with the pressures which even on his own field, the cricket field, maintained a reserve which was more than natural. Ollivierre had done it for Derbyshire after the 1900 tour. S. G. Smith had done it for Northants after the 1906 tour. The story was that Small had been approached to qualify for Sussex (or Hampshire) after the war. But Joe refused. Through cricket, steadiness of character and a limited outlook Joe had made a place for himself that was quite satisfactory to him. St. Hill was a dissatisfied man. In the most animated conversation about John's off-break or J. W. Hearne's googly (Hearne had visited us in 1911), St. Hill, as soon as the discussion flagged, seemed to slip back into some private retreat where he lived alone. A member of my cricket clique once told me that he said to St. Hill, 'Maple would be glad to have a man like you.' The reply was instantaneous. 'Yes, but they wouldn't want my brothers.' His brothers were darker than he and had neither his reputation nor his poise.

He never said a word to me about all this, but his friends must have known. The sonnet he did not mention, though there may have been a shade more warmth in his smile when we met after it appeared. I was, of course, quite certain that he had nothing whatever to do with the request. He wasn't one who asked for anything. He continued to bat divinely. One afternoon I was walking in the country with a bat in my hand when I passed a shoemaker's shop with a few men gossiping by the door. I had gone some yards when the shoemaker himself came running after me, awl in hand. 'Excuse me, sir,' he said, 'but are you Mr. St. Hill?' I looked at the group by the door. All were watching intently. I had to say no, and he was sadly disappointed, as I was. I went back to talk. None of them had ever seen St. Hill, but they worshipped him. They knew my name and that I not only played but wrote in the papers. I told them what I thought of St. Hill's batting. Their enthusiasm boiled over. One said weightily: 'You know what I waitin' for? When he go to Lord's and the Oval and make his century there! That's what I want to see.' I have to repeat: It took me years to understand. To paraphrase a famous sentence: It was the instinct of an oppressed man that spoke. If further proof of this were needed it is the hostility with which anti-nationalists and lukewarm supporters respond to this now so obvious truism. As for those who believe that all this harms cricket, they should produce ways and means of keeping it out. They are blind to the grandeur of a game which, in lands far from that which gave it birth, could encompass so much of social reality and still remain a game.

Which brings me to a long but necessary digression.

Periodically, as I write, I find myself increasingly astonished at the peculiar mental habits of educated English people in the nineteenth and early twentieth centuries. Understatement can be a virtue, but overstatement is surely better than no statement at all. It took an Australian, Philip Lindsay, in a little book on Bradman,[1] published in 1951, to make me fully conscious of what I had always known about our cricket heroes and their worshippers in the West Indies of my day.

Lindsay is a writer who struggled from poverty and even 'pennilessness' to a success that, it seems, has satisfied him. I know nothing about him except this book on Bradman. His style in this book is antipathetic

[1] Phoenix House.

to me. Yet I shall quote extensively from it. For he says what I have not seen said anywhere else, but what was vividly present to my consciousness from the day I left school until I left the island. Perhaps these sentiments exist only in territories at the periphery? I thought so once but I know now that is not true and I shall quietly demonstrate it before I am done.

Lindsay records that in the spring of 1928 cricket in Australia was at a low ebb. Mailey and McDonald had 'deserted' it, one to journalism, the other to England. Gregory was doubtful and only Grimmett remained. Gloom descended over cricketing Australia.

'Yet while we talked, there was one name that often cropped up. Unfortunately, it was not the name of a bowler, a bowler being what we craved most, but that of a batsman. Any name, however, was needed to revive our shrinking egos and on that name we settled, about it we talked, we lovers of cricket, and had there been a god of the game to whom we could have prayed that lad's name would have risen from almost every home in Australia, freighted with a country's hopes, imploring heaven that he would not let us down but would carry to greatness the promise he had already shown.'

That lad was, of course, Don Bradman.

The thing went far beyond cricket. In Australia Lindsay was a struggling young writer who faced failure.

'Reading poetry and watching cricket were the sum of my world, and the two are not so far apart as many aesthetes might believe. . . .'

That has been exactly my experience. But to continue with Lindsay.

'Most of us need an ideal. Nor is it necessary for that ideal to symbolize one's particular ambition. An actor can prove to be the spur, rousing one's spirit to a realization of the greatness in mankind and the latent powers within oneself, but more often it is a work of art, the reading of a poem, the hearing of music, the sight of a great painting . . . and to me Don Bradman became that symbol of achievement, of mastery over fate, all the more powerful because it was impossible for me, a cricketing rabbit, to compare myself with him.'

He came to England and not only starved but hadn't even the money to see his idol play once in 1930. He had to read about it in the public library.

'That during those months of misery I did not lose faith in myself and abandon all hope of success by writing I must thank Don Bradman. That I never made that final desperate choice between hunger and ambition and pawned my typewriter, as often the devil gnawing in my empty belly prompted me to pawn it, I must thank Don Bradman. Not entirely of course. A man's resolutions are made of many promptings and dreams of hopes, but Bradman helped to keep my faith alight, and this association of myself with him as nearly of an age and of the same country made me feel somehow that I must not let him down as he had not let me down. Yes, sport can do that to a young man, to one of those despised inactive watchers so often attacked as being boneless sitters on their bottoms: it can stiffen the backbone and exalt the heart.'

Perhaps it is only we on the periphery who think this way. Perhaps. I do not know of any West Indians in the West Indies to whom the success of a cricketer meant so much in so personal a way. There may be some among the emigrants, but I know that to tens of thousands of coloured Trinidadians the unquestioned glory of St. Hill's batting conveyed the sensation that here was one of us, performing *in excelsis* in a sphere where competition was open. It was a demonstration that atoned for a pervading humiliation, and nourished pride and hope. Jimmy Durante, the famous American comedian, has popularized a phrase in the United States: 'That's my boy.' I am told that its popularity originates in the heart of the immigrant, struggling with the new language, baffled by the new customs. All his pains were transcended by the sight of young hopeful reciting *The Village Blacksmith* or Lincoln's Gettysburg oration, *civis americanus*, on the way from his log cabin to a house which, if not white, would at any rate be big. Wilton St. Hill was our boy.

The West Indies selectors left St. Hill out of the 1923 team. It did not come as a sudden blow. There were two or three trial matches. He failed in them and they left him out. If they had decided to ignore the trial failures not a soul would have said anything. But they left him out and it was as if a destined Prime Minister had lost his seat in the elections. He maintained his usual silence and it was not the sort of thing I would have raised with him. The blow shook him badly, he was a man of exceeding pride, and it is my belief that he never fully recovered from it. I expect that is one of the differences in temperament that make for success or for failure. As for us, his friends and admirers, that wound was never to heal.

This is what we believed. The great West Indian batsman of the day, before the 1923 tour, was Percy Tarilton, not George Challenor. Challenor was his superior in style, and the Barbados masses worshipped him. But Tarilton stood first in reliability and solidity. Next to these two was D. W. Ince, a white left-hander, also from Barbados. British Guiana had another white batsman, M. P. Fernandes. This was the traditional order, a line of white batsmen and a line of black bowlers. Joe Small had made for himself a place as a batsman which could not be denied. Joe was enough. They didn't want any more. Further, Joe was an inoffensive person. St. Hill was not in any way offensive. Far from it. But he was not friendly.

As we pursued our notes and observations after the dreadful event, some of us went further. We became convinced in our own minds that St. Hill was the greatest of all West Indian batsmen and on English wickets this coloured man would infallibly put all white rivals in the shade. And they too were afraid of precisely the same thing, and therefore were glad to keep him out. We were not helped by the fact that in our heart of hearts we didn't know exactly how good he was. We hadn't seen an English team since 1912, and it was only after Challenor's unqualified success in England in 1923 that we had reliable standards to go by. We terribly wanted to say not only to West Indians but to all England, 'That's our boy.' And now we couldn't. On performance Small rivalled St. Hill. But Joe never aroused the excitement that Wilton did.

We were neither mean nor vicious. If Challenor had failed to score in every innings of the trial matches we would have protested loudly against any idea of his exclusion. If through loss of form Challenor or Tarilton could have been included only by dropping St. Hill we would have made faces but we would have swallowed the dose. Furthermore, the case was not at all simple. Jamaica had to have so many, British Guiana had to have its share. We would have been hard put to it to say whom to leave out. We burnt our fingers badly in that very tour. Griffith had made his reputation as a fast bowler in 1921. Griffith had had a secondary education, called nobody mister except the captain, H. B. G. Austin, and had the reputation of being ready to call anybody anything which seemed to him to apply. When the team was selected Griff was out, and an unknown, a bowler at the Austin nets, had been chosen instead. To us it seemed that here was another flagrant piece of class discrimination. But the unknown bowler was soon to make himself known and never to be forgotten. In his first match against Sussex he took ten for 83, in his second against Hampshire, seven for 85, in the third against Middlesex, nine for 120. This silenced us and when the English newspapers came the chorus of praise showed that in preferring Francis to Griffith, Austin had made a judgment which should have its place in history, for in 1923 Griffith was very, very good, as good if not better than he ever was after.

Finally the man whom we chiefly blamed, H. B. G. Austin, could point to West Indies cricket and say with far more justification than Jack: 'This is the house that I built. I know what I am about. I chose young Constantine when on the record most of you would have left him out.' That was true. Few would have been surprised if Constantine had not been selected in 1923. But we were sensitized, on the alert for discrimination. In fact I was so upset and for so long that my friends pointed out to me that in my copies of the *Cricketer* I was underlining everything said against the West Indies team.

We had to shut up on Griffith. But St. Hill's omission remained in our minds. He recovered and in 1926, when the Englishmen came, he was, as we have seen, second to none in the West Indies. He scored heavily in the 1928 trials and came to England. The rest should be silence. He was a horrible, a disastrous, an incredible, failure, the greatest failure who ever came out of the West Indies. I have heard authoritatively that he would not change his style and he has been blamed for it. I don't think he could even if he had wanted to. He was not the type, and after 1923 something had hardened in him. In 1930, when the M.C.C. came again, the eagle had clipped his own wings at last. He stood up for four hours and made a patient century. An English commentator said he was very experienced and showed defence. Of course he had defence, he had always had it. But when he was 'on the go' it was the bowler who needed defence, not he. He died in 1957, and I was sorry I had not yet written this notice of him as I had always planned to do. I think he would have liked to read it. Who knows? He might even have said something about it.

One question will remain with every cricketer who never saw him: How good was he exactly? Doesn't your memory enshrine a striking figure with an enhancing haze? Perhaps. But I don't think so. Around about 1910 St. Hill was a boy of about eighteen. In those days Stingo was the club of bowlers, with George John and six other bowlers, all internationals or intercolonials, men with reputation and with records. Against them St. Hill played an innings of which nearly fifty years later Constantine writes as follows:

'He was smoking as he walked out; he took his stance, still smoking, glanced idly round the field, then threw away his cigarette. George John —also now gone to the "great divide"—one of the most formidable fast bowlers who ever handled a ball, thundered up at the other end and sent down a red lightning flash, atomic if you wish—but the slender boy flicked his wrists and the ball flew to the boundary faster than sound. The next ball went the same way. The boy batted from his wrists, he never seemed to use any force. I don't believe he had the strength even if he so desired. His was just perfect timing. Wilton St. Hill became famous later, but I never saw him or anyone else play a more heart-lifting innings than he did that day.'

Of an innings played in Barbados eighteen years after Constantine writes in a similar strain. Constantine played and bowled with Francis from 1923 to 1933, all over the West Indies, in England and in Australia. Never, he says, did he see any batsman hit Francis as St. Hill hit him, and this was in a trial match on which depended his selection for the English tour. We have heard Lord Harris. I can multiply these testimonies. I shall give only one more. Before their first-class season began the 1928 West Indies team played a two-day game. This is what *The Times* correspondent was moved to say:

'. . . W. H. St. Hill, who can be relied upon to provide the entertainment of the side. He is very supple, has a beautifully erect stance and, having lifted his bat, performs amazing apparently double-jointed tricks with his wrists and arms. Some of those contortions are graceful and remunerative, such as his gliding to leg, but some are unsound and dangerous, such as an exaggerated turn of the wrist in cutting. He will certainly play some big and attractive innings, but some others may be easily curtailed by his exotic fancy in dealing with balls on the off-side.'

How I treasure that notice: The critic had caught St. Hill's quality even in that brief innings. He stood beautifully erect and still and flicked the ball away like a conjuror. His apparently exotic fancies were exotic only when he mistimed them, as he did so often in 1928. Between 1910 and 1926 they were in perfect control by those amazing double-jointed wrists and arms and never more so than on big occasions. For the general, I can sum it up this way. No one batting at the other end could ever have overshadowed him. Of that I am quite certain, and of very few can that be said. It was against the finest bowlers, John, Francis, C. R. Browne, Root, that he was at his best.

For myself, I stick to the technical. He saw the ball as early as anyone. He played it as late as anyone. His spirit was untameable, perhaps too much so. There we must leave it.

# PART THREE

# ONE MAN IN HIS TIME

---

# 8

## *Prince and Pauper*

Aᴌᴌ that we did, thought and hoped for met and crashed in St. Hill. It was carried to the heights by Constantine. Even his countrymen know only the body and not the bones of his career. The rest of the world, England in particular, knows a great and original cricketer, a man of character, shrewd and genial; and, of late years, with a tendency ('rather a pity') to lay emphasis on racial discrimination. Circumstances placed me in a position to observe at its critical stages the development of one of the most remarkable personalities of the day. He belongs to that distinguished company of men who, through cricket, influenced the history of their time. Head and shoulders above all others is W. G. Grace. There is C. B. Fry, Ranjitsinhji, Lord Hawke, Sir Pelham Warner and Sir Donald Bradman. . . .

Constantine, of course, is a lucky man. But for the war, England would have seen Challenor, Tarilton, George John and W. St. Hill in 1913 or 1914. History would have been made. His cricket career, therefore, began at the right time for him, in 1921, and came to an end just at the right time, in 1939. He was lucky, too, in his ancestry. Evans reports a speech of Constantine's brother Elias as follows: 'I'se only hopes, Godfrey, that you happens to be bowling when I'se comes out to bat. Then I shall show you'se how I'se can hit 'em.' Where Evans got that from God only knows. I have never heard *anyone* in the West Indies speak like that. Elias must have been pulling his leg. I knew Elias well.

Another brother attended a secondary school where I taught him Latin and French, algebra and geometry. He played for the school team and was a magnificent boy batsman. Youth though he was, he put the length ball through the covers off his back foot in a manner that made me wonder at the injustice which allows one person to do without effort what others sweat in vain to achieve. He died young.

Constantine, as I say, had ancestry. He came from a good family. His father was an overseer on an estate, often, though not always, a white man's preserve. The job, however, was modest. On it he raised a family of fine children, and at the same time managed to maintain his form as an international batsman for a quarter of a century. It was no easy task. In those days black men were usually bowlers. The boat with the team to England in 1900 had left and 'Cons', as he was called, though chosen, had remained behind. Organization was not what it has become. He was not a rich man who could pay his own way. He was not a professional for whom everything had to be found. He had not gone because he couldn't afford it. People who thought he had gone saw him standing in the street. A public subscription was organized on the spot, a fast launch was chartered and caught the boat before it reached the open sea. Constantine Snr. scrambled on board to hit the first West Indies century made in England (st. Reynolds b. Grace, 113) at Lord's of all places. He made it against W.G., who took five for 56 in the first innings, and Stoddart, who could bowl—he took seven for 92 in the second. Constantine in the first innings went in at No. 8 and made 24 not out. The score was 132 for eight in the second innings when Burton joined him. They put on 162 in 65 minutes and W.G.'s 21 overs cost 87 runs.

Old Constantine was an independent spirit. Cricket must have meant a great deal to him. Yet when some dispute broke out with the authorities he refused to play any more. One who saw it told me how A. E. Harragin left the Queen's Park pavilion, walked over to where Constantine was sitting in the stands and persuaded him to come back. Few people in Trinidad, white or black, could refuse Bertie Harragin anything. He was an all-round athlete of rare powers, of singular honesty and charm. I would have accepted any cricket pronouncement of his at face value. (He was one of the very few white men in the island at the time who never seemed aware of the colour of the person he was speaking to.) Many years later a dispute between Old Cons, captaining Shannon, and the Queen's Park Club arose about an umpire. Old Cons did not want him.

The Queen's Park captain refused to change him. 'Then you can have the match,' said Old Cons, and led his team out of the Oval. On the cricket field the Constantines of Shannon met all other men as equals.

From the time young Constantine knew himself he knew his father as the most loved and most famous cricketer in the island. His mother's brother, Victor Pascall, was the West Indies slow left-hander, a most charming person and a great popular favourite with all classes. We cannot overestimate the influence of all this on young Constantine. He was born to the purple, and in cricket circles never saw himself as inferior to anyone or dependent for anything on anyone.

Constantine is not a pure Negro, if that term has any meaning. Any West Indian who took one glimpse at his father would know that somewhere in his ancestry, and not too far back, there was European blood. The Constantines, however, were black people. Off the cricket field the family prestige would not be worth very much. Constantine was of royal ancestry in cricket, but in ordinary life, though not a pauper, he was no prince. This contrast explains not all, but much.

I saw him for the first time about 1911, a thick-set, rather slow boy. He came to my father's school in St. Ann's, Port of Spain, for a short while. A mob of boys used to play 'pass out' in the school-yard. He was already known as his father's son. What I distinctly recall is that in the scramble for the ball he rather stood aside and watched. I did not know that already his father was coaching him and this rough and tumble probably did not appeal to him. My father's school was a Government school, non-denominational. Learie is a Catholic and he soon left to go to a Catholic school.

I lost sight of him for some years until about the early twenties, when I was playing first-class cricket for Maple and he for Shannon. He bowled at me in a match, fast straight stuff to which one could play forward comfortably. He began to get wickets, make a few runs and, above all, take some catches. Even to my interested eye he was full of promise, but not more. Major Harragin, however, was captaining Trinidad in the evening of his cricketing days. He knew a cricketer when he saw one and he probably could see much of the father in the son. Practically on his own individual judgment he put Learie in the intercolonial tournament of 1921. But for the Major's sharp eye and authority it is most unlikely that he would have got in so early. Apart from a wonderful left-handed catch in the slips, he did nothing unusual. (In his only innings he tried a mighty swipe at, I believe, his first ball and was caught at deep point for nought.) Thus the heir-apparent to his father was godfathered by the most respected and influential cricketers in the island. I have to stress this. From the very beginning he felt himself as good as anyone else. This was a West Indian black man, of the lower middle class, but a man conscious of status.

Now comes the second Constantine characteristic.

John, always belligerent, announced that when he met the new star in the club competition he was going to send his wickets flying and all turned up to see. (Some people had been making provocative comparisons between John and Learie.) Constantine has described the innings more than once—sixty-seven in an hour, composed of classic defence and the most brilliant strokes against fast bowling of the highest class on a matting wicket in the Savannah. More remarkable than the innings was what followed. Nothing followed. Constantine never played another such innings until 1928 in England. In England or Australia such a display would have marked him down as a rare batsman. He would have been selected as such in big games, coached as such, advised as such, made to feel his responsibility as such. Not so in the West Indies of those days and not so for Constantine. The innings was talked about for a while, then forgotten. Constantine put it behind him and went his own carefree way.

The innings against John was an explosion. Now follows another. He goes to British Guiana with the intercolonial team, does nothing to speak of with bat or ball, but, placed by chance at cover-point, by the end of the day emerges as one of the most brilliant covers ever seen in the West Indies.

The princely career continues. H. B. G. Austin, like Major Harragin, knew a cricketer when he saw one, and Constantine was one of his earliest choices for the 1923 tour. Constantine is now sponsored by the man who has more than any other made West Indies cricket what it is. In England he makes useful runs, gets useful wickets and Sidney Pardon calls him an 'amazingly good' cover-point. Mr. Pelham Warner arranges for him to be coached at Lord's. Hobbs tells him that he is yards faster to the ball than anyone he has ever seen; he gives him some hints on technique and finesse which Constantine stores for future use. He is a success, but he has not set the Thames on fire, and, what is more, he hasn't tried to.

He goes back to the West Indies. Although one of the first choices and always doing astonishing things with bat, ball or in the field, his actual performances in big cricket do not single him out in any way. Except for his fielding at cover, where he is now an admitted master. In fact in 1926 he was dropped from the first All West Indies XI against the M.C.C. in Barbados. No Trinidad selection committee would have dared to drop him in Trinidad. Again it was H. B. G. Austin who took him to British Guiana for the All West Indies side. Austin had just fielded out in Barbados to nearly 600 runs, he wanted a cover-point in the team and Constantine by this time had made himself into a cover-point such as no one had ever seen before. He now bowled very well, but he was not really fast. He might make runs or not, more often not. One brief episode, however, in 1926 remains clearly in my mind from the time I saw it to this day.

Late one afternoon he walked in to bat to the bowling of Hammond. Hammond bowled him a ball pitching a foot or so outside the off-stump, breaking in. Constantine advanced his left foot halfway to meet the ball and saw the break crowd in on him. Doubling himself almost into two, to give himself space, he cut the ball a little to the left of point for a four which no one in the world, not even himself, could have stopped. He tried it again next ball, but this time Hammond brought the ball closer to the wicket. He could get only two and was soon out.

What made us sit up and take notice was that he had never in his life made such a stroke before—that came out afterwards—and he had had no premeditated idea of making any such stroke. I do not remember seeing it again. He went in, there was the ball, and on the spur of the moment he responded. Every few years one sees a stroke that remains in the mind, as a single gesture of an actor in a long performance remains in the mind. (It is not always great batsmen who make them: I have seen two at least made by Freddie Trueman.) This one brought back vividly the innings against John. It stamped Constantine as a batsman who could do anything that he wanted to do. But after the Englishmen left he relapsed into his carefree batting. We used to beg him to settle down and bat. He simply wouldn't 'settle down'. When the news of his scoring in 1928 began to reach us we were startled enough, but nothing as startled as when we saw his first innings on his return. He had indeed settled down to bat, but in a manner peculiar to himself; every other stroke seemed an improvization of the type that had flashed before us in 1926. Nobody, not a single soul, had ever seen Constantine bat in the West Indies as he batted in England in 1928. This was the biggest explosion so far. He took 100 wickets, made 1,000 runs and laid claim to being the finest fieldsman yet known. He had changed. If the change had taken place in England it had been well prepared in the West Indies.

Constantine, the heir-apparent, the happy warrior, the darling of the crowd, prize pupil of the captain of the West Indies, had revolted against the revolting contrast between his first-class status as a cricketer and his third-class status as a man. Contrary to all other West Indian cricketers, his development was slow. An occasion presented itself and he added a cubit to his stature. That is the cricketer. That is his character as a man. The restraints imposed upon him by social conditions in the West Indies had become intolerable and he decided to stand them no longer.

Constantine did not explode without ignition. The spark was one of the most highly charged the game has ever known—no less a person than C. G. Macartney. Macartney was in England in 1928, admired the West Indians greatly and saw Constantine's possibilities. 'You hit those bowlers,' he told Constantine. '*Hit* them.' So urged, Constantine went in and hit them. That is where ninety-nine per cent of cricket anecdotes begin and end, which is why they appeal to so few except cricketers. We must look at what had been happening to Constantine off the cricket field.

On leaving school, he went into a solicitor's office to work at the usual small salary. He had a good elementary education, was bright and in time became a wizard on the typewriter. But for a man of his colour, despite his reputation and his father's reputation, there was no job. There were big firms who subscribed heavily to all sorts of sporting events and causes. Anyone of a dozen of them could have given him a job as a clerk. He would have earned his keep. The Constantine they recognized bowled and batted and fielded. He had no existence otherwise. There was the Government. He got an acting post in the Education Office. An acting man does not wish to imperil his chances by asking for leave. So that when Constantine was invited to British Guiana to play for All West Indies against M.C.C. he did not ask for leave. However, H. B. G. Austin, captain of the West Indies, wanted Constantine in his team in British Guiana and was able to get leave for him at full pay. Now H.B.G. was undoubtedly a big man in the West Indies. He was the son of a bishop of the West Indies, business tycoon, Senior Member for Bridgetown in the House of Representatives of Barbados, at one time chairman of the Barbados Board of Education, etc., etc. But there were some very big fish in our Trinidad pond. How came it that none of them could get leave for Constantine to play for the West Indies in the West Indies! The talk about regulations was all eyewash. Austin got the leave all right and with full pay. We looked and noted and swore impotently.

In time the vacancy in the Education Office was filled, not by Constantine. This was not the first time an acting appointment in the Government had ended in failure. Another one in the Registrar's Office had ended in nothing. Constantine, as many young athletes who were black, found refuge in the oilfields. Constantine's new employer was generous, as generous as he could be. But the oilfields administrative staffs were divided into two: white and very light-skinned, and dark. Beyond a certain limit dark could not aspire. Each section was provided with its own sports club and clubhouse.

The matter of no job for Constantine some of us took more seriously than he appeared to do (but we were wrong). If McDonald, the Australian bowler, could find no job in Australia after 1921, and so left Australian Test cricket to play county cricket in England, that, we thought, was all very well for Australia. They were established. We were not. Why in the name of heaven those who could have given him a job in town didn't do so remains beyond all reasonable comprehension. The people would have appreciated them for it.

Constantine was already a national hero, and the pride of the populace. And I was one of the populace. None more so. During the 1926 M.C.C. tour there was, as usual, grumbling about fast bowling aimed at the batsman. Constantine got into it because an English bowler bowled short at H. B. G. Austin. The old warrior (he was forty-eight) was very angry and said to Constantine, 'It is no accident; he is doing it purposely.' Constantine's cricket trinity were his father, H. B. G. Austin and Jack Hobbs. He would make remarks about Austin which showed that he saw him whole. But nobody was going to bowl short at Austin and get away with it in any match that he was playing in. He returned in kind. That was O.K. with me. But in the heat of things he let loose one or two that flew past Calthorpe's head, the Honourable F. S. G. Calthorpe, captain of the M.C.C. touring team. There was a buzz round the field. I was scared stiff, and at the first interval two or three of us went to Constantine. 'Stop it, Learie!' we told him. He replied: 'What's wrong with you? It is cricket.' I told him bluntly: 'Do not bump the ball at that man. He is the M.C.C. captain, captain of an English county and an English aristocrat. The bowling is obviously too fast for him, and if you hit him and knock him down there'll be a hell of a row and we don't want to see you in any such mess. Stop it!' He was rebellious, but we were adamant. He saw what we were driving at, finally agreed and loyally kept the ball out of harm's way.

Others were as watchful. Wilton St. Hill met me and said: 'You heard? Learie is injured playing football.' Yes, I had heard. 'That fool!' he fumed. 'What right has a man like Constantine to be playing football, you tell me!' He was terribly angry. I agreed. I hadn't seen it that way but I saw it now. All of us were looking to him to do great things, greater than had ever been done before.

A national hero must have a nation. The nation as it was could do nothing for the national hero except applaud. I am only guessing when I say that St. Hill decided to go to England and do his best to stay there. With Constantine I am sure. In his autobiography he tells how he made up his mind to do so well in the coming West Indies tour to England that he would be asked to stay. He chose fast bowling as his main weapon and began to develop pace and stamina. He had not hitherto been really fast for any great length of time. He could not be a fast bowler and a cover-point. By hours of labour on the slip-machine, gymnastic exercises and hard thought, he made himself into a slip fieldsman in no way inferior to the cover-point that he already was. No cricketer has worked at his cricket and studied it more than this so original and creative of cricketers. So much for the persistent illusion of West Indian spontaneity.

Cricketers are human. Here are Constantine's own words. Let him who can, separate the cricketing from the personal life.

'The team was chosen and we sailed for England in April. But before I describe that tour I must give a little piece of personal history. Cricketers, like other people, must live. My prospect of becoming a solicitor seemed more and more unrealizable. First I worked in a solicitor's office. Then I acted in the Registrar's Office, and again in the Education Office. The vacancies were filled and I was out of a job.

'It was Mr. H. C. W. Johnson of the Trinidad Leaseholds who gave me a fairly good job, took the greatest interest in my cricket, gave me leave whenever I wanted on half-pay, and when I finally left for

England told me that my job would be left open for me whenever I came back. He was a stranger to Trinidad and a South African besides.

'During my stay at Fyzabad, and finally at Pointe-a-Pierre with the Leaseholds, I did some hard thinking, and not only thinking but some acting too. I set to work at my cricket, and when the trial matches began I waited my chance and let go at George Challenor's off-stump. I had him edging and scraping and chopping down, and missing. I felt satisfied, the more so when Mr. Austin spoke to me that night.

' "Mr. Challenor says that you were as fast today as John or Francis at their fastest."

' "Mr. Challenor is out of form and——"

' "None of that nonsense, Constantine," said my old skipper: there was no fooling him.

'So the bowling was all right, so was the fielding. And the batting? I had made a few big scores between 1923 and 1927. To most cricketers in the West Indies I was only a swiper. But a few friends, among them Cecil Bain than whom there are few sounder judges of the game, used almost to beg me to settle down and bat. They insisted, as Pelham Warner pointed out afterwards more than once, that despite the big hitting, the essentials of my style (based on the coaching of 1923) were correct and that with a little restraint I could score.

'When I landed in England I was as fit a man as I have ever been in my life.'

The key words in this passage are 'a stranger to Trinidad and a South African besides'. What they hint at I have revealed. It is cricket history too, for I believe that if Constantine had had not only honour but a little profit in his own country he never would have settled abroad. True, one great chapter in the history of cricket would never have been written. Another might have been. We who knew his cricket from the beginning believed that in his own good time he would become such a batsman as the world had never seen before. It was not to be, and what was, was not less. The point is that what he did become was the result of personal choice arising from national neglect. Had his skin been white, like George Challenor's, or even light, he would have been able to choose a life at home.

So Constantine went off to Nelson in 1929 amidst mingled cheers and regrets at our losing him. I shared in the first and took no part in the second. It was years before I came to know the facts precisely, but I understood them in general; and I believed then, as I believe now, that if the West Indies cannot afford to keep their great cricketers at home they don't deserve to have them. All the shouting and patting on the back of 'our boys' doesn't mean a thing to me if it cannot be translated into a way of life for them.

Constantine returned to Trinidad often. Whenever he did we continued our discussions and arguments about cricket as energetically as before. Now, however, a new and inexhaustible topic was added—England and the English people. On this we did not argue. He was ready to talk, and I, my head full of English history, English literature, English periodicals, was ready to listen.

In the interval between the end of the season of 1931 and his departure with the West Indies team for Australia he exploded twice.

'I want to write a book. All these things I am telling you, they should be in print. The book could sell and make a lot of money.'

In 1931 cricketers who had not yet retired rarely wrote books. No one in the West Indies that I knew, cricketer or not, was writing books at all; certainly none was being printed abroad. I agreed that it was quite an idea. I agreed to do the actual writing. He began to talk more systematically and I to listen with a writing-pad on my knee. I had all the historical and statistical material in my house. We reviewed the whole of the past and came to terms with it. It turned out to be a preparatory operation. I happened to mention that I too was planning to go to England as soon as I could, to write books. Constantine thought for a second, then said:

'You come on to England. Don't put it off. Do your writing and if things get too rough I'll see you through.'

I accepted the offer, and we agreed to meet in England the following spring. The plans were as rapid in the making as in the telling. At the time he had, I think, dined at my house once. I doubt if his wife and mine had yet met. We didn't know it but we were making history. This transcendence of our relations as cricketers was to initiate the West Indian renaissance not only in cricket, but in politics, in history and in writing.

In March 1932 I boarded the boat for Plymouth. I was about to enter the arena where I was to play the role for which I had prepared myself. The British intellectual was going to Britain. About Britain I was a strange compound of knowledge and ignorance. Luckily, I knew it.

I had read all that it was possible for me to read. All my life I had known Englishmen, and West Indians who had spent years in England. Yet I had met no one, West Indian or English, who had views on which I could build anything substantial. For a non-white colonial to adjust his sights to England and not to lose focus is the devil's own job and the devil pays great attention to it. It is difficult enough today. It was far harder in the thirties. Professional men who had their training in England knew chiefly fellow students. People educated as I had been could move rapidly from uncritical admiration of abstractions to an equally uncritical hostility to the complex reality. Some coloured well-to-do who had been well received in England used their experiences there as a weapon against the backwardness of the local masses, against the arrogance of the English in the colonies and the local whites. Political passion easily submits all other values to its purposes. Reactionaries would hold up the English as models far above us. The incipient nationalists armed themselves with bombs for debunking. In all the drumming and fifing for England I could distinguish no order, no pattern. Constantine, as he came back home year after year, had been far the best. His advantages were many. He had no theory to expound, no abstract studies with which to square what he saw with his eyes and heard with his ears. He was on lunching if not on dining terms with cricketing members of the British aristocracy and big bourgeoisie. He knew cricket officialdom and the Press. He knew Lancashire well: mill-owners, professional men and the great body of the working people, among whom he had his closest but not his only friends. In other walks of English life he had intimates.

Of Constantine's England, however, I had been wary. I didn't know him very well. He had a point of view which seemed to me unduly coloured by national and racial considerations. Many doors in England were open to him. That doors were closed to other West Indians seemed more important to him. He weighed the relative prestige values of black men and Orientals, in relation to the English people and in relation to one another. Like most self-made men, and particularly black men whose life is passed among white people, he is always very conscious of who and what is before him. It is not improbable that he was telling me what I didn't know and ought to know. Long years before I had had an abrupt experience with him on this very topic.

It was just after the 1923 tour. Puritanical as ever, I continued to view with apostolic disfavour any departure from the most rigorous ethics of the game. I was then too naive to know that writers on sport, more particularly writers on cricket, and most particularly English writers on cricket, automatically put what was unpleasant out of sight even if they had to sweep it under the carpet. The impression they created was one of almost perpetual sweetness and light. (Those days, of course, are long past.) Against this background I was holding forth about some example of low West Indian cricket morals when Constantine grew grave with an almost aggressive expression on his face.

'You have it all wrong, you know,' he said coldly.

What did I have all wrong?

'You have it all wrong. You believe all that you read in those books. They are no better than we.'

I floundered around. I hadn't intended to say that they were better than we. Yet a great deal of what I had been saying was just that. Constantine reverted to an old theme.

'I have told you that we *won* that match. We *won* it.'

The conversation broke up, leaving me somewhat bewildered. 'They are no better than we.' I knew we were man for man as good as anybody. I had known that since my schooldays. But if that were the truth, it was not the whole truth. The year before I left, the internal contradictions of this seductive generalization had been laid bare. England went off the gold standard and some local patriots proposed that the Legislature vote a sum of money to send to the Chancellor of the Exchequer. Thus we would show our loyalty by helping to mitigate England's difficulties. An Englishman wrote a furious letter to the Press, denouncing the proposal. In England, he said, the children were getting free lunches, free rides to school, many children in the West Indies had no lunches and no schools. This started off an acrid discussion on the educational opportunities of children in England as compared to ours. As a lecturer at the Teachers' Training College, I knew the ratio of opportunity was somewhere about ten to one. If with all that they were still no better than we, then either we were very good indeed or they were very bad. To say that all we needed was the opportunity, was to say nothing. It was precisely the opportunity that only a few of us got. Time would pass, old empires would fall and new ones take their place, the relations of countries and the relations of classes had to change, before I discovered that it is not quality of goods and utility which matter, but movement; not where you are or what you have, but where you have come from, where you are going and the rate at which you are getting there.

Constantine was quite untroubled by all this and I didn't trouble him with it. His immediate responses were conditioned by his own experience. In a few short years he had met and faced successfully a host of new problems and new people. His sharp eye and native shrewdness, both trained in the demanding social relations of the island, had carried him through. To this day one of his most comical recitals, always richly enjoyed by both of us, is of various public situations in which he was suddenly projected, his watchful reserve, his cautious seizure of an opening, rapid retreat or advance according to how it developed, and, not infrequently, triumph out of what easily might have been disaster. For this, wit and shrewdness were necessary but not sufficient. He had deep convictions. Not simply that he was as good as anybody else—in his own particular field he was better than most. His 'They are no better than we' did not have a particular application. It was a slogan and a banner. It was politics, the politics of nationalism.

In that sense Constantine had always been political, far more than I had ever been. My sentiments were in the right place, but I was still enclosed within the mould of nineteenth-century intellectualism. Unbeknown to me, however, the shell had been cracked. Constantine's conversations were always pecking at it. The people of Trinidad were rougher in their methods.

By the end of the twenties the political situation in the island was developing rapidly. Captain Cipriani, a local white man, was an elected member of the Legislative Council. In that body the Governor had a firm official majority, able to keep the elected members quiet even if they sought to do anything more than talk. Cipriani, however, built a mass labour movement and as this grew so did his power in the Legislature. This was *real*. I was caught up in it like many others and began to take notice. In this troubled situation a distinguished scientist at the Imperial College of Tropical Agriculture foolishly took it upon himself to write an article proving that Negroes were as a race inferior in intelligence to whites. I wasn't going to stand for that and in our little local magazine I tore him apart. I had merely done what seemed to me a routine job, but tinder was around. Students at the Training College spoke to me about the controversy with sparks in their eyes. People stopped me in the street. The article, I discovered, had travelled far and wide. Spending a seaside weekend in the company of a local member of the Executive Council, he learnt that I had the article with me and asked me to read it to him. He listened with what struck me as unusual care, approved of it and let drop a remark or two which he refused to amplify. He had said enough for me to divine that this purely literary dispute on the relative intelligence of races had been judged of sufficient importance to occupy the attention of the Governor in Executive Council. These folks were nervous.

Fate, inspired by the people, conspired to drag me away still farther from Flaubert and C. B. Fry. I gave lessons in English to the —— consul in Trinidad. Most of the time we talked about European history. He was strong on Bismarck's policy towards the East, I on imperialist intrigues resulting in the partition of Africa. He passed disparaging remarks on the colonial policies of Great Britain; I pointed out the similarities with those of his own country. We had a good time and he told me a lot about diplomacy that isn't written in books. After a while we talked quite familiarly. Without due preparation he shifted a conversation to local politics and Captain Cipriani. He was an intimate friend of the Governor and I was at once on my guard. Suddenly he asked me, 'What do you think would happen if the Government arrested Cipriani?' Like a flash it hit me that this step was being discussed in the circles he frequented. 'Arrest Cipriani!' I said, with all the surprise I could summon. 'Why, the people would burn down Government House.' He was impressed with my certainty. I enlarged on some details and invented others. I dropped my strongest card as an afterthought. 'They did it before, you know. Oh, yes, they did. The Governor some years ago provoked them. They rioted, burnt down the Government buildings, and the Governor, Sir Alfred Maloney, escaped from the Legislative Chamber only by disguising himself as a woman.'

The consul seemed to be suitably impressed and I left with the strong impression that he would urge restraint. Cipriani, at any rate, was never arrested.

I began to study the history of the islands. I collected *Hansards*, old White Papers, reports of Royal Commissions. There were plenty around which nobody wanted. It was all very simple and straightforward. For background I had the Whig interpretation of history and the declarations of the British Labour Party. For foreground there were the black masses, the brown professional and clerical middle classes, the Europeans and local whites, Stingo and Shannon, Maple and Queen's Park. My hitherto vague ideas of freedom crystalized around a political conviction: we should be free to govern ourselves. I said nothing to anyone. After all, I was working for the Government. When I told my brother some of my ideas his only comment was: 'You will end up in gaol.'

As I prepared to leave for England, I had to decide what to do with the stuff, very good stuff and new. Cipriani was a national hero. I would write a biography of him and incorporate the material. I went to see him and he agreed cordially. So he too talked and I listened with my writing-pad on my knee.

Some obscure but powerful logic had been at work. I was now on my way to Britain with these two manuscripts. To prepare one I had to review the whole cricket history of the West Indies to date. To prepare the other I had to do the same with the political history. To the activities of two very practical men I had brought literary facility, wide reading and a by now ingrained habit of seeking order, logical sequence, development, perspective, in any group or mass of facts. I was idealistic but no longer naive. The worlds I had explored with Constantine and Cipriani looked very different once you got inside. It was possible to write only a portion of what had been discussed, and that always with caution.

At any rate, as soon as I reached England I would begin to shed these ties. I would listen once more to Constantine with my pad on my knee until that book was finished. I would publish *The Case for West Indian Self-Government* under its West Indian title, *The Life of Captain Cipriani*, and send it back to the West Indies. Then I would be free to get down to my own business. I had a completed novel with me. But that was only my 'prentice hand. Contrary to accepted experience, the real *magnum opus* was to be my second novel.

I landed in Plymouth and ran around London for a few weeks. My money began to give out and Constantine suggested that I come up to Nelson and stay with him as the first step to sorting out my future. Up to that time I doubt if he and I had ever talked for five consecutive minutes on West Indian politics. Within five weeks we had unearthed the politician in each other. Within five months we were supplementing each other in a working partnership which had West Indian self-government as its goal.

# 9

## Magnanimity in Politics

THE mechanics were simple enough. The people in Lancashire had an inordinate appetite for asking Constantine to come to speak to them, most often in church and similar organizations. It was something of a strain on him, but he was always ready to oblige. He began by taking me along to say a few words and soon substituted me whenever possible. By the winter we were in full cry all over the place. Sometimes I was paid and the money was useful. Money or no money we went along. The public meetings were only an extension of the private ones. Besides the people who came continually to the house, whenever we went to have high tea the topics were two: cricket and the West Indies. From my school debating-society days I had never had any difficulty on the public platform and here was an audience eager to listen to whatever I had to say.

The truth was that Constantine by his cricket, by the demeanour of himself and his wife in what all could realize was no easy situation, by 1932 had created an enormous interest in the West Indies and West Indians. Most people were hazy about both the islands and the people. The majority, or at least a great many, thought the West Indies had to do with India. In the park, preparing for a speech that night, a very friendly little boy came up to me, sat on my knee and asked me where was my spear. The children were always intrigued at our unusual appearance and often came up to make acquaintance. Wherefore one evening

Mr. Mayor, overflowing with goodwill, told my audience that when he saw Mr. Constantine and Mr. James with the children he knew . . . I cannot remember the phrase but it was to the effect that we were as human as the rest of them. We put all of that right. So much so that a Lancastrian who had visited the West Indies used to go round telling people: 'All of them are not like Constantine and James. All of them are not like Constantine and James.' Correcting this error, I fell into another one. My reputation as a speaker on this subject spread quickly and some months later I was asked to take part with five distinguished persons in a series on the B.B.C. commemorating the centenary of the abolition of slavery. I heard afterwards that Richard Hughes, the author of *A High Wind in Jamaica*, had been approached first; it turned out that Hughes had never been to the West Indies at all and so I was asked: such were those days. I visualized my audience as people who had to be made to understand that West Indians were a Westernized people. I must have stressed the point too hard, in fact I know I did. Colonial officials in England, and others, began their protests to the B.B.C. almost before I had finished speaking. I countered with a detailed reply of many thousand words which I circulated far and wide. The battle was joined. Constantine and Norma, and many friends and acquaintances in the North of England, listened to the broadcast. Daughter Gloria was allowed to stay up to hear. When I saw Constantine afterwards he was very, very pleased.

That year in Nelson was a year of growth for both of us. He would sit on the platform listening to what he already knew or had heard many times before with the attention of a man hearing it for the first time. For years he must have been longing for someone to do the job which so badly needed doing. There might have been something of an edge to me on the platform, particularly at the beginning. As far as I could see no one ever resented it. If they did there was always Constantine's reassuring presence and a few pleasant and graceful words at the end. Seasoned with a cricketing metaphor or two, they were always uproariously welcomed and put us all back on the home ground. One evening, as soon as I was finished, the chairman rose after applause and said, 'Bless my soul if Mr. James isn't as good at this business as Learie is at his.' The audience responded with a deep hum of approval. It is at such moments you know that old bonds have been cut away and new ones put in their place.

We were educating thousands, including ourselves. Those were the first days that we talked about West Indian politics and began to exchange and to clarify ideas. I discovered his abiding ambition—to use his reputation and the financial competence it gave him as a means of advancing the cause of the West Indian people. He obviously liked me and appreciated my devotion to cricket and admiration of his own play. But his offer to help me was at bottom based upon the fact that he saw in me a West Indian who would do credit to the West Indies abroad.

I would not be surprised if it was at this time that the idea began to take root in Constantine's head, to flower later, that he would use his reputation some day to spread the type of information that occupied us. Neither he nor I had any illusions about the fact that I was travelling in his orbit. As a professional cricketer, he kept out of politics. I was not so bound. I soon made friends in the local Labour Party, attended their meetings, spoke to them. Some of Constantine's intimate friends who came to the house often found congenial company in me, apart from cricket. My Labour and Socialist ideas had been got from books and were rather abstract. These humorously cynical working men were a revelation and brought me down to earth. Learie listened sympathetically, commenting with discretion but laughing a lot. I read some of my manuscript on *The Case for West Indian Self-Government* to him, and told him that I wanted to publish it. With his customary absence of hesitation he said: 'Go ahead. Find out what it will cost and I'll pay. When you sell the copies at home you can pay me back.' The book was published in Nelson; my Labour friends made merry with it. A few people did raise their eyebrows. Constantine pursued his previous way, refusing to be affected one way or the other. Some members of the cricket-club committee were Conservatives. They held their peace and Constantine held his. The book went to the West Indies and was a grand success. When the letters and the notices came Constantine and I rejoiced. Where exactly we were going with all this we didn't know, but we were on our way.

West Indian history now began to assume a new importance. Stuck away in the back of my head for years was the project of writing a biography of Toussaint Louverture—the leader of the revolt of the slaves in the French colony of San Domingo. This revolt and the successful establishment of the state of Haiti is the most outstanding event in the history of the West Indies. I had not been long in Nelson before I began to import from France the books that I would need to prepare a biography of Toussaint. I had no money at all and most of that summer there hung over me the shadow of what I was going to do to earn some, and when. It was cricket, which I had discarded, that came to my rescue.

Sidney Barnes, nearly sixty, played in a league match in Nelson and I went down to see him play. I was profoundly impressed by him, both as a cricketer and as a man. Coming home that evening the old journalistic spirit stirred in me and I wrote down an impression of Barnes in some 1,500 words. I showed the article to Constantine and he told me to send it to Neville Cardus. Constantine knew him well and told me to write as a friend of his. All I asked was that Mr. Cardus should recommend to me a provincial paper which might publish the article. Much to my astonishment, Mr. Cardus replied that the *Manchester Guardian* would publish it. Also he would like to see me when next I was in Manchester. I went, we talked and he told me that he wanted someone to deputize for him when he was engaged otherwise, or there was more than one match which the paper wished fully reported. He thought I would fill the post adequately. Would I be interested in it? I was. He told me to see him again at the beginning of the season; he was confident it could be arranged. So, Sesame! Presto! I had a job, and a good job. I could now look forward with some confidence to the future I had planned. I could relieve Constantine of the burden of supporting me. I could even think of some time repaying him the now considerable sums he had already spent on me. I thought of it even if I did not get much further. *Multum gaudium in castris.* There was much rejoicing in our camp. He had sponsored me and I had got an entry into one of the famous newspapers of the world.

Through the writings of Neville Cardus the *Manchester Guardian* held a unique position in the journalism of cricket. But Constantine more than anyone else would know that, though at the time I had seen but one first-class match in England, I was highly trained and would be able to hold my own. The article on Barnes was useful in other ways. It advertised me for more talks on the West Indies. People who had paid little attention to me before now asked Constantine to bring me round. I was not proud. He and I or I alone went and we talked cricket and the case for West Indian self-government. The case did not have to be forced upon them. They wanted to know.

Earlier I used the term West Indian renaissance. I use it in its literary sense. Constantine's *Cricket and I* came first. To the general it was merely another book on cricket. To the West Indians it was the first book ever published in England by a world-famous West Indian writing as a West Indian about people and events in the West Indies. *The Life of Captain Cipriani* was abridged and published for English readers by the Hogarth Press under its real title, *The Case for West Indian Self-Government*. The abridgment was done in Nelson and I travelled up and down from Nelson to London to make all the arrangements for the publication. The project on Toussaint Louverture, embarked upon in Nelson, was carried through in time. Even my forgotten novel saw daylight. The publisher of my other book heard me talk about it, asked to see it, and published. It was the first of the West Indian novels to be published in Great Britain. Henceforth the West Indies was speaking for itself to the modern world.

Some years later the Trinidad workers in the oilfields moved. They were followed by masses of people in all the other islands, closing one epoch in West Indian history and opening another. One Government commentator, in reviewing the causes, was kind enough to refer to the writings of C. L. R. James as helping to stir up the people. The chief of these was the Nelson publication. These books did more. I continually meet middle-class West Indians and students who say this: When the upheavals did take place these books were high on the list of those few that helped them to make the mental and moral transition which the new circumstances required. At such times literary values are not decisive. There must be new material, new in that its premises are the future, not the past. I have shown the circumstances in which the material was produced. Others may be able to separate from these circumstances cricket and a great cricketer. It should be obvious that for me this is impossible.

All these discoveries and excitements had one disastrous consequence. They ruined Learie's batting for nearly a whole season. Despite the objective circumstances, I believe that the responsibility was largely mine. I was adjusting myself to British life. I was reading hard. Night after night I would be up till three or four. I must have seriously discommoded that orderly household. Often I was abstracted and withdrawn. Literature was vanishing from my consciousness and politics was substituting itself. That was no easy transition. There hung over me for part of the time the great question mark: How was I to earn my living? I committed the unpardonable ingratitude and ill-manners of taking or leaving Learie's cricket as the mood suited me, a violent contrast from my attitude at home. It must have hurt him deeply. Matthew Arnold still had possession. In the book on self-government, throwing every brick to hand at the arrogance of English colonialism, I had indicted the English as a whole of being an unintellectual people.

'Schopenhauer, at dinner in an inn every night, put a gold coin on his table before he began and when he finished put it back into his pocket. The waiter was moved to ask him why. "Do you see those English officers over there?" said the philosopher. "The first night that they speak of something else besides women and horses this gold coin is yours." But the waiter never got it. They spoke of women because they were officers, but they spoke of horses because they were Englishmen. If anyone happens to meet fairly frequently any group of Englishmen, even of university education, he will find that as a rule they dislike civilized conversation and look with suspicion, if not positive dislike, upon anyone who introduces it into their continual reverberations over the football match, the cricket match, the hockey match or the tennis match. How often one meets an Englishman, who, though not a sportsman, tries to make it appear as if he is or has been one.'

The particular target I aimed at was the staff of the Queen's Royal College. The college master who talked more about cricket than I did in the common-room had not been born, if he has been born since. But truth is many-sided. This is what I read to Learie and he paid to print it. At best I could have cut it out. My only excuse is that I firmly believed it.

If I was occupied I might not even go to see a Nelson home match. The damned legal profession shoved its nose in to complicate matters further. It wasn't me this time. Constantine still had his mind set on becoming a lawyer. To enter an Inn he would require a Senior Cambridge Certificate and I began to give him lessons. He wanted these lessons and I was anxious to give them. (That I forced them upon him is a slander.) What with one thing and another, and the disruptive presence of a strange personality in the house, I believe, for the first and only time in all his long years in league cricket, Learie began the season badly and for many weeks could not score. It was a horrible business. He would come back home on Saturday evening, cheerful and taking his failure in good part, too good a part. Norma watched him anxiously. The friends came around that evening or the next day to talk it over. Jack, a municipal worker, was a real comfort. He did not commiserate; neither did he go into whether the ball had kept low or jumped high. 'Nelson needs a new professional,' he would announce on entering the house. Shaking his head from side to side, he would pontificate, 'Norma, your old man is getting down,' all the kindness in the world beaming behind the solemnity of his face. Constantine would perk up at once and the chaff would begin to fly. After half an hour Jack would leave, he and everyone else in wonderful good humour. But, as weeks passed with no change, you could see that Learie was faking it. On Saturday he would leave home full of confidence, by Saturday night it was the same old story. It seemed as if all Nelson and half of Lancashire had nothing else on their minds but Learie's batting failures. He knew that every person he passed in the street thought of it as soon as they saw him. 'Well, it happens to the best!' 'That's cricket, you know' can wear pretty thin in time. I came in for my share of the condolences. Early one week Learie took leave and went off to spend a few days with friends in Nottingham. No use. The lessons discontinued and never began again. Constantine, of course, was worth his place for bowling and fielding and strategy alone. But the carefree batsman of the Trinidad years was no more. He came out of it in the end and I shall always remember Norma's smiling face and shining eyes when he began to score as usual. Jack was his usual contrary self. 'Not a bad innings,' he would say, 'though I have seen better.' And the match would be lived over again. Jack specialized in stories of who had said what and when, around the ropes and in the pavilion or the pub afterwards. The whole episode opened a window into the life of a professional cricketer, especially a league professional. There can be raw pain and bleeding where so many thousands see the inevitable ups and downs of only a game. Learie maintained on the whole an equable front, but I saw him inside. I knew what it did to me.

I used to go around with him, playing friendly and exhibition matches. One afternoon I took some wickets and scored some runs. The club we were playing told Learie to ask me if I would be their professional at £3 10s. a week. I badly needed some money, and I loved to play cricket. But my reply was instantaneous: 'Who? Me! To go out there to bat, knowing that they have paid me, and to make nought. No, thank you!' The words were out before I reflected that there were other aspects of the proposal which needed consideration. If Constantine had told me that I ought to take it I would have agreed. Instead he burst out laughing, could barely stammer, 'O.K., O.K., I'll tell them,' before he was off laughing again, all the time looking at me as if he had never understood that aspect of me before. I expect he was not displeased to see that I respected the responsibilities of a league professional.

Life in Nelson was not easy and could not be otherwise. Apart from someone who went around collecting refuse in an old pushcart, Learie and I were the only coloured men in Nelson. That meant wherever you went (and you had to go somewhere) and whatever you did (and you had to do something) you were automatically under observation. Constantine lived the life placidly enough, but at times he would just pick himself up and on the slightest excuse go off to the anonymity of London, or even Manchester. There had been prejudice at the beginning, but by 1932 the Constantine family were Nelson citizens. When he finally decided to leave, all Nelson asked him to stay. He had conquered the hearts of the Nelson people. That story is sufficiently known. What is not known is that the Nelson people conquered him.

Early one morning a friend turns up, has a chat and a cup of tea and rises to leave. 'Norma, I am just going to do my shopping. If you haven't done yours I'll do it for you.' Later Constantine said to me, 'You noticed?' I hadn't noticed anything. 'Look outside. It is a nasty day. She came so that Norma will not have to go out into the cold.' It was the way he said it that struck me.

We did not lack for friends. Some of the best friends a man could make I made during my first weeks in Nelson. Friends could not prevent instances of prejudice or, worse still, what might or might not be prejudice. We could not get rid of the feeling that whatever we did would be judged as representative of the habits and standards of millions of people at home (and goodness knows where else). You had to be mobilized so as to keep a steady head and not be betrayed into foolishness. The unobtrusive gestures of concern and affection undermined your watchfulness. You were being disarmed. The scepticism in Learie's tone and a resigned look in his eyes indicated that by 1932 the process of disarming was far gone. When the war came in 1939 he stayed. In a national broadcast just before he finally left for home in 1954 he explained that he had earned his living in England and when the country was in trouble he was not going to run out. He phrased his decision in terms of playing the game. That was much, but not all. The league crowds, the

people of the North, all sorts of people all over England, had been generous to him. Together he and Lancashire had had some wonderful years.
But if he had never made a penny in England he would still have stayed.
And by now, almost second nature, as a West Indian in England and a
very distinguished West Indian, he would not flinch from any role which
he thought it his duty to fill. Generous by nature, it is this sense of responsibility which explains much that is inexplicable and sometimes vexing
even to many of his best friends in England.

His sponsorship of me expressed an attitude which appeared in large
things as in small. I turn up in Nelson to say good-bye before I leave for
the United States. I am dressed in my literary-political grey flannels and
sports jacket. Constantine takes one look at me and says, 'You cannot
go to the United States that way.' I protest in vain. 'I know the United
States. It wouldn't do.' He is in his dressing-gown, but he runs upstairs,
dresses and comes down. 'Come on with me to the Co-op.' There he
stocks me out so that I do not know myself. When I am finally dressed
to leave he takes an approving look at me, but is not satisfied. 'Wait,'
he says, and he runs upstairs and comes back with a most expensive camera
in a Newmarket case and straps. I can do as little with a camera as with
an aeroplane. No use. He puts it across my shoulder and is at last satisfied. He wants me to look well because he wishes me well. Nevertheless,
at the back of his mind is the idea that as a representative West Indian
I must be up to mark in the United States.

When I was in Nelson there was an intermittent stream of requests
for help from West Indians, some from people (brown) who at home
would never have asked him to dinner. He and Norma would go over
the pros and cons with a scrupulousness that astonished me. A West
Indian who had made large sums of money in the restaurant business
during the war and spent it freely on political and social causes was in
danger of failing for a sum amounting to thousands of pounds. The
Constantines came to the rescue. When I heard of it the repayment of the
money was in doubt and Constantine does not throw his money around.
Norma said simply, 'We couldn't see —— go down,' and the calm
manner of this gracious woman implied that if the money was lost it was
lost in a good cause. It is the same spirit which motivated his book of
protest against racial discrimination. People have asked me why Constantine, who, of all persons, has been so well received in England, should
show what seems to be such an obsession with racial prejudice. The query

reflects badly on the imagination and public spirit of those who make it. Constantine wanted to use his great reputation in order to clear a road for others. He knew their difficulties, difficulties which his special gifts had enabled him to overcome. The book bowled some wides and quite a few no-balls. That did not matter. It brings home to a lot of people much that they would not have known otherwise but for his name on the cover. His opportunities were greater and he no longer had the responsibility of keeping out of politics.

The Constantine I met again in 1953 was a very different man from the one I had first got to know in 1932. Then we spoke often of 'The Englishman . . .', 'The English . . .', 'In this country, people . . .' After twenty-five years in England that was in the background. Instead he spoke of 'The Government', 'The Colonial Office'. The differences between the 'they' who in 1923 were no better than 'we' seemed to concern him not at all, or very little. 'They' had been narrowed to the sources of power and those who exercised it. I doubt if he was aware of the change.

During the war he served as a welfare officer for West Indian workers in England. He received an M.B.E. from the Government and an illuminated scroll from the men he worked with. About the scroll he held forth to me with more pride than I ever remembered hearing him speak of his cricket feats. When he stopped playing professional cricket he settled down to his long-cherished ambition, passing the Bar examination. It was not easy for one who had done no serious study for thirty years. I looked for his name in the lists more than once and failed to see it. After another disappointment I called him up and commiserated with him. I thought I detected weariness. 'You are not going to give it up?' I asked. He perked up. 'Who? Me! Not on your life!' 'Same as on the cricket field,' I said. 'Ab-so-lutely the same.' That was enough for me. My fears vanished. Next time he came through and set off for the West Indies to take the welfare job he had at first refused.[1]

I have preferred to conclude at once this sketch of his public career thus far (with such personal characteristics as would help to illuminate it). That is because I do not wish any distraction when I discuss his years in the Lancashire League. About this there has been too much froth and too little fact.

[1] Constantine has since gone into West Indian politics. Nothing said here is in any way to be connected with his present political position, attitude and associates. C.L.R.J.

# Wherefore Are These Things Hid?

I T TOOK England to reveal to me the hidden aspects of Constantine's personality, as a politician and as a human being. I thought at any rate that I knew his cricket. I didn't. I couldn't, because he was the same man on the cricket field that he was in our private and public life. The difference was that there, or rather in the Lancashire League, he was able to give his powers full play. To this day, twenty-five years after-wards, the neglect of league cricket, and particularly in the South, passes comprehension. The only reason that makes sense to me is that it is wilful —the South does not want to know. League cricket is not my business here. Constantine is. To say that he is the greatest of all league cricketers is the same as to say that W. G. Grace is the greatest of all cricketers. I shall show later in this book that when you say that about Grace you have only just begun. So it is with Constantine in the league. There were great cricketers in the leagues before him. He paved the way for that stream of Test players from the Dominions and the colonies who for years now have made their gifts familiar to hundreds of thousands who would otherwise have seen nothing or little of them. Constantine put the league on its feet financially when it was balancing on an edge. But his greatest achievement was to create the strategy, the style, the temper and the tone of league cricket. There he found himself. By 1932, when I first saw the league, he was no longer a Test cricketer who played in the league. He was a league cricketer who played in Tests. It was after he became a finished league player that he found his finest form in Tests and big cricket.

If I were on any cricket committee dealing with play on the field, and I had to leave at short notice, I would give my vote to Sir Donald Bradman and tell him to use it as he thought fit. He sees everything that everyone else sees, and much that no one else does. His judgment of cricket strategy and tactics is even more dependable than was his judgment of length with a bat in his hand. I read and re-read his workaday prose with an inner confidence and repose that I give to no other writer on cricket since C. B. Fry. He shocked me when I saw in his autobiography what he thought about league cricket and Constantine.

'One could understand why his name became first on the list of all Lancashire League cricketers. In this class of cricket, where matches are decided in one afternoon, I cannot envisage a player with better qualifications. In a quarter of an hour of terrific speed bowling or unorthodox hitting he could swing the fortunes of a match.'

This misconception is so complete as to be embarrassing. Speed bowling, however terrific, and quarter-hours of unorthodox hitting do not win first place in a league competition seven years out of nine. We are still in the flower garden of the gay, the spontaneous, tropical West Indians. We need some astringent spray.

After ten years of league cricket Constantine played a full season for the West Indies touring team in 1939. He took 103 wickets in 488·4 overs (eight ball). He had four for 42 in one innings of the Manchester Test and five for 75 in one innings of the Oval Test. Against Yorkshire, five for 28, including Yardley and Leyland for small scores; against Middlesex, four for 68, including Edrich and Compton, again for only a few; and so right through the season. He bowled a mixture of all paces with only an occasional fast ball. *The Times* correspondent reported that there was no bowler before the public who was so expert at diddling out batsmen. His previous spell of big cricket had been four years before, in the West Indies 1934–5, when he was still essentially a fast bowler. The new style he had learnt and perfected in the league. His record with it in a bowling side noticeably weak compares favourably with that of any visiting bowler of the century. When I suggested to another famous and successful league cricketer that Sobers and 'Collie' Smith would lose edge through playing in league cricket he was emphatic in his denial of this. 'The conditions vary so much from match to match,' said Frank Worrell, 'that *if you set yourself to master each one* then you maintain your standards and gain in experience.'[1] Constantine set himself to master all conditions. There he made himself into a batsman of a style whose special quality must be recorded. Let me describe one characteristic innings I saw, played against the late Ted McDonald bowling for Accrington.

McDonald in 1932 had retired from Lancashire County. That means only that he cannot stand the grind of three-day county matches day after day. In a half-day match he is still a formidable bowler. Mac has never lost his machine-like run and his perfect action. Today he is at his best, good pace, a slight but late swing from the off-side and periodically one that straightens. All this is on the basis of an impeccable length—Constantine has this effect on most bowlers. Constantine in his turn knows that he cannot afford to get out cheaply; still more, for the sake of the morale of his side, as a professional, he cannot afford to let the opposing professional get him out cheaply. This is a big match, with far more spectators and more tension than two-thirds of the first-class county matches played in a season. For an over or two this sparring continues. The crowd is silent but patient. It knows from long experience that sooner or later Constantine will explode. A length ball straightens, pops and lobs into the slips off the shoulder of Constantine's bat, a catch that eight-year-old Bobby would scorn and ask please to be thrown a real one. First slip all season has been beside himself with anxiety to drop as few as possible of the balls that fly towards him. This lob takes him by surprise and he muffs it. Constantine jumps with joy like an eight-year-old and settles down to take the rest of the over. All the *habitués* know now that the spell has been broken and things will happen soon. Mac too knows. But what? When it does happen no mortal could have foretold it. Constantine takes a long stride with his left foot across the wicket and, leaning well forward glances McDonald from outside the off-stump to long-leg for four. Pandemonium. Mac stands startled, as well he might, if only for one fleeting fraction of a second. He is too experienced a campaigner to attempt to translate his surprise into anything immediate and rash. He does not attempt to bowl any faster; he does not budge an inch from his length. A few balls later Constantine leans forward and

[1] It is the standard of cricket in the West Indies that is lowered.

puts him away again to fine-leg from outside the off-stump. That breaks it. Next over the field is rearranged and Constantine begins to play a normal game, normal for him.

In these two strokes there was not the slightest recklessness or chanciness. The unorthodoxy was carried out with a precision and care fully equal to the orthodoxy of Mac's classical action and perfect length. They were almost as unpredictable, in fact more so, as the strokes against Hammond in 1926. Yet where those were adventures these were strictly business. As far as I remember, the field being opened up, he did not make the stroke again that afternoon. I used to drop in to Lancashire and see league cricket whenever I could. I do not remember ever seeing that stroke again.

These strokes were characteristic of Constantine's batting in the league. That is the way he transferred the liabilities of one-day cricket into assets. Assets for cricket of all days, one as well as five, if that last-named monstrosity continues. It is along that road that the present deadlock in Test cricket will be broken. It is a West Indian heritage. George Challenor in his early days in the West Indies was known for it. Whatever the match, he looked upon a maiden over as a personal affront. For All West Indies in British Guiana he hit inswinger Root for six over cover-point's head in the first over. I have described the way St. Hill shook himself free of Griffith's encirclement. The youthful George Headley was the same, Test match or no Test match. If I am not mistaken, in Sobers, 'Collie' Smith and Kanhai I have seen the same spirit fighting for expression against the heavy burdens that were unexpectedly placed upon them in 1957. In the Lancashire League Constantine developed it to a finished and elaborated method. In his own opinion the finest innings of his career was played against Sidney Barnes in the league with all the dice loaded against him. Barnes pinned him down. To score he had to get the leg-break away through two short-legs and force the off-break through two gullys. Against the break all the time. I did not see the innings, but I can visualize the billiard-like precision and concentration with which it was done. He did not say: 'Ha, this is new and scientific. I am defeated. If I stay I will have achieved.' There are new roads for batsmen to explore.

A great English critic of the arts, perhaps the greatest of this century, has redefined the terms classical and romantic. The control, the mastery, the balance between means and ends which we call classical, these he attributed to the fact that the material which the classical artist handled was traditional. The Romantic was faced with material outside of the traditional. This necessitated new methods, but not romantic methods. Sir Donald Tovey found that the great Romantics invented new means which were so perfectly adapted to their new ends that the only applicable word was classical. We need not accept the analysis. It is sufficient if it throws some light. Batting will handle new material (if it is new) with classical perfection, but only when it is compelled to. As long as it deludes itself that what it has to face is some new science in bowling it will stay where it is and even go backwards. Constantine's leg-glance from outside the off-stump to long-leg was a classical stroke. It was not due to his marvellous West Indian eyes and marvellous West Indian wrists. It was due, if you must have it, to his marvellous West Indian brains. He saw that the best league bowlers were always out to pin him down, and the conditions, including the marvellous league crowds, compelled him to work out new *and safe* ways of countering them. When the Australian team of 1956 wanted to score quickly against the off-breaks of Titmus at Lord's their hoicks to long-on already foreshadowed their doom.

It would be a pity if this aspect of Constantine's best batting in the league were lost. He, of course, whenever the opportunity offered, whacked away as merrily as ever. And most cricketers in the South think of him in terms of his last innings at the Oval in 1939. In Altham and Swanton's history, and other authoritative records, this is a bright page.

'Constantine made 78 runs off less than 12 overs in an unforgettable display of hitting upon which Nichols and Perks, with a demoralized field scattered to all parts of the compass, were quite unable to place even momentary check. Amid a bewildering variety of strokes, surpassing the wildest flights of fancy, one six to the Vauxhall end off the back-foot will never be forgotten by those who saw it.'

That was Learie's quarter of an hour, but in a Test, not a league match. Cricket will always do with such. The danger is to think that this is the only alternative to McGlew.

Swimming in the caves of league cricket between the wars, to this day dark and unfathomed, Constantine strengthened and flexed his strategic muscles. Here are some of his ideas.

· · · · ·

'A great success in county cricket and even moderate success in Test cricket does not qualify a man for success in league cricket. To begin with, on each side will be found one or two or more sound batsmen. Then the bowler, fast, medium or slow, will find more often than not that league batsmen have no respect for him or his reputation. They are out to play Saturday-afternoon cricket beginning at two and ending at seven, 30 runs is a pretty good score, but 20 is by no means to be despised, and the resolute batsman who can hit the ball and is not afraid to take a chance will often get 20 runs. Add to these one or two batsmen who will stand and play the bowling properly, and an absolutely first-class bowler will find his work cut out to prevent an opposing side getting 150 runs—and 150 runs under ordinary circumstances is a winning score.'

Not fast bowling and brilliant quarters of an hour but absolute accuracy and meticulous field-placing were the conditions of consistent success for the player who took his job seriously. Men who had played in both league and county cricket were agreed that it was harder to get 100 wickets in a season of league cricket than in the counties.

'A slow bowler has to be particularly careful. It does not need courage for the batsman to have a hit at him, and he has to think all the time, for wickets must be got. They must be got fairly quickly if he wants to win his match, and yet the score must be kept within reasonably small limits. Sometimes the bowler is a batsman as well, and all the time he is bowling he has to remember that the side is looking to him to cut a large slice out of the runs that are being made.'

Constantine adds, 'It is a thing you have to be in to know.' But why should that be true merely of league cricket? It is true of all other forms.
Finally the league professional, with breadth of view and subtlety, must translate psychology into technique.

'Sometimes the professional has to bat at both ends in order to help a young player round a difficult corner. Sometimes when bowling is easy he has to give the same player as much of it as possible and refrain from hitting it about lest changes be made. Sometimes while bowling the professional sees one of the opposing star bats, especially a brother professional, settled for the day. He may find it worth while to concentrate his attack on a single stump, with field placed to suit and impeccable length. He thus pegs the other professional down, and gives an atmosphere to the game which stimulates his own side and depresses the batsmen on the other. . . . If even the professional is the essence of selfishness, and thinks only of doing well for himself, it will pay him in the end to study and help his side as much as possible; for it is with them that he has to play and no one man can consistently beat eleven others at cricket.'

The years in the Lancashire League were a great chapter in the history of English cricket. I was singularly fortunate in that my first introduction to England was to the working people of the North, and not to the over-heated atmosphere of London. Similarly with cricket. I had seen and grasped league cricket before I became familiar with English county cricket. Constantine seems to believe that the future of cricket lies along the road of the league. On that I have no opinion that matters. Biography is my subject, and the biography of a West Indian. But for Nelson and the league, his cricketing talents would have been wasted. I hope I have preserved some of it here. It can still prove of value. The West Indies had no use for it. Sir Donald Bradman (how certain voices insist on being heard) has in more than one place recorded the unhappiness of a captain who has to lead players older and more experienced than himself. (He was the last man from whom one should have expected these qualms.) From such handicaps West Indian captains between the wars were held to be immune. If need be they would have been recruited from the kindergarten. Constantine could have been valuable in other ways. He is absolutely convinced that if he or George Headley had gone to Australia with the 1951-2 West Indies team they could not possibly have lost the series: his admiration for the technical capacity of the 1950 players is very great. He visited the West Indies in the early fifties. On his return he published a solemn warning that the masses of the people were bitter at racial discrimination in general and specifically at the gymnastics that were being played with the captaincy. He foretold political demonstrations at Test matches. For this reason he refused at the time a job which was offered him as a welfare officer (in the very oilfields of the old days—times had indeed changed, but not enough). The warning passed un-noticed and, I would wager, provoked some solemn frowns. One year later there took place the distressing events which marked the 1953-4

M.C.C. tour. In 1960 the Trinidad crowd stopped a Test by throwing bottles on the field.

Despite the arguments for—and they are powerful—I adhere stubbornly to my juvenile ethics, that the captain should be not a black man but the best man. Talking to Atkinson in Hastings, I found myself glad to hear that he played for Wanderers, the old club of Austin, the Challenors (seven brothers), H. W. Ince and the other heroes of my boyhood days. They made West Indian batting, and Worrell, Weekes and Walcott stand on their shoulders. I would like to believe that with the appointment of Frank Worrell as captain of the West Indies team, all will take a long breath and leave the old days behind. But, as will be amply demonstrated, the circumstances surrounding that appointment show that the price of liberty is still eternal vigilance.

# PART FOUR

# TO INTERPOSE A LITTLE EASE

---

## II

## *George Headley: Nascitur Non Fit*

To THINK about Constantine between the wars is to conjure up the other West Indian master of the period, the one and only George Headley. I write of him purely as a cricketer. And I do so contrary to the pattern of this book, because, first, this West Indian narrowly escapes being the greatest batsman I have ever seen. Pride of place in my list goes to Bradman, but George is not far behind. In fact, it is my belief that if he had lived his cricketing life in England or Australia he would not be behind anyone. Everyone is familiar with his scores. On a world scale his average is, I believe, exceeded only by Bradman and Merchant. His average of one century in every four Test innings is second only to Bradman. In those days there were no Test matches against India and Pakistan and New Zealand. George had to meet the full strength of England and Australia. The second reason why I write about him is that he is a remarkable individual. I believe that every great batsman is a special organism; it must be so, for they are very rare, as rare as great violinists— I doubt if I have known many more than a dozen.

There is a third reason, but that I shall reserve.

I saw George in 1930, I saw him in 1934, I played cricket with him in Lancashire. He had to a superlative degree the three cardinal qualities of the super batsman. He saw the ball early. He was quick on his feet. He was quick with his bat. The most important of all, in my view, is seeing the ball early. In 1953 George told me that from the time he began to play cricket he saw every ball bowled come out of the bowler's hand. He added that if he did not see it out of the bowler's hand he would be at a loss how to play. The conversation began by his telling me of a bowler in league cricket, of no importance, who had bowled him two balls in succession neither of which he saw out of the hand. The experience left him completely bewildered.

He was as quick on his feet as any player I have seen except Don Bradman. To see Bradman get back, his right foot outside the off-stump, pointing to mid-on, and hook a fast bowler was to witness not cricket but acrobatics: you knew he had got there only after he had made the stroke. George's speed of foot was of the same kind. He was as quick with his bat as any. Bowlers, seeing the ball practically on his pad, appealed against him for lbw, only to grind their teeth as the bat came down and put the ball away to the fine-leg boundary. Any single one of these three qualities makes a fine batsman, and courage and confidence are the natural result of having all three.

What I want to draw special attention to here is George's play on wet or uncertain wickets. Here are his scores on such wickets in England.

| 1933 | | Other high scores in the innings |
|---|---|---|
| *v.* Northamptonshire | 52 out of 129 | 32 and 15 |
| *v.* Yorkshire | 25 out of 115 | 25 and 16 |
| *v.* Nottinghamshire | 66 out of 314 | 54 and 51 |
| *v.* Lancashire | 66 out of 174 | 29 and 18 |
| *v.* Leicestershire | 60 out of 156 | 22 and 19 |
| *v.* Leveson-Gower's XI | 35 out of 251 | 70 and 44 |
| | | |
| 1939 | | |
| *v.* Surrey | 52 out of 224 | 58 and 52 |
| *v.* Yorkshire | 61 out of 234 | 72 and 28 |
| *v.* England | 51 out of 133 | 47 and 16 |
| | 5 out of 43   (4w) | 13 and 11 |
| *v.* Somerset | 0 out of 84 | 45 and 17 |
| *v.* Gloucestershire | 40 out of 220 | 50 and 28 |
| | 5 out of 162 | 43 and 26 |

In those 13 innings George passed 50 seven times. Three times only he scored less than double figures, and in his other three innings his scores were 25, 35 and 40. I believe those figures would be hard to beat. Look at a similar list made for Bradman by Ray Robinson in his fascinating book *Between Wickets*.

| | Match | Total | Bradman | Top Scorer |
|---|---|---|---|---|
| 1928 | Brisbane Test | 66 | 1 | Woodfull 30 n.o. |
| 1929 | Sydney | 128 | 15 | Fairfax 40 |
| 1930 | Notts Test | 144 | 8 | Kippax 64 n.o. |
| | Northants | 93 | 22 | Bradman 22 |
| | Gloucester | 157 | 42 | Ponsford 51 |
| | | 117 | 14 | McCabe 34 |
| 1932 | Perth | 159 | 3 | McCabe 43 |
| | Melbourne | 19 (2w) | 13 | |
| 1933 | Sydney | 180 | 1 | Rowe 70 |
| | | 128 | 71 | Bradman 71 |
| 1934 | Lord's Test | 118 | 13 | Woodfull 43 |
| 1936 | Brisbane Test | 58 | 0 | Chipperfield 36 |
| | Sydney Test | 80 | 0 | O'Reilly 37 n.o. |
| 1938 | Middlesex | 132 | 5 | Chipperfield 36 |
| | Yorkshire | 132 | 42 | Bradman 42 |

In fifteen innings Bradman passed 50 only once, 40 only twice and 15 only four times. His average is 16·66. George's average is 39·85. You need not build on these figures a monument, but you cannot ignore them.

Bradman's curious deficiency on wet wickets has been the subject of much searching comment. George's superior record has been noticed before, and one critic, I think it was Neville Cardus, has stated that Headley has good claims to be considered *on all wickets* the finest of the inter-war batsmen. I would not go so far. It is easy to give figures and make comparisons and draw rational conclusions. The fact remains that the odds were 10 to 1 that in any Test Bradman would make 150 or 200 runs, and the more the runs were needed the more certain he was to make them. Yet if Bradman never failed in a Test series, neither did George. I believe Bradman and Headley are the only two between the wars of whom that can be said. (Hammond failed terribly in 1930 in England and almost as badly in the West Indies in 1934–5.)

But there is another point I wish to bring out. Between 1930 and 1938 Bradman had with him in England Ponsford, Woodfull, McCabe, Kippax, Brown, Hassett. All scored heavily. In 1933 and 1939 West Indian batsmen scored runs at various times, but George had nobody who could be depended on. In 1933 his average in the Tests was 55·40. Among those who played regularly the next average was 23·83. In 1939 his average in the Tests was 66·80. The next batsman averaged 57·66, but of his total of 173 he made 137 in one innings. Next was 27·50. It can be argued that this stiffened his resistance. I don't think so. And George most certainly does not. 'I would be putting on my pads and sometimes before I was finished I would hear that the first wicket had gone.' This is what he carried on his shoulders for nearly ten years. None, not a single one of the great batsmen, has ever been so burdened for so long.

He had characteristics which can be attributed to less than half a dozen in the whole history of the game. He has said, and all who know his play can testify, that he did not care who bowled at him: right hand, left hand, new ball, old ball, slow, fast, all were the same. He loved the bad wickets. And his reason is indicative of the burden he carried. 'On a bad wicket it was you and the bowler. If he pitched up you had to drive. If he pitched short you had to turn and hook. No nonsense.' I sensed there a relief, a feeling that he was free to play the only game which could be successful under the circumstances, but this time his own natural game.

George was a quiet cricketer. So quiet that you could easily underestimate him. One day in 1933 West Indies were playing Yorkshire at Harrogate, the wicket was wet and Verity placed men close in, silly mid-off and silly point I think. The West Indian players talked about bowlers who placed men close in for this batsman and the other batsman. George joined in the reminiscences. Someone said, 'George, if Verity put a man there for you——'

A yell as of sudden, intense, unbearable pain burst from George, so as to startle everyone for yards around.

'Me!' he said. 'Put a man there for me!'

They could talk about it for other players, Test players, but that anyone should even think that such fieldsmen could be placed for him— that was too much for George. The idea hurt him physically.

George was a great master of the game in many senses. He landed in Australia (1931–2) a boy of twenty-one who had never played or seen cricket out of the West Indies. As he has told me in great detail: 'I was an off-side batsman, drive, cut and back-stroke through the covers. Of course, I also could hook.' Australian critics were startled at his mastery of batting and of an innings of 131, played at Victoria in less than even time, one critic who had seen all the great players of the previous thirty years said that no finer innings had ever been seen on the Melbourne ground. An innings of 82 against New South Wales evoked the same admiration. Then, as he says, the word went round: keep away from his off-stump and outside it, you will never get him there. Henceforth in every match, on every ground, it was a leg-stump attack and an on-side field. George was baffled and I remember how anxious we were at a succession of failures. What he did, under fire, so to speak, was to re-organize his batting to meet the new attack.

This is what happened to George in Australia: 25, 82, 131, 34. Then he failed steadily: 27 run out and 16; 0 and 11 (Test, to Grimmett both times); 3; 14 and 2 (Test); 19 and 17. Nine successive failures. It is only by the Third Test that George is once more in control of the situation: 102 not out out of 193 (next highest score 21), and 28 out of 148 (again top score); 77 and 113; 75 and 39; 33 out of 99 (top score) and 11 out of 107 (Fourth Test); 70 run out and 2; 105 and 30 (Fifth Test).

He had so mastered the new problems that Grimmett considers Headley to be the greatest master of on-side play whom he ever bowled against, and he bowled against both Hobbs and Bradman. Yet of George's 169 not out in the Manchester Test of 1934, A. Ratcliffe, reviewing modern cricket (*The Cricketer Annual*, 1933–4), says, 'His cuts off the slow bowling were a strange sight to see and I had only seen such strokes once before when Woolley cut Roy Kilner's slow deliveries to the boundary time after time.'

George Headley, this West Indian, would be my candidate for a clinical study of a great batsman as a unique type of human being, mentally and physically. So far as I know no one has probed into this before.

Mentally. George is batting against an Australian slow bowler, probably Grimmett. To the length ball he gets back and forces Grimmett away between mid-wicket and mid-on or between mid-wicket and square-leg. He is so quick on his feet and so quick with his bat that Grimmett simply cannot stop ones and twos in between the fieldsmen. Every time Grimmett flights the ball, out of the crease and the full drive. Grimmett, that great master of length, can't even keep George quiet. He has a man at fine-leg. He shifts him round to square and moves square to block up the hole. Next ball is just outside the leg-stump. George, gleeful at the thought that fine-leg is no longer there, dances in front of the wicket 'to pick up a cheap four'. He glances neatly, only to see Oldfield, the wicketkeeper, way over on the leg-side taking the catch. The two seasoned Australians have trapped him. That sort of thing has happened often enough. Now note George's reaction.

'I cut that out.'

'What do you mean, you cut it out?'

'I just made up my mind never to be caught that way again.'

'So you do not glance?'

'Sure I glance, but I take care to find out first if any of these traps are being laid.'

'Always?'

'Always.'

And I can see that he means it.

Mark Twain was once a pilot on the Mississippi. The bed of that river is always changing and a man is sounding all the time and calling out the changes. Mark Twain says that a pilot, whether on duty or not, is always hearing these soundings. Even when playing poker his mind registers them automatically and days after uses the latest results when piloting. Great batsmen are the same, they are not like you or me. An experience is automatically registered and henceforth functions as a permanent part of the organism.

Similarly with placing. For George, to make a stroke was to hit the ball (he had a loud scorn for 'the pushers') and to hit it precisely in a certain place. He couldn't think of a stroke without thinking of exactly where it was going. Whenever he had scored a century and runs were not urgent, he practised different strokes at the same ball, so as to be sure to command the placing of the ball where there was no fieldsman. Those who know George only after the war don't really know him. In 1939 he was, in addition to on-side play, a master of the cut, both square and late, and though he was, like Bradman, mainly a back-foot player, half-volleys did not escape him. This placing to a shifting field must also be to a substantial degree automatic. Having taken a glance round, *and sized up what the bowler is trying to do*, the great batsman puts the ball away more by reflex than conscious action.

George had one quality that was paralleled by no one except Bradman.

When he was run out in the Oval Test in 1939 he had scored 65 and, as one reporter wrote, if he hadn't been run out nothing was more certain than that he would make a century. He was not on the defensive but, according to *Wisden*, was cutting, forcing off his legs and driving.

Now physically. Headley has told me that the night before a Test he rarely slept more than an hour or two. (The night before the second century in the Test at Lord's he never slept at all.) But he isn't suffering from insomnia, not in the least. This fantastic man is busy playing his innings the next day. The fast bowler will swing from leg. He plays a stroke. Then the bowler will come in from the off. He plays the stroke to correspond. The bowler will shorten. George hooks or cuts. Verity will keep a length on or just outside the off-stump. George will force him away by getting back to cut and must be on guard not to go too greedily at a loose ball—that is how in Tests he most fears he will lose his innings (a revealing commentary on his attitude to bowlers). Langridge will flight the ball. Down the pitch to drive. So he goes through every conceivable ball and makes a stroke to correspond. This cricket strategist obviously works on Napoleon's maxim that if a general is taken by surprise at anything that occurs on a battlefield then he is a bad general.

Morning sees him in the grip of processes he does not control. He rises early and immediately has a bowel motion. At ten o'clock he has another. And then he is ready. He is very specific that these automatic physiological releases take place only on big-match days. He is chain-smoking in the dressing-room. But once he starts to walk down the pavilion steps he would not be able to recognize his father if he met him halfway. Everything is out of his mind except batting. Bumpers? Bodyline? He is not concerned. He gets out to good balls (or bad), but such is his nervous control that no bowler as such has ever bothered him. Near the end of an English tour he is physically drained except for batting. He has a few days' leave, he sits and smokes. His companions plan expeditions, make dates to go out with girls. George sits and smokes. From where he sits he doesn't want to budge an inch. But when they return to the tour, as soon as he has a bat in his hands, he is as fit as ever; fit, however, for nothing else except batting. When the season is over the fatigue remains and it takes him weeks to recover his habitual self. I watched the West Indians in the nets at Lord's in 1933 before the tour began. George never to my knowledge practised seriously. He fooled around playing the ball here and there. It was his first visit to England, but he was as sure of himself as if he were in Jamaica. In 1933 he ended the season with scores of 79, 31 (run out), 167, 95, 14 and 35. He was third in the averages for the season, Hammond and Mead averaging 67 to his 66. If he had thought about it in 1933 he would have made the runs needed. With him batting was first, not second, nature. In 1939 he was 72 with Hammond next at 63. He was a fine fieldsman and of the great batsmen of his day only Bradman was faster between the wickets.

His only unhappiness on the cricket field was that he was allowed to bowl only on the rarest occasions. George used to watch batsmen and detect their weak points. But from there he went on to think that he could get them out with his leg-break. Which does not at all follow. In 1933 he took 21 wickets. Alas! in 1939 he was allowed to bowl only 10 overs for the whole season. He spoke of it with feeling. In 1948, in a series of intercolonial matches in Jamaica, George made, out of 356, 203 not out; out of 151 for five, 57 not out; out of 456, 79 retired hurt. But he also took four for 40 and three for 53. Whereby I deduce that George captained the Jamaica side.

What does he remember most? Or rather what do I remember most about his talk on cricket? George rarely raises his voice. He never raised it louder than when he spoke of the West Indian failure in Australia to deal with the bumpers of Lindwall and Miller. 'West Indians couldn't hook,' he says, his eyes blazing. *'West Indians!'* To this day he remains adamant in his view that as far as he is concerned bowlers can drop the ball where they like and put fieldsmen where they like. 'If they catch it when I hit it they are welcome.' There is not the slightest trace of braggadocio; I have not known a more genuinely modest cricketer. For all I know, George may be quite wrong in his views of short fast balls, though he had plenty of them in his time and dealt faithfully by them. He speaks as he does because it is part of his outlook: never to have his equanimity disturbed by anything that a bowler may do.

That is why he speaks so soberly of the two balls which he did not see out of the bowler's hand. He had a kind of nightmare vision of having to bat without seeing the ball out of the hand. And one more catastrophe, a real one. A celebration match in one of the leagues. Mayors and corporations, dignitaries and their ladies. George, the star attraction, opens the innings, taking the first ball. An unknown medium-paced bowler sends one right up on middle-and-leg. Right up. George plays comfortably forward, a thing he rarely does, only to see the ball move away in the last inches and hit his off-stump. George is horrified. He has disappointed everybody. But there is more to it. He goes behind and observes the bowler carefully. Yes, it was not an accident, he is swinging the ball very late. George makes enquiries. Yes, he is a good league bowler, always moves the new ball well. It is years since it has happened. But George cannot get over it. He has been caught napping. He should never have assumed that any bowler with a new ball in whatever kind of cricket was not able to move it so late. Ordinary humans don't play cricket that way. Few people in this world do anything that way.

Such strange human beings as George Headley fascinate me not only for what they do but in themselves. There was a time when I read every biography of Napoleon I came across, and I still read some. He looks over a map of gun emplacements on the coast of France and points out that the investigators have left out two. I have known a few men who could do similarly. He could sleep instantaneously at any time for any length of time available. I have never met a man who could do that. And I have met very few men who can concentrate on anything as George concentrated on batting. I am sure he never had to learn it. I wonder if he had gone to America to study medicine (and had got interested in it) if he would have become a great surgeon, seeing everything, remembering everything, hands deft and sure, without nerves before the most distressing case. These qualities were not remote from those which made George the batsman he was.

I once talked for two hours with C. B. Fry. Technicalities all the time. But I added to my store of curiosa. While we talked there was cricket on television, a rather small screen. He looked at me and gesticulated a great deal, watching the cricket, if at all, only out of the corner of his eye. But he seemed to see and judge every stroke and he always showed why a batsman got out. He was at the time over eighty and was not wearing glasses. It was Mississippi piloting in London, N.W.2. (When I was leaving he told me, 'Come in again.') To many thousands of people a great batsman is a man who makes a lot of runs. Not to me. A really great batsman (*there are not many*) is to me as strange a human being as a man seven feet tall or a man I once heard of who could not read but spoke six languages. It is, however, only when you are aware of this that you begin to see. In scientific investigation you see as a rule only what you are looking for.

147

I read many books on cricket about and by great batsmen. Even the very few good ones tell more about the writer than the player. If life were not so urgent I would be willing to spend a year talking to a great batsman, asking him questions and probing into all sorts of aspects of his life on and off the cricket field. If he and I hit it off the result would be a book such as had never yet been written, which physiologists, anthropologists and psychologists would read more eagerly than cricketers. Such an investigation of Worrell, Walcott and Weekes would tell us as much about the past and future of the people of the West Indies as about cricket. But it will not be done. Late and soon, the world is too much with us.

No, I have not forgotten the third reason why I wanted to write about George Headley. And note it well, you adventurous categorizers. I know Constantine and Headley pretty well, as cricketers and as human beings. Contrary to all belief, popular and learned, Constantine the magician is the product of tradition and training. It is George the maestro who is an absolutely natural cricketer. We West Indians are a people on our way who have not yet reached a point of rest and consolidation. Critics of a sociological turn of mind had proved that we were a nation which naturally produced fast bowlers, when in 1950 Ram and Val, both under twenty-one, produced the greatest slow-bowling sensation since the South African team of 1907. We are moving too fast for any label to stick.

# PART FIVE

# W.G.: PRE-EMINENT VICTORIAN

—————

## 12

# *What Do Men Live By ?*

MOST of the summers between 1933 and 1938 I spent reporting cricket, first for the *Manchester Guardian* and then for the *Glasgow Herald*. They were happy days and if I were writing the usual type of cricket reminiscences I would have plenty to say. But though I read that sort of book I have no intention of writing one.

Fiction-writing drained out of me and was replaced by politics. I became a Marxist, a Trotskyist. I published large books and small articles on these and kindred subjects. I wrote and spoke. Like many others, I expected war, and during or after the war social revolution. In 1938 a lecture tour took me to the United States and I stayed there fifteen years. The war came. It did not bring soviets and proletarian power. Instead the bureaucratic-totalitarian monster grew stronger and spread. As early as 1941 I had begun to question the premises of Trotskyism. It took nearly a decade of incessant labour and collaboration to break with it and reorganize my Marxist ideas to cope with the post-war world. That was a matter of doctrine, of history, of economics and politics. These pursuits I shared with collaborators, rivals, enemies and our public. We covered the ground thoroughly.

In my private mind, however, I was increasingly aware of large areas of human existence that my history and my politics did not seem to cover. What did men live by? What did they want? What did history show that they had wanted? Had they wanted then what they wanted now? The men I had known, what had they wanted? What exactly was art and what exactly culture? I had believed that, more or less, I knew. Years afterwards I was to see my preoccupations formulated clearly if crudely in the pages of Old Solemnity itself, the *Times Literary Supplement.* I was to read:

'. . . For example, in an age of market research and public opinion polls what exactly *do* men—and women—want from work, money, life? Has any British political party ever conducted a sample enquiry, as a good manufacturer must do to design and sell his wares? Again, if by materialism be meant a dominant individual and social urge for material good things, it has never in history precluded deep spirituality, better arts and the fuller realization of human personality. A strong case could be made for the exact opposite.'

Better arts? What is a better art? Better than what? To be investigated presumably by sample polls, organized by a political party, with spirituality taken in passing. I was travelling in a different direction.

A glance at the world showed that when the common people were not at work, one thing they wanted was organized sports and games. They wanted them greedily, passionately. So much so, that the politicians who devoted themselves to the improvement of the condition of the people, the disciples of culture, the aesthetes, all deplored the expenditure of so much time, energy, attention and money on sports and games instead of on the higher things. Well, presumably it could not be helped. It had always been so and was likely to continue for a long time. But that was quite untrue. Organized games had been part and parcel of the civilization of Ancient Greece. With the decline of that civilization they disappeared from Europe for some 1,500 years. People ran and jumped and kicked balls about and competed with one another; they went to see the knights jousting. But games and sports, organized as the Greeks had organized them, there were none. More curious still to the enquiring eye, after this long absence they seemed all to have returned within about a decade of each other, in frantic haste, as if there were only limited space and those who did not get in early would be permanently shut out. Golf was known to be ancient. The first annual tournament of the Open Championship was held only in 1860. The Football Association was founded only in 1863. It was in 1866 that the first athletic championship was held in England. The first English cricket team left for Australia in 1862 and a county championship worthy of the name was organized only in 1873. In the United States the first all-professional baseball team was organized in 1869. One of the most popular of modern games, lawn tennis, was actually invented and played for the first time in Wales in 1873 and was carried next year to the United States by a solitary young lady who had acquired the equipment from a British Army supply store in Bermuda. The public flocked to these sports and games. All of a sudden, everyone wanted organized sports and games.

But in that very decade this same public was occupied with other organizations of a very different type. Disraeli's Reform Bill, introducing popular democracy in England, was passed in 1865. In the same year the slave states were defeated in the American Civil War, to be followed immediately by the first modern organization of American labour. In 1864 Karl Marx and Frederick Engels founded the First Communist International and within a few years Europe for the first time since the Crusades saw an international organization comprising millions of people. In 1871 in France Napoleon III was overthrown and the Paris Commune was established. It failed, and popular democracy in France seemed doomed for many decades. In only four years it had returned and the Third Republic was founded. So that this same public that wanted sports and games so eagerly wanted popular democracy too. Perhaps they were not exactly the same people in each case. Even so, both groups were stirred at the same time.

The conjunction hit me as it would have hit few of the students of society and culture in the international organization to which I belonged. Trotsky had said that the workers were deflected from politics by sports. With my past I simply could not accept that. I was British and the history of those decades in Britain was very familiar to me, both the politics and the sport. The organizational drive for sport had come from Britain. It was from Britain that cricket, and soccer more than cricket, had spread as nothing international had ever spread for centuries before. (Even as I write some little Spanish boys in a little Spanish village are kicking a ball on a rough open space and shouting, '*Gol*', '*Penálti*' and '*Corni*'.) I read and thought and read and unearthed a grievous scandal. This was that not a single English scholar, historian or social analyst of repute had deemed it worth his while to pay even the most cursory attention to these remarkable events in which his own country played so central, in fact the central, role. Books on the Olympic Games of Greece are few in any language. You would expect that here English scholarship was particularly fitted to shine. In the catalogues under Games, Olympic, you found little. When you examined what you had found there was less.

I could, of course, wait for the Conservative Party or the Labour Party to organize a sample poll. A poll on art. A sample poll! A sample poll can investigate only what the pollsters know, and it cannot do even that properly.

What I myself wanted out of life was no help. I was not a good subject even for my own poll. The ordinary man did not ask himself the questions I was always asking. But I had not always asked myself these questions. There had been a time when I took the world for granted. What had I wanted then? I believed that if when I left school I had gone into the society of Ancient Greece I would have been more at home than ever I had been since. It was a fantasy, but for me it had meaning. The world we lived in, and Ancient Greece. If I had been French or German or African I would have thought differently. But I was British, I knew best the British way of life, not merely in historical facts but in the instinctive responses. I had acquired them in childhood and, without these, facts are merely figures. In the intervals of my busy days and nights I pondered and read and looked about me and pondered and read again. Sport and politics in Ancient Greece. Sport and politics in nineteenth-century Britain. Over the second half of the nineteenth century, sparking the great international movement, drawing all eyes to it, startling millions who otherwise would have taken no notice, creating the myth and the legend, there began to loom the gigantic black-bearded figure of W. G. Grace. All my half-forgotten past in Trinidad, and now my probing into what men live by, had sensitized me to see cricket with fresh eyes as soon as I had begun to think for myself about it. The first task was to get Greece clear.

Greco-Roman we are, and, as the years of crisis deepen, the heritage of imperial Rome becomes more than ever a millstone around our necks and ball and chain on our feet. On the other hand, as we intensify our countless billions of candle-power so that they threaten to consume us, the luminous glow of the Greek city-state seems to penetrate more searchingly into every corner of our civilization. Into the immeasurable chaos of his *Guernica*, lit by the electric chandelier, Picasso introduces a Greek face with an extended arm which holds a primitive oil-lamp.

The Greek lamp burns today as steadily as ever. They who laid the intellectual foundations of the Western world were the most fanatical players and organizers of games that the world has ever known.

The first recorded date in European history is 776 B.C., the date of the first Olympic Games. The Greek states made unceasing war against one another. But when the four-yearly games approached they declared a national truce, the various competitors assembled at Olympia, the games were held and when these were over the wars began again. Olympia, the site of the games, was a national shrine of Zeus and was maintained as such. The games, however, were a form of worship of Zeus, and the whole gigantic organization centred on the preparation and conduct of the games. To every Greek city and every colony (as far away as Italy, Sicily, Africa, Egypt and Marseilles) the envoys went from Olympia with the invitations, and the communities sent their representatives and their official deputations. Forty thousand pilgrims would assemble, including the most distinguished members of Greek society. Plato and Pythagoras were always in the front seats. Socrates, Anaxagoras, Demosthenes, Pindar, Herodotus and even Diogenes came to the games. The barbarians could not understand why the Greeks spent so much time and energy on what seemed to them these childish pursuits; why they should put aside their serious affairs and sweat and strain on the running track, batter their faces and break their limbs and even lose their lives in the boxing and wrestling matches, and run the risk of frightful accidents in the chariot races. Lucian in one of his dialogues puts the answer in the mouth of Solon, the famous political regenerator of Greece and the symbol of wisdom. To this day Solon's answer is unsurpassed. You would have to be there, he tells the puzzled barbarian.

'By seeing what was going on you would be able to appreciate that we are quite justified in expending so much ardour on these spectacles. I cannot find words to give you an idea of the pleasure that you would have if you were seated in the middle of the anxious spectators, watching the courage of the athletes, the beauty of their bodies, their splendid poses, their extraordinary suppleness, their tireless energy, their audacity, their sense of competition, their unconquerable courage, their unceasing efforts to win a victory. I am sure that you would not cease to overwhelm them with praise, to shout again and again, to applaud.'

·        ·        ·        ·        ·

Lucian, the Bernard Shaw of his day, like many other Greek philosophers and intellectuals, sneered at the games. He sneered, but he could
not keep away.

Two aspects of the games have a special meaning for us. The Greeks
were the most politically minded and intellectually and artistically
the most creative of all peoples. It is surprising to find that they hero-
worshipped the athletes to a degree which would shock our modern
seekers after autographs. To our hypocritical 'only a game', they would
have replied with scorn and their quick anger. The Greeks believed that
an athlete who had represented his community at a national competition,
and won, had thereby conferred a notable distinction on his city. His
victory was a testament to the quality of the citizens. All the magnates of
the city welcomed him home in civic procession. They broke down a
part of the wall for him to enter: a city which could produce such
citizens had no need of walls to defend it. For the rest of his life he ate at
the public expense. He was given a job, usually director of the city
gymnasium. The gymnasium was not a barn for callisthenics and drilling.
It was the resort of old and young for physical and intellectual recreation.
As great honour as any, his fellow citizens or his friends were allowed to
erect a statue in the precincts of Olympia itself, a distinction which
emperors and conquerors could get only in the days of Olympia's decline.
These statues were the work of the greatest sculptors of the day. Odes
were composed to the athletes by poets, and Pindar, the greatest of
Greek lyric poets, was in constant demand for such odes. One can only
envy the Greeks their freedom from intellectual snobbery. Diagoras of
Rhodes had been an Olympic champion in his youth. Later he took to
Olympia his two sons, each of whom won a prize. The two young men
crowned their father with the wild olive and carried him around the
arena in triumph while the pilgrims covered the happy old man with
flowers. 'Die, Diagoras,' some of the enthusiasts called to him. 'Die now,
life has nothing more to offer you.' Overcome with joy, the good old
man collapsed and died.

The second startling feature of the games for us is that they became a
centre for the intellectual life of Greece. The philosophers, the scientists,
the extreme democrats, began to hold their conferences and give demonstrations there during the period of the games. To the assembled thousands, orators delivered orations, poets read their pieces. It was at Olympia
that Herodotus tried out the new art of history by reading his early

chapters to the crowd. In time governments ratified and deposited treaties at Olympia. They built treasuries, small temples, to house their sacred documents, and by the beauty of their design and the richness of their ornamentation these did honour to Olympia and to the donors. It was at the Olympic Games that the individualistic city-states and colonies asserted the national unity of Greek civilization and the consciousness of themselves as separate from the barbarians who surrounded them.

To the extent that a historical parallel is suggestive, to that very degree it is dangerous. The games were *not* introduced into Greece by the popular democracy. In fact, when the democracy came into power it lifted another type of celebration to a position of eminence to which the games soon took second place.

The Olympic Games had been a festival of the feudal aristocracy and the bourgeoisie of Greece. Only the bourgeoisie had the money to stand the expense of the competitors, which were heavy. Only the aristocratic families were in a position to take part in the chariot races. Olympia was not a city. It was a combination of Canterbury Cathedral and Lord's situated in a remote part of Greece. To get there needed money and leisure, which the ordinary Greek citizens did not have. There were other guests, but Olympia in particular was not for the common man. Most of the pilgrims had to camp out.

The fifth century B.C. was the period of great democratic revolutions, beginning in Athens and followed by other city-states. The democrats did not come to power all at once. In the name of the popular masses, Peisistratus the tyrant suppressed the power of the ruling aristocrats. It is not infrequently said that he looked around for means of binding the city masses more closely to his regime. Perhaps he recognized that a new regime needed new festivals. Whatever his reason, it was under his regime that the Athenian tragic drama in primitive form began to play before the Athenian citizens. By the time the democracy had definitively established itself Aeschylus had written the first genuine tragedies. Original and never to be surpassed, they were popular. The dramatists and actors were subsidized by the state or under the aegis of the state. The people did not have to travel anywhere. They paid a few pennies and took their seats. The Athenian drama was competitive, and the populace who attended were moved to laughter and tears, terror and pity; but also they applauded their favourites and howled down their dislikes in much the same way as did the crowd at the Olympic Games. W. H. Auden compares the Greek crowd to a Spanish crowd at a bullfight. Aeschylus, Sophocles and Euripides were not culture. It seems that at first the crowd itself decided who was the victor. Later, when the judges were chosen by lot, the crowd did its best to intimidate them. Though the Olympic Games lasted for centuries after the rise and decline of the democracy, it is legitimate to say that the democracy needed a new means of expression for its new status and found it in the tragic drama. Once every year for four days the tens of thousands of Athenian citizens sat in the open air on the stone seats at the side of the Acropolis and from sunrise to sunset watched the plays of the competing dramatists. All that we have to correspond is a Test match. The manner in which the drama arrived will tell us something valuable about Test matches and (for the moment let us whisper it) the way Test matches arrived may start a trail into that vexed question: the origin of Greek drama. There are so many that another wouldn't hurt.

# 13

## *Prolegomena to W.G.*

A FAMOUS Liberal[1] historian can write the social history of England in the nineteenth century, and two famous Socialists[2] can write what they declared to be the history of the common people of England, and between them never once mention the man who was the best-known Englishman of his time. I can no longer accept the system of values which could not find in these books a place for W. G. Grace. Despite the intensification of the means and modes of modern publicity, he still stands high in the historical memory of the British people and all who have been brought into close relations with their branch of Western civilization. Between those who, writing about social life in Britain, can leave him out, and myself, there yawns a gulf deep and wide. Filled it is unlikely to be, but I can at least sketch the outline of a bridge.

W. G. Grace was a Victorian, but the game he transformed into a national institution was not Victorian either in origin or essence. It was a creation of pre-Victorian England, of the two generations which preceded the accession of the Queen, the England of the early Dickens and of William Hazlitt. It was an England still unconquered by the Industrial Revolution. It travelled by saddle and carriage. Whenever it could it ate and drank prodigiously. It was not finicky in morals. It enjoyed life. It prized the virtues of frankness, independence, individuality, conviviality.

[1] G. M. Trevelyan.
[2] Raymond Postgate and G. D. H. Cole.

There were rulers and ruled, the educated and the uneducated. If the two groupings could be described as two nations they were neither of them conscious of the division as a state of things which ought not to be. You can see that clearly in the finest prose-writer of the time. Hazlitt was an intellectual to his fingertips, and a militant, an extreme democrat who suffered martyrdom for his opinions. Yet he is not a divided man, he has no acute consciousness either of class or of divided culture. He discusses with equal verve the virtues of a classical education and the ignorance of the learned. It is impossible to distinguish any change in his style whether he writes on William Cobbett, on his First Acquaintance with Poets, on John Cavanagh, the Fives Player, or on the Fight between Bill Neate and the Gas-man. It would be comparatively simple to maintain that his essay on The Fight is his finest piece. It is what he called 'a complete thing', giving such a picture of the England of his time as can nowhere else be found in such a narrow compass. Wide as is his range, unlike the late Robert Lynd or A. G. Gardiner (to mention two at random), he does not fit his subject into a practised pattern. He takes his whole self wherever he goes; he is ready to go everywhere; every new experience renews and expands him. He writes as freely and as publicly of a most degrading love-affair as of Elizabethan literature. The possibility of such completeness of expression ended with him and has not yet returned.

Hazlitt's strength and comprehensiveness were the final culmination of one age fertilized by the new. In prose, in poetry, in criticism, in painting, his age was more creative than the country had been for two centuries before and would be for a century after. This was the age that among its other creations produced the game of cricket.

In all essentials the modern game was formed and shaped between 1778, when Hazlitt was born, and 1830, when he died. It was created by the yeoman farmer, the gamekeeper, the potter, the tinker, the Nottingham coal-miner, the Yorkshire factory hand. These artisans made it, men of hand and eye. Rich and idle young noblemen and some substantial city people contributed money, organization and prestige. Between them, by 1837 they had evolved a highly complicated game with all the typical characteristics of a genuinely national art form: founded on elements long present in the nation, profoundly popular in origin, yet attracting to it disinterested elements of the leisured and educated classes. Confined to areas and numbers which were relatively small, it contained all the premises of rapid growth. There was nothing in the slightest degree Victorian about it. At their matches cricketers ate and drank with the gusto of the time, sang songs and played for large sums of money. Bookies sat before the pavilion at Lord's openly taking bets. The unscrupulous nobleman and the poor but dishonest commoner alike bought and sold matches. Both Sir Donald Bradman and Mr. Neville Cardus think that cricket is too complex a game to encourage betting. The history of the game is against them. There is nothing too complex for men to bet on. Cricket took its start from the age in which it was born, both the good and the bad. That the good could predominate was a testimony to the simple men who made it and the life they lived.

The class of the population that seems to have contributed least was the class destined to appropriate the game and convert it into a national institution. This was the solid Victorian middle class. It was accumulating wealth. It had won its first political victory in the Reform Bill of 1832 and it would win its second with the Repeal of the Corn Laws in 1846. It was on its way. More than most newcomers it was raw. Unlike the French bourgeoisie of the eighteenth century, it had no need to create a new political and philosophical system to prepare itself for power. Its chief subjective quality was a moral unctuousness. This it wore like armour to justify its exploitation of common labour, and to protect itself from the loose and erratic lives of the aristocracy it was preparing to supplant. Matthew Arnold, twenty years later, was to win a reputation by denouncing it as Philistine and cataloguing its deficiencies with an almost pathological malice. The Victorian middle classes paid little attention to him, and rightly so. They knew what was wrong with them. A far greater man than Arnold had told them almost from the beginning, had shown them themselves, not with intellectual fastidiousness, but in terms of human character and human relations. The Victorian middle classes read Dickens, loved Dickens, worshipped Dickens as few writers have been before or since. It is a very bold assumption that they did not understand what Dickens was saying. By 1850 he had already drawn Pecksniff, Dombey and the horrible Mr. Murdstone. In 1854 *Hard Times* showed labour rebellious and despairing against the conditions imposed upon it by the new industrial processes.

Dickens saw Victorian England always with the eyes of a pre-Victorian. His ideal England was the England of Hazlitt and of Pickwick. Man of genius as he was, the Victorians were more perspicacious than he. They were not looking backwards. They wanted a culture, a way of life of their own. They found it symbolized for them in the work of three men, first in Thomas Arnold, the famous headmaster of Rugby, secondly in Thomas Hughes, the author of *Tom Brown's Schooldays*, and lastly in W. G. Grace. These three men, more than all others, created Victorianism, and to leave out Grace is to misconceive the other two. That the Victorian middle classes found in these three what they had been waiting anxiously for is proved first by the extraordinary enthusiasm of the reception they gave to them, and secondly by the manner in which they took from each exactly what they needed to create a whole and rejected the rest. Cricket, we may note in passing, was in 1837 still no more than a camp-follower in the life of the nation. Money was on the order of the day and in 1846 William Clarke organized the first itinerant All England XI to make money—he said so plainly. Morals (or rather moralism) being part of the climate of the time, cricket purged itself of its matches at £500 a side; both organizationally from above and by internal discipline it rid itself of bookies and those who sold matches for money. Unwittingly it was girding itself for the destiny that Arnold, more than any other man, was unwittingly preparing for it.

Thomas Arnold is one of the few enduring figures of the Victorian era. Carlyle and Ruskin, Tennyson and Browning, continue to fill space and occupy time even though diminishing. All of them put in one scale do not weigh down the achievement and the influence of the redoubtable Thomas. He did not do exactly what he set out to do, but then few who set out to remake a nation ever do.

Wordsworth had said that England needed manners, virtue, freedom, power. Arnold saw that it had power. Freedom for him was embodied in the first Reform Act. But manners and virtue he was sure were absent and he was equally sure that their continued absence from the realm would end in the destruction of both power and freedom. Mealy-mouthed generations have watered him down as they have watered down Charles Dickens. Arnold was a man of tempestuous temperament. He was tormented all his life by the fear that England (in fact the whole modern world) would be cracked wide open by social revolution and end either in ruin or military dictatorship. It was to counter this that he did what he did. He aimed to create a body of educated men of the upper classes who would resist the crimes of Toryism and the greed and vulgarity of industrialists on the one hand, and the socialistic claims of the oppressed but uneducated masses on the other. Never the slave of political shibboleths, he did not so much mind Peel and Wellington. What he hated was 'the tribe of selfish and ignorant lords, and country squires and clergymen, who would irritate the feelings of the people to madness'. This is but a modest sample of the habitual violence of his language whenever he referred to Toryism. Benthamism as a solution to social problems he despised and thought Bentham 'a bad man'.

Though always willing to try to educate the masses, he considered them as essentially uneducable. Universal suffrage he equated with universal plunder. The trade unions he saw as 'a fearful engine of mischief, always ready to riot and to assassinate'. Ruin, convulsion, irreparable destruction of civilized society, these were the habitual constituents of his mind. As late as 1840, only two years before his death, he confessed that he had often thought of going to New Zealand 'if there was any prospect of rearing any hopeful form of society'.

This was the world in which he lived.[1] The only solution he saw was in the actual union of church and state, a moral political body which would institute the rule of God upon earth. He was no mere thought-provoker. He began with what he had before him, the boys of Rugby School. He taught them discipline and self-reliance, to govern themselves so as to be able to govern men. He taught the fear of God and the love of truth. What he aimed at is familiar enough. How he sought to achieve it gives a better picture of his essential kinship with the great political organizers. He ruthlessly excluded from the school all the boys who did not fit in. 'Till a man learns that the first, second, and third duty of a schoolmaster is to get rid of unpromising subjects, a great public school will never be what it might be, and what it ought to be.' Unpromising was a term he used in a sense peculiar to himself. There were boys of unusual gifts and character whom he recommended as sure to do well in another environment, for example the university. In the school, however, they were out of place, and though he gave sympathetic advice to the parents, out they had to go. Arnold was not a pioneer who had to draw the plans and lay the foundation stone. He was happy to relate that when he went to Rugby he found there already much that he believed in. His appointment was not in any way fortuitous. He was recommended to the Board on the ground that he would alter the whole public-school system in England. Obviously there were people who thought the whole

---

[1] Arnold's world was not a temperamental idiosyncrasy. It was essentially the world of Marx and of de Tocqueville, two of the acutest minds of the time.

system needed to be altered. His method spread to school after school in England with a rapidity that can be accounted for only by the fact that the people whom it was to serve were ready and ripe for it. The supreme irony, however, is that what they took was not what Arnold gave. Arnold believed in religion and he believed in character. Scarcely less powerful in his conceptions was the role of the intellect. One of the great moments of his own vigorous intellectual life is his discovery that he must teach not knowledge but the power of acquiring it. For Arnold intellectual excellence was inseparable from the moral.

What actually happened is one of the most fantastic transformations in the history of education and of culture. The English ruling classes accepted Arnold's aims and accepted also his methods in general. But with an unerring instinct they separated from it the cultivation of the intellect and substituted for it organized games, with cricket at the head of the curriculum. It seems that it is the historian of sport who is best able to see with open eyes what took place.

'The next step came with the realization that football and other games were not merely useful as substitutes for undesirable activities but might be used to inculcate more positive virtues—loyalty and self-sacrifice, unselfishness, co-operation and *esprit de corps*, a sense of honour, the capacity to be a "good loser" or to "take it" (if we may use anachronistically two colloquialisms of later, but different, dates). This way of looking at games is more or less taken for granted now, at any rate in schools, but it was a novelty then. With it seems to have grown up the notion that the English nation derives some of its peculiar virtues from addiction to games—a thesis which appears far from obvious now, but may contain a grain of truth.'

Arnold would have repudiated this.

'The playing fields did indeed now become in some cases the centre of school life, and in the hands of fanatical masters games came to dominate everything else. Many of these enthusiasts forgot that games had originally been fostered for a purpose: cricket and football were treated as ends in themselves, and the desirability of forcing them on pupils was never questioned.'

     •      •      •      •      •

There is an implication here of coercion. Some boys undoubtedly suffered. But under any system some suffer. We are nearer the truth with reminiscences of Earl Attlee at a function of the Cricket Society a year or two ago when he said that for him and his school-fellows cricket was a religion and W.G. stood next to the Deity. This was what became of the system of Arnold, a man who had only the most casual interest in cricket and football, if the word interest can be used at all for watching the Schoolhouse at football and family cricket with the children on the lawn.

Nothing is more convincing of how sure parents and masters were of what they were doing than the reiteration that they did not want scholars. in 1856 the then headmaster of Rugby published the *Rugby School Book* as an authoritative memorial of what Rugby stood for. There it is categorically stated: 'We are not students in England. Great Englishmen (generally speaking) are great in some departments of practical life, great in statesmanship, jurisprudence or war. Their nature is abhorrent of the Study. With the Germans it is otherwise.' The writer of this (probably the headmaster himself) vilifies the history of thought and of his own country. Whenever a great European nation has found it necessary to think and to study it has done so. Hobbes, Locke, Newton and Milton were men of the study because the times demanded it. The Victorians took Carlyle and Ruskin in their stride. What really interested them was Arnold's moral excellence and character training. His intellectual passion they had no use for. They found ample scope for character training and the inculcation of moral excellence in the two games, football and cricket, and of one of them, cricket, they made the basis of what can only be called a national culture. 'A straight bat' and 'It isn't cricket' became the watchwords of manners and virtue and the guardians of freedom and power. All sneering at these as cant or hypocrisy is ignorance or stupidity. 'Cant,' says Hazlitt, 'is the voluntary overcharging or prolongation of a real sentiment; hypocrisy is the setting up of pretension to a feeling you never had and have no wish for.' It is possible to speak of cant in regard to cricket only within the last thirty years, and then with caution; to speak of hypocrisy is to ignore completely the solid needs and interests which these ideas and terminology served.

I have said that this transformation of Arnold's methods was instinctive. By this I mean that it was not the result of conscious manipulation. I describe it also as unerring. The term is precise but must be purged of possible ambiguity. There are people who, looking at history in much the same way as I do, are inclined to see in what happened to Arnold's ideas little more than a clever manœuvre. By it a ruling class disciplined and trained itself for the more supple and effective exercise of power. This is not even good invective. It is mere railing because it is completely unhistorical. The translators and emasculators of Arnold were the vanguard of a world-wide movement.

The world-wide renaissance of organized games and sports as an integral part of modern civilization was on its way. Of this renaissance, the elevation of cricket and football to the place that they soon held in English life was a part; historically speaking, the most important part. The system as finally adopted was not an invention but a discovery, or rather a rediscovery. Arnold might give a grudging recognition to Dissent. Yet every renewal of English life so far has gone back to the Puritan past, and his system was Puritan or it was nothing. Cricket and football provided a meeting place for the moral outlook of the dissenting middle classes and the athletic instincts of the aristocracy. Finally, cricket was one of the most complete products of that previous age to which a man like Dickens always looked back with such nostalgia. It had been formed by rural and artisan Englishmen who had aimed at nothing but the creation of an activity which would disinterestedly express their native artistic instincts. If it could so rapidly be elevated to the status of a moral discipline it was because it had been born and grew in an atmosphere and in circumstances untainted by any serious corruption. The Victorians made it compulsory for their children, and all the evidence points to the fact that they valued competence in it and respect for what it came to signify more than they did intellectual accomplishment of any kind. The only word that I know for this is culture. The proof of its validity is its success, first of all at home and then almost as rapidly abroad, in the most diverse places and among peoples living lives which were poles removed from that whence it originally came. This signifies, as so often in any deeply national movement, that it contained elements of universality that went beyond the bounds of the originating nation. It is the only contribution of the English educational system of the nineteenth century to the general educational ideas of Western civilization. Chambertin, to whom more than any other man we owe the Olympic Games, was primarily an educationist. He came to England to study the English educational system as it had originated at Rugby School. And he himself has testified to the role which this visit played in his final decision to organize the games and his struggles to achieve it.

Every movement must have its sacred book, its testament. By it the faithful can renew their faith and the young be moulded without pain. The testament came in 1857—*Tom Brown's Schooldays* by Thomas Hughes. No one will call Hughes a great writer. For the literary critic he is a minor figure. Yet Bagehot's dictum that if a man writes a book then he is such a man as could write that book is here useful. This makes it only more difficult to reconcile a simplicity amounting almost to naivety with the firm grasp on shifting conditions of social life, the invention and skill with which they are presented and the author's independence of mind. For consider what he has to say, directly or indirectly, about all the matters this chapter has been probing into.

The book is justly celebrated for its portrait of the Doctor. Whatever Arnold said or did would have meant little unless it had been vitalized by an inspiring personality. No print, no report, no message, could ever convey what the Doctor's actual presence conveyed. This Hughes knows, says, sets out to demonstrate and succeeds.

The moral excellence and character training of Arnold's system are the backbone of the book. Hughes, however, is no blind follower. Tom Brown's father and Tom himself are quite positive that proficiency in the school curriculum is of little interest to them. 'Were I a private schoolmaster, I should say, let who will hear the boys their lessons, but let me live with them when they are at play and rest.' Private school or public, the attitude is the same. The *Rugby School Book* of 1856 might say that literature is the crown of an educated man. Among all the characters in *Tom Brown* the only one with any sensitivity to literature or the classics is young Arthur. It could not be by chance that Arthur is a frail, sickly boy, who, despite his intellectual and moral depth and sensitivity, is dependent for his place in school life on the cricketing Tom. Arthur's first timid friendship is with a boy of remarkable scientific gifts. He is known as the Madman and is persecuted by all his fellows until, for Arthur's sake, Tom comes to the rescue. Art and science depend for their very existence on physical strength and character.

Arnold has seen the salvation of society in a body of God-fearing men who would hold the balance between ruthless industrialism and rebellious labour. Such a one is Arthur's father, a curate who attempts to do just this in one of the industrial towns. The effort kills him.

Arnold had hoped for a society in which each type of man would find his proper place and do his work, conscious that whatever that work was, it contributed to the common good. It was not an ideal. Arnold believed that unless this was achieved society was doomed. Hughes transforms this into a vision, a dream. It is when Arthur, the sensitive scholar, is at death's door that he dreams this dream. The vision not only pulls him back from death but reconciles him to it, reconciles him also to the possible deaths of his friends at the school.

Arnold had hoped that the mechanics' institutes and other workers' associations (purged of their atheistic socialism) would contribute towards the education of the workers. Hughes dismisses this out of hand and here he speaks with the very voice of Victorian England: the organizers of such institutions must find some substitute for the games of the old country 'veast'; something to put in the place of the old back-swording and wrestling and racing; something to try the muscles of men's bodies and the endurance of their hearts, and to make them rejoice in their strength. Otherwise they will fail or end in intellectual priggishness. Arnold did not, could not, think in this way. Hughes and the people for whom he spoke saw more deeply into the needs of the people of England than Arnold did. If the Industrial Revolution organized into a concerted whole the particular movements of the artisans who practised a trade, cricket organized into a whole the elementary tensions and stresses of back-swording, wrestling, racing and the other games of the 'veast'.

Hughes was not a reactionary. He was a Dickensian without the social passion of Dickens, and therefore with a surer eye for society as it was and not as it might be. His love of Dickens appears in his sentiment, his sentimentality, even in phrases and cadences—'had never tasted such good potatoes or seen such jolly boys'. He was a Dickensian in a far deeper sense; the old England was very dear to him.

He begins his book with a description of the Browns, sturdy, individualistic, quarrelsome, clannish, generous. Nothing he does is better than his description of the old village life which is lived by Tom's father, the squire, and the villagers. All through the book he hankers after these good days with the rough, kindly, simple life, the loving exploration of every square inch of the neighbourhood, the village sports, the delights and hardships of the mail coach. He pours nostalgic scorn on the luxuries of railroad and foreign travel now enjoyed by the young men of his day. He has more than sympathy with the spontaneity, not to say violence and lawlessness, of those early days. But Hughes knows that they are gone. He knows that a new age requires a new discipline and that Arnold is the protagonist of that discipline. But either instinctively or by design he sees that discipline as arising from an adaptation of as much as possible of pre-Victorian England into the public school, the private school and the mechanics' institutes. Hence the power of his famous descriptions of the football match, the cross-country run, the cricket match, the fight between Tom Brown and Slogger Williams.

In the *History of Football* by Mr. Morris Marples one can read more of the social history of England than in many large and learned tomes. There he shows that for his description of the games Hughes has leaned heavily on three essays signed W.D.A. which had appeared the year before in the *Rugby School Book*. Hughes's debt to at least two of them is certainly heavy. Their author was none other than W. D. Arnold, son of Thomas and brother of Matthew. If Hughes borrowed heavily it was from a stock that was held in common by very different types of people. The same nostalgia for the old which so distinguishes Hughes pervades the essays of W.D.A.

W. D. Arnold was a soldier. Though he was only fourteen when his father died he was a true disciple of Thomas. His ethical sense was strong and he seems to have tried to inculcate it in military society in India. As Director of Public Education he founded schools in the Punjab. He translated from the German a thesis on English education. He had his father's wide intellectual interests, lecturing and publishing on the caste system in India, the Palace of Westminster and the discovery of America. Yet he contributed as much as any to the transformation which overtook his father's system of which he was so eminent an example. He was one of the three who drew up the Rugby Football Rules in 1845. His beautifully written and deeply felt essays on the cross-country run and the Schoolhouse against the School at football live in Hughes's book and the 10,000 books and stories for which it served as the model. He interests me much more than does his famous brother Matthew. His influence was greater and more valuable than Matthew's philistine ideas about sweetness and light.

For general ideas, perspective, an ideal, a model, Hughes followed Thomas Arnold. The grandeur of these ideas, their moral elevation, their seductiveness, never shifted Hughes from his acute sense of transition from one age to another, which had been the central experience of his youth. His feeling for what was or should be transitory and what was permanent in English life was sure and strong. He was completely free from the abstractions of Carlyle's thunders and Ruskin's lamps.

The book was one of the great successes of the century. That could only have been because it put into compact form the ideas and feelings that were stirring in the upper classes of England ever since Arnold had been appointed headmaster of Rugby twenty-five years before.

Hughes did not think that trade unions were engines of mischief, always ready for riot and assassination. He had sympathy for their aims and wished them success. Chartism had died down, and with it the fear of social revolution. If the upper classes were acquiring stability and perspective, the working classes, or at least organized labour, were doing the same. The old England had indeed gone. By 1857 a majority of the population lived in cities. This was the generation, the first of many to come, which was, in the words of Mr. Marples, 'cut off from the natural country pursuits and amusements which had been the heritage of Englishmen for centuries'. They probably felt the loss far more than the public-school boys of Hughes. In the ten years that followed the Factory Act of 1847 there had come into existence an enormous urban public, proletarian and clerical lower middle class. They had won for themselves one great victory, freedom on Saturday afternoons. They were 'waiting to be amused'. The phrase is Mr. Marples's and for the moment let it serve.

The decade of the sixties, with its rush to organize sports associations of every kind, was just round the corner. In 1862 the first team of English cricketers sailed for Australia, in 1863 the M.C.C. authorized over-arm bowling, thus removing the last barrier to the development of the game's full potentialities. In 1863 W.G., then fifteen years old, played in a first-class game. He had made his first appearance on a stage which all classes in the nation had helped to build, and which was just about ready for the performance W.G. was to give. Prolegomena is a tough word, but my purpose being what it is, it is the only one I can honestly use. It means the social, political, literary and other antecedents of some outstanding figure in the arts and sciences. Grasp the fact that a whole nation had prepared the way for him and you begin to see his stature as a national embodiment.

# 14

# *W.G.*

THROUGH W. G. Grace, cricket, the most complete expression of popular life in pre-industrial England, was incorporated into the life of the nation. As far as any social activity can be the work of any one man, he did it. Perhaps the best way to introduce him is to tabulate what he did. He did not merely bring over what he inherited. Directly and indirectly he took what he found and re-created it. It is not certain that the game would so easily and quickly have gained and held its place without the technical transformation and the *réclame* he gave to it. This total success might have come in a different way. It came his way, at the perfect historical moment, and it came completely. Any extended cricket analysis which is not based on historical facts or the technique of the game tells more about the writer than what he is writing about. Let us begin, therefore, unusually, with his influence on bowling.

It is a cricket commonplace that he killed the professional fast bowling of the sixties. For twenty years a line of fast bowlers had dominated play. On the many rough wickets of the day they were often unplayable. W.G. so mastered them that after a time they were almost afraid to bowl within his reach. Looking back, one of the players of the day wondered how he escaped being permanently maimed or killed. In 1857, against some of the fastest bowlers of the day, on the always lively Lord's wicket, Reginald Hankey for the Gentlemen played an innings which immediately became famous, and has remained so to this day. He made only 70. W.G. first played for the Gentlemen in 1865, not yet seventeen. Beginning in 1871 he scored against the Players, in consecutive innings, 217, 77 and 112, 163, 158 and 70. He put an end to the brute strength which had survived from the previous era. Even in those days bowling was in the hands more of professionals than amateurs. To deal with W.G. the professional bowlers had to develop new skills, new arts. Chiefly they learned from the Australians, but it is ironical that W.G. himself was one of the pioneers of change.

He had been one of the fast slingers and a very successful one. As he grew older and wickets began to get better he bowled slow round the wicket. As late as 1887 A. G. Steel calls him the best change bowler in England 'bar none'. Eight years later, when he is three years short of fifty, he bowls Ranjitsinhji, well set, with the first ball he bowls to him. Ranjitsinhji repeats the 1887 judgment of Steel. The same critic discusses the new phenomenon of balls curling in the air and prophesies that when the practice is perfected it will make batting more difficult than ever. Among those he mentions as being able to do the new trick is W. G. Grace. Steel, Ranjitsinhji, Pelham Warner. They cover a long period in the history of cricket; what between them they do not know is not knowledge. This is Sir Pelham Warner writing many years after, in fact in the memorial biography:

'Of all the feats I witnessed by W.G., the one that most surprised me was a bowling one. It was in 1902—he was then nearly fifty-four—against the Australians when Trumper was at his very best. The Old Man took the ball and I thought we were in for it. Instead the Australians were—five for 29; marvellously baffling, too, not a pinch of luck to help an analysis of which Tom Richardson would have been proud.'

This is the bowling record of the greatest batsman the world has ever known, the creator of modern batting. (He was, by the way, in his younger days, the greatest all-round fieldsman of his time.) His bowling record tells us much about him. His greatest gift was in his head, where resided a genius for the game. He had a general's rapid eye. He saw a boy of eighteen batting at the nets one day at Lord's in 1906 and asked who he was. George Challenor from the West Indies, he was told. 'Take note of him,' said W.G. 'You will hear of him one day.' His marvellous physique was a priceless asset, but it was the lesser half, and later 1 shall examine this phrase, colossal physique, so glibly used.

W.G.'s batting figures, remarkable as they are, lose all their true significance unless they are seen in close relation with the history of cricket itself and the social history of England. Unless you do this you fall head foremost into the trap of making comparisons with Bradman. Bradman piled up centuries. W.G. built a social organization.

Despite the impression of continuity and expansion which the histories of cricket give, there is little evidence to show that it was widely played or that it was a common public entertainment before the decade in which W.G. first appeared. The histories will say that the University match has been played since 1827. Yet up to 1862 (only 100 years ago) the Oxford University Cricket Club was run by three treasurers, no one knew exactly who was to collect the eleven and, *mirabile dictu*, there was never a definite captain. There were often two captains, both directing the field and changing the bowling; each of the treasurers had some sort of right, *ex officio*, to play in the eleven, even to the exclusion of better players. One conclusion is inescapable—such doings were responsible to no public interest or public opinion. Cricket at Cambridge was not quite so haphazard but only that. Of the counties only Surrey had been long established. W.G.'s own county, Gloucestershire, was formally founded only in 1871. Despite the long and famous record of Hampshire cricketers, the Hampshire County Cricket Club was founded only in 1863 and it was twenty years before the cricket of this county was established on a sound footing. The Lancashire county club came into existence only in 1864. The same decade saw the birth of Middlesex and Yorkshire. Most indicative is the history of so famous a cricketing county as Kent. Late in the century it was once more organized and then had no more than 300 members. There is no need to go through the list. When in 1871 W.G. made 2,739 runs, with an average of 78·9, he played but five matches for Gloucestershire and one of these was against M.C.C. and Ground. His season comprised matches against the Players, for South *v.* North, for Gentlemen of the South *v.* Players of the South. One of the early Australian teams advertised in the papers for fixtures. A county championship was organized only in 1873. The whole imposing structure and organization of first-class cricket as we know it today we owe to W.G. The crowds flocked to see him play. Batsmen followed in his footsteps and became great. He swelled the treasuries of the counties and earned thousands of pounds for professionals in benefit matches.

Most dramatically, he had sprung on to the field fully fledged. He blew a note to signal that he had arrived, and no brass band or orchestra could keep up with him. In 1864, brought by his older brother Henry from South Wales to play against Surrey in London and against Gentlemen of Sussex at Hove, he made only 5 and 38 at the Oval, and his captain wanted to drop him. He was saved by the protests of his brother Henry. The boy made 170 and 56 not out, the second score against the clock. The next season he scored five centuries, including a 224. In two years, not yet twenty years old, he was the greatest batsman in England, scoring as no one had ever scored before and batting as no one had ever batted before. He was news, and as he continually broke all precedents (even his own) before he had passed the middle twenties, each amazing new performance told the public, cricketing and otherwise, that here was one of those rare phenomena, something that had never been seen before and was not likely to be seen again.

In 1868 he scored a century in each innings of a match. This had been done once, and as long ago as fifty years past. When he made 2,739 runs in a season no batsman had ever made 2,000. No wonder the record stood unbroken for twenty years. In that year the batsman second to him made about half as many as W.G.'s total. To visualize what he did and the impression it made we must imagine a contemporary batsman making over 5,000 runs in a season, with an average of 200. In 1874 he made 1,000 runs and took 100 wickets, the first man ever known to do so. In 1876 he scored the first 300 ever made in first-class cricket. This was in the East, in Canterbury, on August 11th and 12th. He travelled by train to the West and on the 14th he made 177 for Gloucestershire against Notts. He set off to the North and at Sheffield against Yorkshire made another 300. In seven days, covering ground like some Alexander, he had made 839 runs. In 1880 the first Test match against Australia in England was played. England won by five wickets, Grace 152. He went twice to Australia, where he often faced conditions as bad if not worse than those of the Hambledon men 100 years before. No matter. He was the champion there as well as on the perfect Oval turf. He was only thirty-one when he was the recipient of a national testimonial including a cheque for nearly £1,500. He created the technique of the modern game and he created the arena in which it could thrive. The county clubs and the organization of cricket as a national institution followed in his wake. Of how many Englishmen in the nineteenth century could anything similar be said?

What manner of man was he? The answer can be given in a single sentence. He was in every respect that mattered a typical representative of the pre-Victorian Age.

The evidence for it abounds. His was a Gloucestershire country father who made a good wicket in the orchard and the whole family rose at dawn to get in a few hours of cricket. Their dogs were trained to act as retrievers. They organized clubs and played matches all over their part of the country. W.G. was taking part from the time he was nine. It is 1857, but one is continually reminded of Tom Brown's childhood thirty years before. The back-swording, running and wrestling have been replaced by a game which provides all that these gave in a more organized manner befitting a new age. But the surroundings are the same, the zest, the concentration, the desire to excel, are the same. The Grace family make their own ground at home. I am only surprised that they did not make their own bats, there must have been much splicing and binding. If they try to play according to established principles, well, the father is a trained man of science. Four sons will become doctors. The wicket the father makes is a good one. The boys are taught to play straight. With characteristically sturdy independence, one brother hits across and keeps on hitting across. They let him alone while W.G. and G.F. are encouraged to stick to first principles. Such live and let live was not the Victorian method with youth.

W.G.'s fabulous stamina was not a gift from the gods. Boys of the Grace clan once walked seven miles to school in the morning, seven miles home for lunch, seven miles back to school and seven miles home in the evenings. Decadence was already creeping in and made this seem excessive. So the midday fourteen miles was cut out. That was the breed, reared in the pre-Victorian days before railways. He was not the only pre-Victorian in the family. His elder brother E.M. was even more so than he. The records show that the family in its West Gloucestershire cricketing encounters queried, disputed and did not shrink from fisticuffs. To the end of their days E.M. and W.G. chattered on the field like magpies. Their talking at and even to the batsman was so notorious that young players were warned against them. They were uninhibited with each other and could be furious at fraternal slights or mistakes. They were uninhibited in general. The stories of W.G. which prove this are among the best about him. There is room here for only one.

W.G. enquired about a new bowler from the opposing captain and was told enigmatically, 'He mixes them up.' The Old Man watched the newcomer carefully for a few overs. Then he hit him far away and as he ran between the wickets shouted to his partner: 'Run up. Run up. We'll mix 'em up for him. We'll mix 'em up for him.' It is quite impossible even to imagine anyone shouting such a remark in a big match today. It was most probably out of place already when W.G. made it.

In his attitude to book-learning he belonged entirely to the school of the pre-Arnold Browns. He rebuked a fellow player who was always reading in the dressing-rooms: 'How do you expect to score if you are always reading?' Then follows this priceless piece of ingenuous self-revelation: 'I am never caught that way.' It would be idle to discount the reputation he gained for trying to diddle umpires, and even on occasions disputing with them. He is credited with inducing a batsman to look up at the sun to see a fictitious flight of birds and then calling on the bowler to send down a fast one while the victim's eyes were still hazy. Yet I think there is evidence to show that his face would have become grave and he would have pulled at his beard if a wicket turned out to be prepared in a way that was unfair to his opponents. Everyone knows such men, whom you can trust with your life, your fortune and your sacred honour, but will peep at your cards when playing bridge at a penny a hundred. His humours, his combativeness, his unashamed wish to have it his own way on the field of play, his manœuvres to encompass this, his delight when he did, his complaints when he didn't, are the rubs and knots of an oak that was sound through and through. Once only was he known to be flustered, and that was when he approached the last few runs of his hundredth century. All who played with him testify that he had a heart of gold, loyal, generous to the end of his life, ready to place his knowledge, his experience and his time at the disposal of young players, even opponents. He is all of one piece, of the same family as the Browns with whom Thomas Hughes begins his book.

W.G. was a pre-Victorian. Yet a man of his stature does not fit easily into any one mould. When we look at the family again we see that there was a Victorian in it. The mother was one of those modern women who being born before their time did what was expected of them in the sphere to which they had been called, but made of it a field for the exercise of qualities that would otherwise have been suppressed. The prototype of them all is Florence Nightingale. Mrs. Grace's place was in the home, which included the orchard. She mastered the game of cricket, was firm, not to say severe, with W.G. for not catching on quickly enough to her instructions as to how to play a certain stroke. She kept books, the scores of the family in their early matches. She wrote to the captain of the All England XI recommending her son E.M. for a place in his side. She took the opportunity to say a word for W.G., who, she said, would be the best of the Graces—his back-play showed it. The boy, it seems, was *taught* to play forward and back. Until she died the boys wired match scores and their personal scores to her at the end of each day's play. There was much of his mother in W.G.

The three Grace brothers became famous cricketers. The Walker brothers were more than twice as many as the Graces. Yet they do not give the impression of being a clan as the three brothers E.M., W.G. and G.F. (There were two others, Henry and Alfred, who were good, but not great cricketers.) From all accounts E.M. on the cricket field was a card and it would be interesting to know what he was like on the bench: he was a coroner. G.F. appears to have been thoughtful and reserved, and died young. W.G. was close enough to E.M., yet is said to have felt the death of G.F. more than he felt most other bereavements. Linked together, they were yet three individual men. W.G., the greatest of the three, most completely embodied the family qualities. This has been often observed in great men.

We can sum up. He seems to have been one of those men in whom the characteristics of life as lived by many generations seemed to meet for the last, in a complete and perfectly blended whole. His personality was sufficiently wide and firm to include a strong Victorian streak without being inhibited. That I would say was his greatest strength. He was not in any way inhibited. What he lacked he would not need. All that he had he could use. In tune with his inheritance and his environment, he was not in any way repressed. All his physical and spiritual force was at his disposal to do what he wanted to do. He is said on all sides to have been one of the most typical of Englishmen, to have symbolized John Bull, and so on and so forth. To this, it is claimed, as well as to his deeds, he owed his enormous popularity. I take leave to doubt it. The man usually hailed as representative is never quite typical, is more subtly compounded than the plain up-and-down figure of the stock characteristics. Looking on from outside and at a distance it seems to me that Grace gives a more complex impression than is usually attributed to him. He was English undoubtedly, very much so. But he was typical of an England that was being superseded. He was the yeoman, the country doctor, the squire, the England of yesterday. But he was no relic, nor historical or nostalgic curiosity. He was pre-Victorian in the Victorian Age but a pre-Victorian militant.

There he was using his bat like an axe, building as much of that old world as possible into the new, and fabulously successful at it. The more simple past was battling with the more complex, more dominant, present, and the present was being forced to yield ground and make room. In any age he would have been a striking personality and vastly popular. That particular age he hit between wind and water. Yet, as in all such achievements, he could conquer only by adopting the methods of the new.

Cricket is an art. Like all arts it has a technical foundation. To enjoy it does not require technical knowledge, but analysis that is not technically based is mere impressionism. That W.G. was a pre-Victorian who made a pre-Victorian game a part of the Victorian era appears nowhere so clearly as in the technique he introduced. It had the good fortune (rare with him) to be beautifully stated.

It is as a batsman that he is best known and surely what he did should take its place in the co-ordination which seeks to plot the process by which the arts develop. Batsmen before him were content to specialize in what suited them best. One great player used the forward style. Another was distinguished for his mastery of back-play. Equally the cut as the leg-hit had its particular exponents. There were aggressive players and players defensive. There were players who were good on good wickets. There were others at their best on bad. Whether on the village green or at Lord's, this was in essence cricket of the age of the Browns.

Practically from his very first appearance W.G. put an end to all this categorization. He used all the strokes, he played back or forward, aggressively or defensively, as the circumstances or the occasion required. As he approached forty he confessed to preferring a good slow wicket to a good fast one. In his prime it did not matter to him, and in these days when a jumping or turning wicket is regarded as a reversal of the order of nature, he shares with Victor Trumper and J. B. Hobbs the distinction of being batsmen who at their best were least concerned about the state of the pitch. The crowd at Lord's once rose at him for stopping four shooters in succession. In 1896 on a bad wicket at Sheffield Park the Australian fast bowler Jones frightened out a magnificent batting side. The batsmen went in with the obvious intention of getting out as fast as possible. W.G., then forty-eight, shared with F. S. Jackson the only batting honours of the day. This then, in the classic passage from Ranjitsinhji's *Jubilee Book of Cricket*, was his achievement. I give it in full.

'Before W.G. batsmen were of two kinds, a batsman played a forward game or he played a back game. Each player, too, seems to have made a specialty of some particular stroke. The criterion of style was, as it were, a certain mixed method of play. It was bad cricket to hit a straight ball; as for pulling a slow long-hop, it was regarded as immoral. What W.G. did was unite in his mighty self all the good points of all the good players, and to make utility the criterion of style. He founded the modern theory of batting by making forward- and back-play of equal importance, relying neither on the one nor on the other, but on both. Any cricketer who thinks for a moment can see the enormous change W.G. introduced into the game. I hold him to be, not only the finest player born or unborn, but the maker of modern batting. He turned the old one-stringed instrument into a many-chorded lyre. And, in addition, he made his execution equal his invention. All of us now have the instrument, but we lack his execution. It is not that we do not know, but that we cannot perform. Before W.G. batsmen did not know what could be made of batting. The development of bowling has been natural and gradual; each great bowler has added his quota. W.G. discovered batting; he turned its many narrow straight channels into one great winding river. Anyone who reads his book will understand this. Those who follow may or may not get within measurable distance of him, but it was he who pioneered and made the road. Where a great man has led, many can go afterwards, but the honour is his who found and cut the path. The theory of modern batting is in all essentials the result of W.G.'s thinking and working on the game.'

The age of the Browns is left behind. What they had created is now organized and sublated. Note particularly the words 'thinking and working on the game': remember what he added to bowling. We can be so dazzled by the splendours of his youth that we are apt to forget the mental labours that made him what he was and kept him there.

It is not merely that he cleared the road along which all succeeding batsmen have travelled. He met and conquered such a succession of conditions and bowlers, strategy and tactics, as it has never fallen to the lot of any batsman to face. Late in life he met the googly and was said to be troubled by it. Sir Donald Bradman claims that O'Reilly was a greater bowler than George Lohmann, because O'Reilly bowled the googly and Lohmann did not. All such reasonings and ratings are low tide against the rock of Grace's batsmanship. Trumper used to say that if you got to the pitch of the ball it did not matter which way it was breaking. In his early days W.G. also used to run out of his crease and hit the slow bowlers all over the place. No batsman was more scientific than W.G. and science was his servant, not his master. He was not one who by unusual endowment did stupendously what many others were doing well. He did what no one else had ever done, developed to a degree unprecedented, and till then undreamt of, potentialities inherent in the game. And it was this more than anything else which made possible W.G.'s greatest achievement. It was by modern scientific method that this pre-Victorian lifted cricket from a more or less casual pastime into the national institution which it rapidly became. Like all truly great men, he bestrides two ages. It is at the very least obvious that he was not the rather simple-minded smiter of a cricket ball which is the usual portrayal of him.

So far the best that has been said of W.G. as a historical personage is this, by a bishop:

'Had Grace been born in Ancient Greece the *Iliad* would have been a different book. Had he lived in the Middle Ages he would have been a Crusader and would now have been lying with his legs crossed in some ancient abbey, having founded a great family. As he was born when the world was older, he was the best known of all Englishmen and the King of that English game least spoilt by any form of vice.'

At least it is not unworthy of its subject. Which is precisely why it does W.G. the greatest injustice of all.

When the Bishop implies that W.G.'s gifts would have served him

to a more distinguished place in another age he did at least put his finger
on the heart of the matter. My contention is that no crusader was more
suited to his time than was W.G. to his own; none rendered more service
to his world. No other age that I know of would have been able to give
him the opportunities the Victorian Age gave him. No other age would
have been able to profit so much by him. In the end judgment depends
not on what you think of Grace but on the role you give to sports and
games in the lives of modern people. As usual, it is Mr. Neville Cardus,
in his vivid darting style, who has got closest to W.G.: 'The plain, lusty
humours of his first practices in a Gloucestershire orchard were to be
savoured throughout the man's gigantic rise to a national renown.' Only
it was not the plain, lusty humours of an orchard, but of a whole way of
life. 'He rendered rusticity cosmopolitan whenever he returned to it.
And always did he cause to blow over the fashionable pleasances of St.
John's. . . .' There they needed it least. It was to bleak Sheffield, to dusty
Kennington and to grim Manchester that W.G. brought the life they
had left behind. The breezes stirred by his bat had blown in their faces,
north, south and east, as well as in the west.

This way of looking at W.G. is not as simple as it may appear. Let
me give some idea of what is hidden below the deceptively placid surface.

There are unfortunately none still living who can recall the success
of Harriet Beecher Stowe's *Uncle Tom's Cabin* a hundred years ago. Mass
emotions have centred on a single figure in no more mystifying quantity
and quality than on the figure of Eliza escaping across the ice from
slavery to freedom. Melodramas built around this episode played to
packed houses in the United States, and the pursuers were shot down to
the cheers and tears of thousands who in real life would have nothing
whatever to do with such violent disturbances of the established order.
The book sold in millions all over Europe. An emotion not dissimilar
and no less unaccountable in strictly rational terms seems to have seized
vast numbers of people in Britain a generation before, regarding slaves
in the West Indies. To many the ferocity of the emotions was inexplicable.
American scholarship has found sufficient to give a starting point for
investigation.

Industrialism was closing in on an American population that had
lived the American version of English rural life. They were aware of
their plight in innumerable ways, unverbalized but no less real. To them
Eliza was a symbol of escape from furies vague but pursuing. In Europe,

where industrialism was adding new pressures to those of an already oppressive feudalism, the hopeful immigrant saw in Eliza's dramatic escape the promise of his own eventual escape to the same wide and hospitable land. What was in the minds and hearts of the people of Victorian England which made them see W.G. as they did I cannot say for certain, as there is much in this sketch that I do not say for certain. But the passions and forces which are embodied in great popular heroes —and W.G. was one of the greatest of popular heroes—these passions and forces do not yield their secrets to the antiquated instruments which the historians still cling to. Wilton St. Hill and Learie Constantine were more than makers of runs and takers of wickets to the people of Trinidad and Tobago. Who will write a biography of Sir Donald Bradman must be able to write a history of Australia in the same period. I have indicated what I think W.G. signified in the lives of the English people, not in what politicians did for them or poets wrote of them or what Carlyle and Ruskin preached to them, but in the lives that they themselves lived from day to day. We shall know more what men want and what they live by when we begin from what they do. They worshipped W.G. That is the fact. And I believe that we have never given this fact the attention it deserves. Some day we shall. Of that I have no doubt. For the time being it is enough to say once more: he brought and made a secure place for pre-industrial England in the iron and steel of the Victorian Age.

We have peered below the surface at what W.G. did for the people. When we try to find what the people did for him we begin with a blank sheet. They went to see him, they cheered him on the field, they walked behind him in the streets. It is accepted that the athlete, the entertainer, the orator, is spurred to excel himself by the applause and excitement of his audience. We apostrophize his marvellous physique. There was more to it than muscle and sinew.

We have seen the state of cricket when he began, with its first tentative attempts at county, not even national, organization. He loved the game passionately and always served it. The proof is in the fact that all the success and all the adulation never turned his head. As he made his tremendous scores he could see the game visibly growing and expanding around him. In 1857 the Cricketers' Fund Friendly Society was started. It could not supply the requirements of the ever-growing body of professionals. W.G. was greatly in demand to play in benefit matches. Their success depended on him and in them he was always at his best. In 1871 he played in three and scored 189 not out, 268 and 217. Thus stimulated by a specific need, he obviously mobilized himself specially to satisfy it. When he made his first triple century in Kent, followed it with a century not out in Gloucestershire and took guard in Yorkshire, I do not see him as merely judging the length, driving and cutting, his personal powers supplying the resources. Such records are not built on such limited premises. He was strong with the strength of men who are filling a social need. Every new achievement made a clearing in the forest, drew new layers of the population, wiped off debts, built pavilions. How warmly the county secretaries and treasurers must have met him at the gates; how happy his fellow Gentlemen must have looked in the dressing-room as they prepared to add another victory over the Players to atone for their long list of defeats; how the crowds must have roared as they saw his gigantic figure with the red-and-yellow cap and black beard emerge from the pavilion to start an innings. The point is that whatever his fatigue, he could not take notice of it. The crowds and the people made of every innings a Test innings. Professor Harbage has boldly written that half the credit for Shakespeare's plays must go to the skilled artisans, the apprentices and the law students (the groundlings), who for twenty years supported him and Burbage against all rivals. Anyone who has participated in an electoral campaign or observed closely key figures in it will have noted how a speaker, eyes red with sleeplessness and sagging with fatigue, will rapidly recover all his power at an uproarious welcome from an expectant crowd. If Grace could be so often and so long at his best it was because so much depended on it, so many hundreds of thousands of people, high and low, were expecting him to be at his best, even to exceed it, as he had so often done in the past. Except for commonplaces and pseudo-scientific misuse of terms (father image), we know as yet very little of the nourishment given to the hero by the crowd. Here it must have been very great—Grace's career was exceptionally long. At times he must have been very tired of it all. Once he even thought of retiring. He didn't. Such a decision could not rest on his individual judgment or inclination.

In the spring of 1895 he was nearly forty-seven. He had scored 98 centuries. Not merely he but the whole country was wondering if, how and when he would add the other two. Eighteen-ninety-four had been a miserable year for everybody. He had scored as well as most of the others, with a total of 1,293 runs, average 29·38, number of centuries three. Only Brockwell with five had scored more. In fact, except for Robert Abel, no one else had scored as many. The centuries scored in the season were 52, no one had scored over 200, there were only five innings which totalled over 400. There had been years in which the Old Man had scored no century at all. His county, Gloucestershire, formerly at the top, was now often at the bottom of the list. As usual he started to practise in March and ran into form early. A whole season and just two more centuries! He had the habit of rising to the occasion and then shooting far above it.

I do not propose to recapitulate in any detail what he did in May. Those who know it know it by heart. Those who don't could spend time worse than in finding out. What I want to stress is that in the words of H. D. G. Leveson-Gower: 'Nothing W. G. Grace ever did, nothing any other champion at any other game ever achieved such widespread and well deserved enthusiasm as his batting in May, 1895, when he was in his forty-eighth year and so burly in figure.'

Burly as the figure was, it was sustained and lifted higher than ever before by what has been and always will be the most potent of all forces in our universe—the spontaneous, unqualified, disinterested enthusiasm and goodwill of a whole community. The spontaneity was only in appearance. Once he had scored the 99th century in the second match of the season, the thirty years of public service and personal achievement gathered themselves together in the generations, willing him to complete the edifice with a crown worthy of it and of them. He did not keep them long. Two modest innings against Yorkshire alone intervened before a magnificent 283. Followed 257 and 73 not out against Kent when he was on the field for every minute of the game, and on the last playing day of May he reached and passed the thousand runs, the first player in the game ever to do so. (It gives us an insight into his mind that in deference to his weight and age he scored heavily by hitting balls on the wicket or outside the off-stump over to the on-side.)

Never since the days of the Olympic champions of Greece has the sporting world known such enthusiasm and never since. That is accepted and it is true and it is important—I am the last to question that. What I take leave to ask even at such a moment is this: On what other occasion, sporting or non-sporting, was there ever such enthusiasm, such an unforced sense of community, of the universal merged in an individual? At the end of a war? A victorious election? With its fears, its hatreds, its violent passions? Scrutinize the list of popular celebrations, the un-official ones; that is to say, those not organized from above. I have heard of no other that approached this celebration of W.G.'s hundredth century. If this is not social history what is? It finds no place in the history of the people because the historians do not begin from what people seem to want but from what they think the people ought to want.

He finished as grandly as he had begun. That year of 1895 he made nine centuries. Abel was next with five and all the others made fewer still. Next year he was one of the three who scored over 2,000 runs and he made another triple century. As late as 1902 he was still high on the list of heavy scorers for the season. On his fifty-eighth birthday he played for the Gentlemen at the Oval. He made 74 and hit a ball out of the ground. When he hit a stroke for three he could only run one, and the runs were worth a century. Of all his innings this is the one I would choose to see. He had enriched the depleted lives of two generations and millions yet to be born. He had extended our conception of human capacity and in doing all this he had done no harm to anyone. He is excluded from the history books of his country. No statue of him exists.[1] Yet he continues warm in the hearts of those who never knew him. There he is safe until the whole crumbling edifice of obeisance before Mammon, contempt for Demos and categorizing intellectualism finally falls apart.

[1] The Grace Gate at Lord's, with its chaste inscription 'TO WILLIAM GILBERT GRACE, THE GREAT CRICKETER', is the nearest he has come to a monument.

# 15

## *Decline of the West*

NOT only did W.G. establish cricket as a national institution. The evidence seems to show that but for him its public-school career would never have achieved security and dominance. Up to and including 1865, the first year he played for them, the Gentlemen had been repeatedly routed and often disgraced by their professional opponents. W.G., and W.G. single-handed, altered this. The Players won at the Oval in 1865 and did not win again until 1880. Between 1866 and 1874, apart from three drawn matches, the Players lost twelve matches in succession. Of forty matches between 1865 and 1881 the Gentlemen won twenty-seven and lost only five. To repeat a worthy phrase—for the dull monotony of professional victory was exchanged the dull monotony of professional defeat. Those were the critical years. It is not possible that cricket would have reached and held the position it did among the upper classes if the Gentlemen, that is to say the products of the public schools and the universities, had been as consistently and cruelly beaten as they had been by the professionals before W.G. began. By the fifties the great public schools had begun what was to become compulsory games with their elaborate systems of coaching. The system produced players like Yardley and Steel, the Players were disorganized, but nevertheless it is clear that Grace won the matches for the Gentlemen. We need not give the figures. He not only smashed what had been the Players' greatest strength, fast bowling. He so established the morale of the Gentlemen that though the Players recovered, it was many years before it was possible to look upon the Players as the more likely winners. If between 1865 and 1880 the cricketing amateurs had experienced nothing but a continuation of defeats by the professionals, the least we can say is that the organized games of the public-school system would have been considerably disorganized and the morale demoralized. Gentlemen would not have continued to win the Battle of Waterloo on the playing fields of Eton if they had continued to meet annual Waterloos at Lord's and the Oval.

What has happened to the house built by Arnold, Thomas Hughes and W.G.? The history of its decline is a fascinating (and as unexplored) as the history of its rise.

By 1887, when the *Badminton Book of Cricket* was published, cricket as a guardian of morals was at its best and most prosperous. That book is evidence sufficient. It was beautifully written and to this day is as entertaining and instructive as anything that has ever been published on the game. It had style, it had confidence. The writers had no doubt of what the status of a professional cricketer was and why it should be so. They could tell the Australians frankly that they didn't want them back for another five years: they were bored with the personnel of the England-Australia games, they wanted time to set the internal business of English cricket in order. The book is utterly free of cant. The one blatant moralism seems to have been tacked on to the end of a chapter as an afterthought. They had the thing itself and they did not need to sing, i.e. to cant about it. Ten years later, by the *Jubilee Book of Cricket*, 1897, the guardians were conscious of profane murmurings. Cricket, says a writer in the *Jubilee Book*, is very valuable, but he confesses that he finds it hard to explain why. Nevertheless, cricket as a cult was preserved intact up to 1913. Like the special interests which had made it their own, it received a violent shock from the war of 1914-18. Country house cricket was after 1918 but a shadow, the University match was barely holding its own, the long struggle of the amateur against extinction began. The game, however, was now part of the national life, it maintained its special connotations in the public schools, despite the sniping of the Waughs, the Graveses, the Sassoons.

The blow from which 'It isn't cricket' has never recovered came from within and it came in 1932. This was body-line.

J. H. Fingleton, the Australian journalist, has written an excellent and necessary book on the body-line controversey. He takes an historical view, but in the end he makes out the cause of body-line to be the phenomenal batting of Bradman and the search of English selectors for means to overthrow him. I believe that there was more than that to body-line. And, more important, I believe that what body-line signified is still with us.

Body-line was not an incident, it was not an accident, it was not a temporary aberration. It was the violence and ferocity of our age expressing itself in cricket. The time was the early thirties, the period in which the contemporary rejection of tradition, the contemporary disregard of means, the contemporary callousness, were taking shape. The totalitarian dictators cultivated brutality of set purpose. By now all of us have supped full with horrors. Today cruelties and abominations which would have immeasurably shocked and permanently distressed earlier ages are a commonplace. We must toughen our hides to live at all. We are now like Macbeth in his last stage:

> 'The time has been my senses would have cool'd
> To hear a night-shriek, and my fell of hair
> Would at a dismal treatise rouse and stir
> As life were in't. I have supped full with horrors;
> Direness, familiar to my slaughterous thoughts,
> Cannot once start me.'

It began in World War I. Exhaustion and a fictitious prosperity in the late twenties delayed its maturity. It came into its own in 1929. Cricket could no more resist than the other organizations and values of the nineteenth century were able to resist. That big cricket survived the initial shock at all is a testimony to its inherent decency and the deep roots it had sunk.

The violence of the cricket passions unloosed in the thirties is what strikes the observer today. There was no absolute necessity for Voce and Larwood to take the actions that they did on their return from Australia. Rather than submit to the opinions of a large majority, A. W. Carr preferred to go out of the game altogether. Jardine seemed to be at war not with the Australian eleven but all Australia. The history books tell us that he carried his relentlessness to India: there were no Bradmans in India. What objective necessity was there to introduce body-line into

England after the Australian tour? Yet the attempt was made. Jardine soon went, never to return. Ponsford abandoned the game when he was only thirty-four. Sir Donald Bradman assures us that but for the intervention of the war, 1938 would have been his last visit to England, and he contemplated only one more season in Australia. He was younger than Ponsford. No balls had whizzed past his head for years. Yet he had had enough.

It is in Bradman's autobiography that we can today see conveniently the mentality of the time. The most remarkable page in that remarkable book is his account of his feelings after he had completed his hundredth century. He had played big cricket for nearly twenty years. In that time he had scored as no one had ever scored before. He had made his runs at the rate of fifty an hour. He had scored centuries and double centuries and treble centuries in cricket of the most demanding type. He had conquered bowlers and decided series. Yet what are his sentiments after he had made the hundredth run of the hundredth century? He felt it incumbent upon him, he says, to give the crowd which had so cheered his achievement some reward for its wonderful feelings towards him. He therefore proceeded to hit 71 runs in 45 minutes. This, he adds, is the way he would always wish to have batted if circumstances had permitted him. However, as circumstances did at last permit him the luxury, he classed 'that particular section of my innings as the most satisfying of my career'. In all the years that I have been reading books on cricket this remains the strangest statement that I have ever read, and one to which I frequently return; to it, and to the writer. If Sir Donald Bradman was able to play 'in the way I would always have loved to do had circumstances permitted' only after he had made one hundred centuries, we have to ask ourselves: What were these inhibiting circumstances?

This much at least is obvious. The game he had played between 1928 and 1947 was a game quite different from the one that had been played by Grace and Shrewsbury, Trumper and Ranjitsinhji, Hobbs and Rhodes, the game we had played in the West Indies. Grace, Ranjitsinhji, Trumper and their fellows who had played with them lost infinitely more matches and series than Sir Donald Bradman ever lost. They were painstaking men who gave all they had to cricket. Yet I cannot conceive of any of them thinking of batting in the way Sir Donald thought of it. He has been blamed for machine-like play. He has been blamed for the ruthlessness with which he piled up big scores. This is absurd. I have seen some of his greatest innings and I do not wish to see anything finer. George Headley has explained to me that people speak of Sir Donald's heavy scoring as if each and every great batsman was able to do the same, but refrained for aesthetic or chivalrous reasons which Sir Donald ignored. Speaking with authority, Headley is lost in admiration and even in wonder at the nervous stamina and concentration which Sir Donald displayed in making these mammoth scores so consistently over so long a period. In the autobiography Sir Donald maintains that he played cricket according to the rules as he saw them. There is no need to question this. Every page of his book shows that he has been deeply hurt by what he considers unfair criticism. Every accusation that I have ever heard made against him he has taken care to answer. The slightest wound still gives pain to this tough, relentless opponent. He is conscious of righteousness. His sincerity is patent. He feels himself a victim, and a victim he is, but not of petty jealousies of individual men. The chronicles of the time (far more then than now), when re-read today in the light of after events, tell the story clearly enough. The 1930 Australian team which broke all previous records took a little time to get going and was left in no doubt as to what spectators and pressmen thought.

By 1928, when he began, big cricket was already being played everywhere with the ruthlessness that Bradman is saddled with. He never knew any other kind of cricket. Ponsford and his triple and quadruple centuries had set the tone for Bradman. If Bradman made 974 runs in Tests in 1930 he had experienced when a boy of eighteen a far more merciless 905 from Hammond in the season of 1928–9. His gifts and his cricket personality matured at a time when the ethics, the morals, the personal impulses and desires of cricketers were quite different from those who had played the game in the decades that had preceded. Cricketers already mature when Bradman appeared might want to play like Bradman. They couldn't. They hadn't the outlook. They hadn't the temper. They had inhibitions Bradman never knew.

The new ones could learn. Hutton at the Oval in 1938 showed that he had learnt well. I have never had so painful an experience at any cricket match as when watching Hutton and Hardstaff together during the England innings of 903 for eight declared. Body-line may have vanished. Its temper remained. Other men had stood out above their fellows. W.G. had. But 1865 was not 1930. The spirit which Sir Donald Bradman could release only after a hundred centuries was present, I am sure, in every single one of the hundred centuries that W. G. Grace made, was always present in Trumper and Ranjitsinhji, Fry and Hobbs. That spirit was dead. If Hobbs had been born in 1910, or later, England would have bred another Bradman. Sir Donald first ran the cricket mile in under four minutes and unloosed the floodgates. Circumstances conspired to place the blame on him. I have gathered that even in Australia the attitude to him is ambivalent. They admire him, they are grateful to him, they love him, but they know that the disregard of the compulsions of everyday life, the chivalry that was always a part of the game, began to fade at the time he came into it. Sir Donald is not to blame. He was unfortunate in his place and time. The fact remains that he was in his own way as tough as Jardine.

This was the situation faced by 'It isn't cricket' in 1930. It was not only a Test series at stake. Everything that the temple stood for seemed threatened within and without. If Bradman continued his portentous career a way of life, a system of morals, faced the possibility of disgrace and defeat just at the particular time when more than ever it needed the stimulus of victory and prestige. The men who had made it their special preserve were threatened not only in cricket. They were threatened everywhere. As is usual in such cases, they fought back blindly and were driven into extravagance and immorality. The body-line upheaval shocked everyone and made the cricket world pull itself up and tread carefully. The spirit was not exorcized. The Oval match of 1938 was followed by the long-drawn-out seige in Durban. Luckily the war put an abrupt end to cricket as it was being played in the thirties. The relief was only temporary. Today the same relentlessness is abroad. Cricketers try to preserve the external decencies. The tradition is still strong. But instead of 'It isn't cricket', now one hears more frequently the cynical 'Why isn't it cricket?' Scarcely a tour but hits the headlines for some grave breach of propriety on and off the cricket field. The strategy of Test matches is the strategy of stalking the prey: you come out in the open to attack only when the victim is wounded. No holds are barred. Captains encourage their bowlers to waste time. Bowlers throw and drag. Wickets are shamelessly doctored. Series are lost or believed to be lost by doubtful decisions and immoral practices, and the victims nurse their wrath and return in kind. Writing in the *Cricketer* in the early twenties MacLaren said that in all his career he had known batsmen duck short balls only on two or three occasions. In the West Indies up to when I left in 1932 you took the short ball round to the leg-boundary (or you underwent repairs). Today statisticians and metaphysicians seek to impose a categorical imperative on the number of bumpers the fast bowler may bowl per over. To legislators for relief batsmen of all nations, like Cherubim and Seraphim, continually do cry.

A corps of cricket correspondents functions as an auxiliary arm of their side, but is ready to turn and rend it at the slightest opportunity. What little remains of 'It isn't cricket' is being finally stifled by the envy, the hatred, the malice and the uncharitableness, the shamelessness of the memoirs written by some of the cricketers themselves. Compared with these books, Sir Donald's ruthless autobiography of a dozen years ago now reads like a Victorian novel. How to blind one's eye to all this? Body-line was only a link in a chain. Modern society took a turn downwards in 1929 and 'It isn't cricket' is one of the casualties. There is no need to despair of cricket. Much, much more than cricket is at stake, in fact everything is at stake. If and when society regenerates itself, cricket will do the same. The Hambledon men built soundly. What Arnold, Hughes and W.G. brought is now indelibly a part of the national life and character, and plays its role, the farther it is away from the pressure of publicity. There it is safe. The values of cricket, like much that is now in eclipse, will go into the foundations of new moral and educational structures. But that they can be legislated to what they used to be is a vain hope which can only sour on the tongue and blear the eye. The owl of Minerva flies only at dusk. And it cannot get much darker without becoming night impenetrable.

# PART SIX

# THE ART AND PRACTIC PART

---

## 16

## *'What is Art ?'*

I HAVE made great claims for cricket. As firmly as I am able and as is here possible, I have integrated it in the historical movement of the times. The question remains: What is it? Is it mere entertainment or is it an art? Mr. Neville Cardus (whose work deserves a critical study) is here most illuminating, not as subject but as object. He will ask: 'Why do we deny the art of a cricketer, and rank it lower than a vocalist's or a fiddler's? If anybody tells me that R. H. Spooner did not compel a pleasure as aesthetic as any compelled by the most cultivated Italian tenor that ever lived I will write him down a purist and an ass.' He says the same in more than one place. More than any sententious declaration, all his work is eloquent with the aesthetic appeal of cricket. Yet he can write in his autobiography: 'I do not believe that anything fine in music or in anything else can be understood or truly felt by the crowd.' Into this he goes at length and puts the seal on it with 'I don't believe in the contemporary idea of taking the arts to the people: let them seek and work for them.' He himself notes that Neville Cardus, the writer on cricket, often introduces music into his cricket writing. Never once has Neville Cardus, the music critic, introduced cricket into his writing on music. He finds this 'a curious point'. It is much more than a point, it is not curious. Cardus is a victim of that categorization and specialization, that division of the human personality, which is the greatest curse of our time. Cricket has suffered, but not only cricket. The aestheticians have scorned to take notice of popular sports and games—to their own detriment. The aridity and confusion of which they so mournfully complain will continue until they include organized games *and the people who watch them* as an integral part of their data. Sir Donald Bradman's technical accomplishments are not on the same plane as those of Yehudi Menuhin. Sir John Gielgud in three hours can express adventures and shades in human personality which are not approached in three years of Denis Compton at the wicket. Yet cricket is an art, not a bastard or a poor relation, but a full member of the community.

The approach must be direct. Too long has it been impressionistic or apologetic, timid or defiant, always ready to take refuge in the mysticism of metaphor. It is a game and we have to compare it with other games. It is an art and we have to compare it with other arts.

Cricket is first and foremost a dramatic spectacle. It belongs with the theatre, ballet, opera and the dance.

In a superficial sense all games are dramatic. Two men boxing or running a race can exhibit skill, courage, endurance and sharp changes of fortune; can evoke hope and fear. They can even harrow the soul with laughter and tears, pity and terror. The state of the city, the nation or the world can invest a sporting event with dramatic intensity such as is reached in few theatres. When the democrat Joe Louis fought the Nazi Schmelling the bout became a focus of approaching world conflict. On the last morning of the 1953 Oval Test, when it was clear that England would win a rubber against Australia after twenty years, the nation stopped work to witness the consummation.

These possibilities cricket shares with other games in a greater or lesser degree. Its quality as drama is more specific. It is so organized that at all times it is compelled to reproduce the central action which characterizes all good drama from the days of the Greeks to our own: two individuals are pitted against each other in a conflict that is strictly personal but no less strictly representative of a social group. One individual batsman faces one individual bowler. But each represents his side. The personal achievement may be of the utmost competence or brilliance. Its ultimate value is whether it assists the side to victory or staves off defeat. This has nothing to do with morals. It is the organizational structure on which the whole spectacle is built. The dramatist, the novelist, the choreographer, must *strive* to make his individual character symbolical of a larger whole. He may or may not succeed. The runner in a relay race must take the plus or minus that his partner or partners give him. The soccer forward and the goalkeeper may at certain rare moments find themselves sole representatives of their sides. Even the baseball-batter, who most nearly approaches this particular aspect of cricket, may and often does find himself after a fine hit standing on one of the bases, where he is now dependent upon others. The batsman facing the ball does not merely represent his side. For that moment, to all intents and purposes, he is his side. This fundamental relation of the One and the Many, Individual and Social, Individual and Universal, leader and followers, representative and ranks, the part and the whole, is structurally imposed on the players of cricket. What other sports, games and arts have to aim at, the players are given to start with, they cannot depart from it. Thus the game is founded upon a dramatic, a human, relation which is universally recognized as the most objectively pervasive and psychologically stimulating in life and therefore in that artificial representation of it which is drama.

The second major consideration in all dramatic spectacles is the relation between event (or, if you prefer, contingency) and design, episode and continuity, diversity in unity, the battle and the campaign, the part and the whole. Here also cricket is structurally perfect. The total spectacle consists and must consist of a series of individual, isolated episodes, each in itself completely self-contained. Each has its beginning, the ball bowled; its middle, the stroke played; its end, runs, no runs, dismissal. Within the fluctuating interest of the rise or fall of the game as a whole, there is this unending series of events, each single one fraught with immense possibilities of expectation and realization. Here again the dramatist or movie director has to strive. In the very finest of soccer matches the ball for long periods is in places where it is impossible to expect any definite alteration in the relative position of the two sides. In lawn tennis the duration of the rally is entirely dependent upon the subjective skill of the players. In baseball alone does the encounter between the two representative protagonists approach the definitiveness of the individual series of episodes in cricket which together constitute the whole.

The structural enforcement of the fundamental appeals which all dramatic spectacle must have is of incalculable value to the spectator. The glorious uncertainty of the game is not anarchy. It would not be glorious if it were not so firmly anchored in the certainties which must attend all successful drama. That is why cricket is perhaps the only game in which the end result (except where national or local pride is at stake) is not of great importance. Appreciation of cricket has little to do with the end, and less still with what are called 'the finer points', of the game. What matters in cricket, as in all the arts, is not finer points but what everyone with some knowledge of the elements can see and feel. It is only within such a rigid structural frame that the individuality so characteristic of cricket can flourish. Two batsmen are in at the same time. Thus the position of representative of the side, though strictly independent, is interchangeable. In baseball one batter bats at a time. The isolated events of which both games consist is in baseball rigidly limited. The batter is allowed choice of three balls. He must hit the third or he is out. If he hits he must run. The batter's place in the batting order is fixed —it cannot be changed. The pitcher must pitch until he is taken off and when he is taken off he is finished for that game. (The Americans obviously prefer it that way.) In cricket the bowler bowls six balls (or eight). He can then be taken off and can be brought on again. He can bowl at the other end. The batting order is interchangeable. Thus while the principle of an individual representing the side at any given moment is maintained, the utmost possible change of personnel compatible with order is allowed. We tend to take these things for granted or not to notice them at all. In what other dramatic spectacle can they be found built-in? The greatness of the great batsman is not so much in his own skill as that he sets in motion all the immense possibilities that are contained in the game as structurally organized.

Cricket, of course, does not allow that representation or suggestion of specific relations as can be done by a play or even by ballet and dance. The players are always players trafficking in the elemental human activities, qualities and emotions—attack, defence, courage, gallantry, steadfastness, grandeur, ruse. This is no drawback. Punch and Judy, *Swan Lake*, pantomime, are even less particularized than cricket. They depend for their effect upon the technical skill and creative force with which their exponents make the ancient patterns live for their contemporaries. Some of the best beloved and finest music is created out of just such elemental sensations. We never grow out of them, of the need to renew them. Any art which by accident or design gets too far from them finds that it has to return or wither. They are the very stuff of human life. It is of this stuff that the drama of cricket is composed.

If the drama is very limited in range and intricacy there are advantages.

These need not be called compensating, but they should not be ignored. The long hours (which so irritates those who crave continuous excitation), the measured ritualism and the varied and intensive physical activity which take place within it, these strip the players of conventional aspects, and human personality is on view long enough and in sufficiently varied form to register itself indelibly. I mention only a few—the lithe grace and elegance of Kardar leading his team on to the field; the unending flow of linear rhythm by which Evans accommodated himself to returns from the field; the dignity which radiates from every motion of Frank Worrell; the magnificence and magnanimity of Keith Miller. There are movie stars, world-famous and rightly so, who mumble words and go through motions which neither they nor their audience care very much about. Their appeal is themselves, how they walk, how they move, how they do anything or nothing, so long as they are themselves and their particular quality shines through. Here a Keith Miller met a Clark Gable on equal terms.

The dramatic content of cricket I have purposely pitched low—I am concerned not with degree but kind. In addition to being a dramatic, cricket is also a visual art. This I do not pitch low at all. The whole issue will be settled here.

The aestheticians of painting, especially the modern ones, are the great advocates of 'significant form', the movement of the line, the relations of colour and tone. Of these critics, the most consistent, the clearest (and the most widely accepted), that I know is the late Mr. Bernhard Berenson. Over sixty years ago in his studies of the Italian Renaissance painters he expounded his aesthetic with refreshing clarity. The merely accurate representation of an object, the blind imitation of nature, was not art, not even if that object was what would commonly be agreed upon as beautiful, for example a beautiful woman. There was another category of painter superior to the first. Such a one would not actually reproduce the object as it was. Being a man of vision and imagination, the object would stimulate in him impulses, thoughts, memories visually creative. These he would fuse into a whole and the result would be not so much the object as the totality of the visual image which the object had evoked in a superior mind. That, too, Mr. Berenson excluded from the category of true art (and was by no means isolated in doing so): mere reproduction of objects, whether actually in existence or the product of the sublimest imaginations, was 'literature' or 'illustration'. What then was the truly artistic? The truly artistic was a quality that existed in its own right, irrespective of the object represented. It was the line, the curve, its movement, the drama it embodied as painting, the linear design, the painterly tones and values taken as a whole: this constituted the specific quality of visual art. Mr. Berenson did not rank colour very high; the head of a statue (with its human expression) he could usually dispense with. It was the form as such which was significant.

Mr. Berenson was not at all cloudy or mystifying. He distinguished two qualities which could be said to constitute the significance of the form in its most emphatic manifestation.

The first he called 'tactile values'. The idea of tactile values could be most clearly grasped by observing the manner in which truly great artists rendered the nude human body. They so posed their figures, they manipulated, arranged, shortened, lengthened, foreshortened, they so articulated the movements of the joints that they stimulated the tactile consciousness of the viewer, his specially artistic sense. This significance in the form gave a higher coefficient of reality to the object represented. Not that such a painting looked more real, made the object more lifelike. That was not Mr. Berenson's point. Significant form makes the painting life-giving, life-enhancing, *to the viewer*. Significant form, or 'decoration', to use his significant personal term, sets off physical processes in the spectator which give to him a far greater sense of the objective reality before him than would a literal representation, however accurate.[1] Mr. Berenson does not deny that an interesting subject skilfully presented in human terms can be interesting as illustration. He does not deny that such illustration can enhance significant form. But it is the form that matters. Mr. John Berger of the *New Statesman*, ardent propagandist of socialist realism in art, claims that what is really significant in Michelangelo is his bounding line. The abstract artists get rid of the object altogether and represent only the abstract form, the line and relations of line. If I understand Mr. Berger aright he claims that all the great representational paintings of the past live and have lived only to the degree that their form is significant—that, however, is merely to repeat Mr. Berenson.

[1] If I do Mr. Berenson any injustice it can be corrected in the reprint of his history, third edition, 1954, and his *Des Arts Visuels* (Esthétique et Histoire), Paris, 1953, where the original thesis is restated. (I am not being pedantic. In these metaphysical matters you can misplace a comma and be thereby liable to ten thousand words of aesthetic damnation.)

The second characteristic of significant form in Mr. Berenson's aesthetic is the sense of 'movement'.

We have so far been wandering in chambers where as cricketers we are not usually guests. Fortunately, the aesthetic vision now focuses on territory not too far distant from ours. In his analysis of 'movement' Mr. Berenson discussed the artistic possibilities and limitations of an athletic event, a wrestling match. His exposition seems designed for cricket and cricketers, and therefore must be reproduced in full.

'Although a wrestling match may, in fact, contain many genuinely artistic elements, our enjoyment of it can never be quite artistic: we are prevented from completely realizing it not only by our dramatic interest in the game, but also, granting the possibility of being devoid of dramatic interest, by the succession of movements being too rapid for us to realize each completely, and too fatiguing, even if realizable. Now if a way could be found of conveying to us the realization of movement without the confusion and the fatigue of the actuality, we should be getting out of the wrestlers more than they themselves can give us—the heightening of vitality which comes to us whenever we keenly realize life, such as the actuality itself would give us, *plus* the greater effectiveness of the heightening brought about by the clearer, intenser and less fatiguing realization. This is precisely what the artist who succeeds in representing movement achieves: making us realize it as we never can actually, he gives us a heightened sense of capacity, and whatever is in the actuality enjoyable, he allows us to enjoy at our leisure. In words already familiar to us, he *extracts the significance of movements*, just as, in rendering tactile values, the artist extracts the corporal significance of objects. His task is, however, far more difficult, although less indispensable: it is not enough that he should extract the values of what at any given moment is an actuality, as is an object, but what at no moment really is—namely, movement. He can accomplish his task in only one way, and that is by so rendering the one particular movement that we shall be able to realize all other movements that the same figure may make. "He is grappling with his enemy now," I say of my wrestler. "What a pleasure to be able to realize in my own muscles, on my own chest, with my own arms and legs, the life that is in him as he is making his supreme effort! What a pleasure, as I look away from the representation, to realize in the same manner, how after the contest his muscles will relax, and the rest trickle like a refreshing stream through his nerves!" All this I shall be made to enjoy by the artist who, in representing any one movement, can give me the logical sequence of visible strain and pressure in the parts and muscles.'

Now here all of us, cricketers and aesthetics, are on familiar ground. I submit that cricket does in fact contain genuinely artistic elements, infinitely surpassing those to be found in wrestling matches. In fact it can be said to comprise most of those to be found in all other games.

I submit further that the abiding charm of cricket is that the game has been so organized that the realization of movement is completely conveyed despite the confusion and fatigue of actuality.

I submit finally that without the intervention of any artist the spectator at cricket extracts the significance of movement and of tactile values. He experiences the heightened sense of capacity. Furthermore, however the purely human element, the literature, the illustration, in cricket may enhance the purely artistic appeal, the significant form at its most unadulterated is permanently present. It is known, expected, recognized and enjoyed by tens of thousands of spectators. Cricketers call it style.

From the beginning of the modern game this quality of style has been abstracted and established in its own right, irrespective of results, human element, dramatic element, anything whatever except itself. It is, if you will, pure decoration. Thus we read of a player a hundred years ago that he was elegance, all elegance, fit to play before the Queen in her parlour. We read of another that he was not equal to W.G. except in style, where he surpassed The Champion. In *Wisden* of 1891 A. G. Steel, a great player, a great judge of the game and, like so many of those days, an excellent writer, leaves no loophole through which form can escape into literature:

'The last-named batsman, when the bowling was very accurate, was a slow scorer, *but* always a treat to watch. If the present generation of stone-wall cricketers, such as Scotton, Hall, Barlow, A. Bannerman, nay even Shrewsbury, possessed such beautiful ease of style the tens of thousands that used to frequent the beautiful Australian ground would still flock there, instead of the hundred or two patient gazers on feats of Job-like patience that now attend them.'

In 1926 H. L. Collins batted five hours for forty runs to save the Manchester Test and Richard Binns wrote a long essay to testify among much else that Collins was never dull because of his beautiful style. There is debate about style. Steel's definition clears away much cumbersome litter about left shoulder forward and straight bat: 'no flourish, but the maximum of power with the minimum of exertion'. If the free-swinging off-drive off the front foot has been challenged by the angular jerk through the covers off the back foot, this last is not at all alien to the generation which has experienced Cubism in posters and newspaper advertisements.

We are accustomed in cricket to speak of beauty. The critics of art are contemptuous of the word. Let us leave it aside and speak of the style that is common to the manifold motions of the great players, or most of them. There are few picture galleries in the world which effectively reproduce a fraction of them—I am sticking to form and eschewing literature and illustration. These motions are not caught and permanently fixed for us to make repeated visits to them. They are repeated often enough to become a permanent possession of the spectator which he can renew at will. And having held our own with the visitor from the higher spheres, I propose to take the offensive.

And first I meet Mr. Berenson on his own ground, so to speak. Here is John Arlott, whose written description of cricket matches I prefer to all others, describing the bowling action of Maurice Tate.

'You would hardly have called Maurice Tate's physique graceful, yet his bowling action remains—and not only for me—as lovely a piece of movement as even cricket has ever produced. He had strong, but sloping shoulders; a deep chest, fairly long arms and—essential to the pace bowler—broad feet to take the jolt of the delivery stride and wide hips to cushion it. His run-in, eight accelerating and lengthening strides, had a hint of scramble about it at the beginning, but, by the eighth stride and well before his final leap, it seemed as if his limbs were gathered together in one glorious wheeling unity. He hoisted his left arm until it was pointing straight upwards, while his right hand, holding the ball, seemed to counter-poise it at the opposite pole. Meanwhile, his body, edge-wise on to the batsman, had swung its weight back on to the right foot: his back curved so that, from the other end, you might see the side of his head jutting out, as it were, from behind his left arm. Then his bowling arm came over and his body turned; he released the ball at the top of his arm-swing, with a full flick of the wrist, and then plunged through, body bending into that earth-tearing, final stride and pulling away to the off side.

'All these things the textbook will tell you to do: yet no one has ever achieved so perfectly a co-ordination and exploitation of wrist, shoulders, waist, legs and feet as Maurice Tate did. It was as if bowling had been implanted in him at birth, and came out—as the great arts come out—after due digestion, at that peak of greatness which is not created—but only confirmed—by instruction.'

Because most people think always of batting when they think of cricket as a visual art another description of a bowler in action will help to correct the unbalance.

'From two walking paces Lindwall glides into the thirteen running strides which have set the world a model for rhythmic gathering of momentum for speed-giving power. Watching him approach the wicket, Sir Pelham Warner was moved to murmur one word, "Poetry!"

'The poetry of motion assumes dramatic overtones in the last couple of strides. A high-lifted left elbow leads Lindwall to the line. The metal plate on his right toe-cap drags through the turf and across the bowling crease as his prancing left foot thrusts directly ahead of it, to land beyond the popping crease. This side-on stretch brings every ounce of his thirteen stone into play as his muscular body tows his arm over for the final fling that shakes his shirtsleeve out of its fold. In two more strides his wheeling follow-through has taken him well to the side of the pitch. Never had plunging force and science formed so deadly an alliance.'

We may note in passing that the technique of watching critically, i.e. with a conception of all the factors that have contributed to the result, can be as highly developed and needs as many years of training in cricket as in the arts. But I do not want to emphasize that here.

What is to be emphasized is that whereas in the fine arts the image of tactile values and movement, however effective, however magnificent, is permanent, fixed, in cricket the spectator sees the image constantly re-created, and whether he is a cultivated spectator or not, has standards which he carries with him always. He can re-create them at will. He can go to see a game hoping and expecting to see the image re-created or even extended. You can stop an automobile to watch a casual game and see a batsman, for ever to be unknown, cutting in a manner that recalls the greatest exponents of one of the most difficult movements in cricket. Sometimes it is a total performance branching out in many directions by a single player who stamps all he does with the hallmark of an individual style—a century by Hutton or Compton or Sobers. It can be and often is a particular image—Hammond's drive through the covers. The image can be a single stroke, made on a certain day, which has been seen and never forgotten. There are some of these the writer has carried in his consciousness for over forty years, some in fact longer, as is described in the first pages of this book. On the business of setting off physical processes and evoking a sense of movement in the spectator, followers of Mr. Berenson's classification would do well to investigate the responses of cricket spectators. The theory may be thereby enriched, or may be seen to need enrichment. To the eye of a cricketer it seems pretty thin.

It may seem that I am squeezing every drop out of a quite casual illustration extracted from Mr. Berenson's more comprehensive argument. That is not so. Any acquaintances with his work will find that he lavishes his most enthusiastic praise on 'Hercules Strangling Antaeus' by Pollaiuolo, and the same artist's 'David Striding Over the Head of the Slain Goliath'. In more than one place 'The Gods Shooting [arrows] at a Mark' and the 'Hercules Struggling With a Lion', drawings by Michelangelo, are shown to be for him the ultimate yet reached in the presentation of tactile values and sense of movement, with the consequent life-giving and life-enhancing stimulation of the spectator. Mr. Berenson, in the books I have mentioned, nowhere analyses this momentous fact: the enormous role that elemental physical action plays in the visual arts throughout the centuries, at least until our own. Why should he believe that Michelangelo's projected painting of the soldiers surprised when bathing would have produced the greatest masterpiece of figure art in modern times? I have been suggesting an answer by implication in describing what W.G. brought from pre-Victorian England to the modern age. I shall now state it plainly.

If we stick to cricket it is not because of any chauvinism. The analysis will apply to all games. After a thorough study of bull-fighting in Spain, Ernest Haas, the famous photographer, does not ignore the violence, the blood, the hovering presence of death, the illustration. Aided by his camera, his conclusion is: 'The bull fight is pure art. The spectacle is all motion. . . . Motion, the perfection of motion, is what the people come to see. They come hoping that this bull-fight will produce the perfect flow of motion.' Another name for the perfect flow of motion is style, or, if you will, significant form.

Let us examine this motion, or, as Mr. Berenson calls it, movement. Where the motive and directing force rests with the single human being, an immense variety of physical motion is embraced within four categories. A human being places himself physically in some relation of contact or avoidance (or both) with another human being, with an animal, an inanimate object, or two or more of these. He may extend the reach and force of his arms or feet with a tool or device of some kind. He propels a missile. He runs, skips, jumps, dives, to attain some objective which he has set himself or others have set for him. In sport there is not much else that he can do, and in our world human beings are on view for artistic enjoyment only on the field of sport or on the entertainment stage. In sport cricket leads the field. The motions of a batter in baseball, a player of lawn tennis, hockey, golf, all their motions added together do not attain the sum of a batsman's. The batsman can shape to hit practically round the points of the compass. He can play a dead bat, pat for a single, drive along the ground; he can skim the infielders; he can lift over their heads; he can clear the boundary. He can cut square with all the force of his wrists, arms and shoulders, or cut late with a touch as delicate as a feather. He can hit to long-leg with all his force or simply deflect with a single motion. He can do most of these off the front foot or the back. Many of them he can do with no or little departure from his original stance. The articulation of his limbs is often enough quite visible, as in the use of the wrists when cutting or hooking. What is not visible is received in the tactile consciousness of thousands who have themselves for years practised the same motion and know each muscle that is involved in each stroke. And all this infinite variety is from one base, stable and fixed, so that each motion in its constituent parts can be observed in its detail and in its entirety from start to finish.

The batsman propels a missile with a tool. The bowler does the same unaided. Within the narrow territory legally allowed to him there is, as Mr. Arlott on Tate has shown, a surprising variety of appeal. He may bowl a slow curve or fast or medium, or he may at his pleasure use each in turn. There have been many bowlers whose method of delivery has seemed to spectators the perfection of form, irrespective of the fate which befell the balls bowled. Here, far more than in batting, the repetition conveys the realization of movement despite the actuality. Confusion is excluded by the very structure of the game.

As for the fieldsmen, there is no limit whatever to their possibilities of running, diving, leaping, falling forward, backwards, sideways, with all their energies concentrated on a specific objective, the whole completely realizable by the alert spectator. The spontaneous outburst of thousands at a fierce hook or a dazzling slip-catch, the ripple of recognition at a long-awaited leg-glance, are as genuine and deeply felt expressions of artistic emotion as any I know.

You will have noted that the four works of art chosen by Mr. Berenson to illustrate movement all deal with some physical action of the athletic kind. Mr. Berenson calls the physical process of response mystical.[1] There I refuse to go along any further, not even for the purpose of discussion. The mystical is the last refuge, if refuge it is. Cricket, in fact any ball game, to the visual image adds the sense of physical co-ordination, of harmonious action, of timing. The visual image of a diving fieldsman is a frame for his rhythmic contact with the flying ball. Here two art forms meet.

I believe that the examination of the stroke, the brilliant piece of fielding, will take us through mysticism to far more fundamental considerations than mere life-enhancing. We respond to physical action or vivid representation of it, dead or alive, because we are made that way. For unknown centuries survival for us, like all other animals, depended upon competent and effective physical activity. This played its part in developing the brain. The particular nature which became ours did not rest satisfied with this. If it had it could never have become human. The use of the hand, the extension of its powers by the tool, the propulsion of a missile at some objective and the accompanying refinements of the mechanics of judgment, these marked us off from the animals. Language may have come at the same time. The evolution may have been slow or rapid. The end result was a new species which preserved the continuity

[1] Mr. Berenson's aesthetics do not by any means exhaust the subject. Mr. Adrian Stokes, for example, on Michelangelo, is suggestive of much that is stimulating to any enquiry into the less obvious origins of a game like cricket. Further I find it strange that (as far as I know) so ardent an apostle of mass culture and non-representational art as Sir Herbert Read has never probed into the question whether the physical modes so beloved by Michelangelo and the physical movements of popular sports and games so beloved by the millions do not appeal to the 'collective unconscious' more powerfully than the esoteric forms of, for example, Mr. Henry Moore. The difficulty here, it seems to me, is not merely the habit of categorizing into higher and lower. The aesthetics of cricket demand first that you master the game, and, preferably, have played it, if not well, at least in good company. And that is not the easy acquisition outsiders think it to be.

of its characteristics and its way of life. Sputnik can be seen as no more than a missile made and projected through tools by the developed hand.

Similarly the eye for the line which is today one of the marks of ultimate aesthetic refinement is not new. It is old. The artists of the caves of Altamira had it. So did the bushmen. They had it to such a degree that they could reproduce it or, rather, represent it with unsurpassed force. Admitting this, Mr. Berenson confines the qualities of this primitive art to animal energy and an exasperated vitality. That, even if true, is totally subordinate to the fact that among these primitive peoples the sense of form existed to the degree that it could be consciously and repeatedly reproduced. It is not a gift of high civilization, the last achievement of noble minds. It is exactly the opposite. The use of sculpture and design among primitive peoples indicates that the significance of the form is a common possession. Children have it. There is no need to adduce further evidence for the presupposition that the faculty or faculties by which we recognize significant form in elemental physical action is native to us, a part of the process by which we have become and remain human. It is neither more nor less mystical than any other of our faculties of apprehension. Neither do I see an 'exasperated vitality' in the work of the primitive artists. The impression I get is that the line was an integral part of co-ordinated physical activity, functional perhaps, but highly refined in that upon it food or immediate self-preservation might depend.

Innate faculty though it might be, the progress of civilization can leave it unused, suppress its use, can remove us from the circumstances in which it is associated with animal energy. Developing civilization can surround us with circumstances and conditions in which our original faculties are debased or refined, made more simple or more complicated. They may seem to disappear altogether. They remain part of our human endowment. The basic motions of cricket represent physical action which has been the basis not only of primitive but of civilized life for countless centuries. In work and in play they were the motions by which men lived and without which they would perish. The Industrial Revolution transformed our existence. Our fundamental characteristics as human beings it did not and could not alter. The bushmen reproduced in one medium not merely animals but the line, the curve, the movement. It supplied in the form they needed a vision of the life they lived. The Hambledon men who made modern cricket did the same. The bushmen's motive was perhaps religious, Hambledon's entertainment. One form was fixed, the other had to be constantly re-created. The contrasts can be multiplied. That will not affect the underlying identity. Each fed the need to satisfy the visual artistic sense. The emphasis on style in cricket proves that without a shadow of doubt; whether the impulse was literature and the artistic quality the result, or vice-versa, does not matter. If the Hambledon form was infinitely more complicated it rose out of a more complicated society, the result of a long historical development. Satisfying the same needs as bushmen and Hambledon, the industrial age took over cricket and made it into what it has become. The whole tortured history of modern Spain explains why it is in the cruelty of the bull-ring that they seek the perfect flow of motion. That flow, however, men since they have been men have always sought and always will. It is an unspeakable impertinence to arrogate the term 'fine art' to one small section of this quest and declare it to be culture. Luckily, the people refuse to be bothered. This does not alter the gross falsification of history and the perversion of values which is the result.

Lucian's Solon tells what the Olympic Games meant to the Greeks. The human drama, the literature, was as important to them as to us. No less so was the line, the curve, the movement of the athletes which inspired one of the greatest artistic creations we have ever known—Greek sculpture. To this day certain statues baffle the experts: are they statues of Apollo or are they statues of athletes? The games and sculpture were 'good' arts and popular. The newly fledged democracy found them insufficient. The contrast between life under an ancient landed aristocracy and an ancient democratic regime was enormous. It can be guessed at by what the democracy actually achieved. The democracy did not neglect the games or sculpture. To the contrary. The birth of democracy saw the birth of individualism in sculpture. Immense new passions and immense new forces had been released. New relations between the individual and society, between individual and individual, launched life on new, exciting and dangerous ways. Out of this came the tragic drama. After a long look at how the creation of the Hambledon men became the cornerstone of Victorian education and entertainment, I can no longer accept that Peisistratus encouraged the dramatic festival as a means of satisfying or appeasing or distracting the urban masses on their way to democracy. That would be equivalent to saying that the rulers of Victorian England encouraged cricket to satisfy or appease or distract the urban masses on their way to democracy. The Victorian experience with cricket suggests a line of investigation on the alert for signs both more subtle and more tortuous. It may be fruitful to investigate whether Peisistratus and his fellow rulers did not need the drama for themselves before it became a national festival. That at any rate is what happened to the Victorians.

The elements which were transformed into Greek drama may have existed in primitive form, quite apart from religious ceremonial—there is even a tradition that peasants played primitive dramas. However that may be, the newly fledged Greek democrat found his need for a fuller existence fulfilled in the tragic drama. He had no spate of books to give him distilled, concentrated and ordered views of life. The old myths no longer sufficed. The drama recast them to satisfy the expanded personality. The end of democracy is a more complete existence. Voting and political parties are only a means. The expanded personality and needs of the Victorian aspiring to democracy did not need drama. The stage, books, newspapers, were part of his inheritance. The production of these for democracy had already begun. What he needed was the further expansion of his aesthetic sense. Print had long made church walls and public monuments obsolescent as a means of social communication. Photography would complete the rout of painting and sculpture, promoting them upstairs. The need was filled by organized games.

Cricket was fortunate in that for their own purposes the British ruling classes took it over and endowed it with money and prestige. On it men of gifts which would have been remarkable in any sphere expended their powers—the late C. B. Fry was a notable example. Yet even he submitted to the prevailing aesthetic categories and circumscribed cricket as a 'physical' fine art. There is no need so to limit it. It is limited in variety of range, of subject-matter. It cannot express the emotions of an age on the nature of the last judgment or the wiping out of a population by bombing. It must repeat. But what it repeats is the original stuff out of which everything visually or otherwise artistic is quarried. The popular democracy of Greece, sitting for days in the sun watching *The Oresteia*; the popular democracy of our day, sitting similarly, watching Miller and Lindwall bowl to Hutton and Compton—each in its own way grasps at a more complete human existence. We may some day be able to answer Tolstoy's exasperated and exasperating question: What is art?—but only when we learn to integrate our vision of Walcott on the back foot through the covers with the outstretched arm of the Olympic Apollo.

# 17

# The Welfare State of Mind

*Manchester Guardian*
October 7th, 1953

'In 1938 I went to the United States and my long and close association with cricket was broken—I did not see a cricket match for fifteen years. I returned to England in the middle of the summer and have seen much of the Leeds Test on television, the Oval Test in the flesh, and a number of county matches. I have devoured *Wisden* for the years between. How does the game look after this long interval?

'The most startling new feature is the routine leg-side slip field for fast bowlers. I have never seen this before, and I am immensely impressed with it. I say this because in the old days many an innings did not edge to the slips a single fast ball swinging away. But almost every batsman I have seen play this strange attack has made one or more streaky strokes through these leg-side fieldsmen or played at balls at which, it seemed, he did not want to play.

'It is batting, however, which has undergone a revolution. The basis of defence to slow bowlers seems to have shifted from back play to bringing the left foot forward and from there watching the ball off the pitch carefully on to the bat. It is for me, with 1936 on my mind, a most uncomfortable thing to look at. L. N. Constantine, with whom I have discussed it, is full of arguments against the technique, but I notice that when I question him about this or that slow bowler whom I have not seen he says as often as not, "You have to play him out here," and out-lines the slow forward motion.

'There are usually good reasons for what a lot of experts do, but every mode has its advantages and disadvantages and I shall have to watch a long time before I can accustom myself to it and come to some balanced judgment. . . .'

Cautiously as I expressed myself (having been away so long), I had made clear my dislike of the long, slow, forward defensive stroke which so many were using. Perhaps it was my absence from cricket for so many years that brought home so clearly the qualitative difference between cricket in the thirties and in the fifties. The trouble was that while the chorus of dissatisfaction grew year after year until the whole cricket firmament rang with it, no one seemed able to go beyond exhortation and legislation—and both Sir Donald Bradman and Sir Leonard Hutton led the way in drastic proposals which would have altered the game without in any way guaranteeing its emergence from the rut into which it had sunk. By 1957 I had come to my own conclusions and they were published in the *Cricketer*. Today, five years after, I have no need to change a word.

*Cricketer*
June 22nd, 1957

'First-class cricket is under such severe scrutiny as has never befallen it in all the centuries of its existence. First, to review briefly the known facts. *Political and Economic Planning* have done it the honour of an investigation (*The Cricket Industry*) in which it comes to the conclusion that only two courses are open, "to remove first-class cricket from the commercial sphere altogether and to rely primarily on membership, as the non-competitive clubs do; or to organize cricket more fully as an entertainment and to rely more heavily on gate and ticket money". But whichever course is adopted, it would seem, according to P.E.P., that there is a strong case for weekend cricket only. For this season the M.C.C. have proposed and the counties have adopted the rather desperate devices of prescribing the number of fielders on the leg-side and limiting the boundary to seventy-five yards. But these proposals are viewed with scepticism, if not hostility, by many ardent supporters of the game.

'In South Africa last winter Tayfield bowled fourteen overs of eight balls each without a run being scored and he was *not* bowling in the negative style. That is disturbing enough, but what is even more disturbing is that while every single commentator has for years prescribed the obvious remedies, batsmen must use their feet, etc., the batsmen resolutely refuse to follow this unanimous chorus of advice.

'What exactly is wrong? It seems to me that most of the commentators and analysts do not pay sufficient attention to a very important aspect of the game, the way in which at any particular period it reflects tendencies in the national life. It is admitted that the Golden Age lasted from about 1890 to the beginning of the First World War. It produced men who to this day are names to conjure with, C. B. Fry, Ranjitsinhji, G. L. Jessop, Victor Trumper, Frank Woolley. They and their contemporaries were not only men of exceptional skill, they were what the modern audience finds so lacking in contemporary players, men of dazzling personality, creative, original, daring, adventurous. I have never seen it stated anywhere that these men displayed on the cricket field the same characteristics that distinguished their contemporaries in other fields. 1890–1914 was the age of Joseph Chamberlain, F. E. Smith and David Lloyd George; of Northcliffe and Beaverbrook, the creators of modern journalism; of Cecil Rhodes and Lord Lugard; of personalities like Bernard Shaw and G. K. Chesterton; even in crime it produced the unique figure of Horatio Bottomley.

'The solid Victorian age was breaking up, the contemporary pattern had not yet taken shape, and in the interim, 1890–1914, we have these dynamic explosions of individual and creative personalities expressing themselves to the utmost limit in a manner impossible today, when the patterns of social existence are more firmly and precisely fixed. In social and political life the Edwardian age was possible only on the solid accumulations of the Victorian era. In cricket it was the same. These explorers, who extended the scope of the game so marvellously, built upon the solid accumulation and consolidation established by W. G. Grace, Arthur Shrewsbury, Alfred Shaw and the great orthodox players of the period 1870–90. If, in general, the achievements that I call Edwardian can be questioned, that in this context is neither here nor there. In cricket the results were brilliant, spectacular, and enriched the game and the national life. We should not underestimate the type of social force which created it. Not only their cricketing styles, but the personal careers of men like Ranjitsinhji and Fry outside the cricket world show how bold and restless was the spirit that expressed itself in their play. Perhaps the most striking of them as a cricketer was Jessop. It demanded a unique self-confidence, and a receptive environment, even to conceive of batting as he did.

'The outstanding proof of the way these men approached the game is in the very technique they adopted. They were *not* primarily back-players in defence, as they are currently reported to be. The books of Fry, Ranjitsinhji, MacLaren and Noble, to mention only a few; their pronouncements, all accounts of their play, show the foundation of their style was: play back *or go to the pitch and drive*. The generation of 1930–9, taking them as a whole, were the genuine back-foot players. The batsmen of the Golden Age limited themselves in no such fashion. They moved with equal facility forward and back, thus dictating the length to the bowler. For Fry back-play was a daring adventure, you watched the ball actually break and gauged its new direction before you moved the back foot. And MacLaren made a distinction between the hook and the pull which today is lost. The stroke we commonly call the hook he insisted was a short-arm pull; the genuine hook stroke was played with an almost straight bat, with as much shoulder as wrist. And he believed it was a stroke that only young men could play. The jump, or the run to drive, was not a stroke they remembered only when they found themselves tied up by a length bowler. They set themselves to master it as an indispensable element in their play. And this stroke, too, demands courage and daring and perfect fitness. They went out to drive along the ground, to lift high or to skim the infielders. Thus their batting was a constant dynamic reaching out in every direction. The question is often asked: what would the leg-glancing Ranjitsinhji have done against Laker's short-legs?

'We underestimate the men of those days in not assuming that they would have tried to block the stroke. They did. And *Wisden* of 1902 gives us Ranjitsinhji's answer: "Opposing teams endeavoured to cramp his game by putting on additional short-legs, but, without abandoning his delightful strokes on that side of the wicket or his beautifully timed cuts, he probably got the majority of his runs by drives—a notable change indeed from his early years as a great cricketer." Yet county cricket shows us today any number of mediocre slow bowlers who can bowl for hours without a fieldsman more than fifty yards from the batsman, the most revealing sight on the modern cricket field.

'From the constant movement back or forward of 1890–1914, we progressed (or rather regressed) to the reliance on the movement back

(1918–39) and now to the long forward-defensive push. The Australians in 1956 seemed to rely more on back-play than the average English county player, but what ruined them was not so much the back stroke as such, but their predisposition to get in front of the wicket before the ball was bowled, and their refusal or inability to drive Laker through or over the off-side field. They could never attempt to drive Laker because the primary condition of success was to get *to the pitch*. And the habit of getting to the pitch has been lost. When the old hands complain that the batsmen of their day would have murdered Ramadhin and put Laker on the defensive they have right on their side. Their only mistake is to believe that that style of play can be invoked at will. It was more than a method, it was a philosophy of life, a large phrase but the only one that is conveniently to hand. The Golden Age was great in batting and in innovations of bowling as well, as the styles of Barnes, Noble, Laver, Bosanquet, Schwartz, Faulkner and Vogler show. You cannot re-create that by adding to the wicket, or taking away from the bowling crease, or experimenting with limiting the numbers of men on the leg-side.

'If the glory of the Golden Age is to be found in the specific mental attitudes of the men who made it what it was, the drabness of the prevailing style of play should be sought in the same place.

'The prevailing attitude of the players of 1890–1914 was daring, adventure, creation. The prevailing attitude of 1957 can be summed up in one word—security. Bowlers and batsmen are dominated by it. The long forward-defensive push, the negative bowling, are the techniques of specialized performers (professional or amateur) in a security-minded age. As a corollary, we find much fast bowling and brilliant and daring close fielding and wicketkeeping—they are the only spheres where the spirit of adventure can express itself. The cricketers of today play the cricket of a specialized stratum, that of functionaries in the Welfare State. When many millions of people all over the world demand security and a state that must guarantee it, that's one thing. But when bowlers or batsmen, responsible for an activity essentially artistic and therefore individual, are dominated by the same principles, then the result is what we have.

'And it is clear that those who support the Welfare State idea in politics and social life do not want it on the cricket field. They will not come to look at it.

'Many critics seem to think the domination of the game by "professionals" is responsible. The word is often very loosely used. The professionals of 1956 are vastly different from the professionals of 1906 and even of 1926. They set the tone today. But the stroke-makers of the thirties, and their survivors into the post-war period, were professionals: Hammond, Barnett, Hardstaff, Hutton, Washbrook, Compton, to name the most obvious. The South African batsmen, the Indian and Pakistan batsmen, are not professionals, yet their play is as characteristic of the age as any of the professionals. And it is an England team which for the first time for many years contains five amateur batsmen which, during the recent season in South Africa, shared honours with the South Africans for the slowest rate of scoring within living or recorded memory.

'Cowdrey is a striking example of how an individual who in another age would have flourished like the green bay tree is profoundly affected by the contemporary pressures. Graveney, if I am not mistaken, is another, and May who, despite the supposed difficulties of the late swing, is one of the finest all-round drivers the game has known, has had to develop his on-side play and is being slowly tamed to the prevailing pattern.

'If this is the true condition of affairs, legislation or rules will not alter it. The remedy must be adequate to the disease. And it must begin in Britain which, for a variety of reasons, has a predominant influence. The remedy is somehow to abolish not professionals but the specialized character of first-class cricket, whether professional or amateur. It would seem that at a certain stage of their development some games require professionals, or men entirely devoted to them, to develop all the inherent possibilities. That stage in cricket is now past, and came to an end in 1914. The cricketer needs to be returned to the community (as so many of our professional experts in so many different spheres of modern life need to be returned). He must do a job of work with his fellows so that cricket, essentially an artistic expression of life, becomes an artistic expression of life, becomes an artistic expression of his own individual life. We read that in this or that Test series, Trumper, and in that, Macartney, were out of form because, the Tests coinciding with a period of intense work in the office where they worked, their sight was affected. They did not suffer, because for them cricket was a recreation. More recent is the case of the Rev. D. S. Sheppard, whose striking success in 1956 should have punctured many cherished theories. There was a spirit about his play that would have been absent if, though playing as an amateur, he had gone through the routine of half a dozen contemporary seasons.

'It is quite remarkable that it is England's captain in 1957 who has made the most drastic proposals so far for the reorganization of the game. He proposes to abolish the distinction between amateurs and professionals; to abolish the County Championship as we have known it for so long and to play instead only at the weekend, Saturday, Sunday and Monday; to divide the counties into zones, and to make corresponding changes for international tours. I think two of his sentences are worth quotation: "All cricketers would be paid by the match (as in Australia) and would be able to have outside jobs as well." And, more important: "I have expressed the opinion that a revision of our first-class programme to be based on weekend matches only (except in the case of Test and representative fixtures) might well raise standards, both technical and financial." Put in social terms, this means that May sees the rejuvenation of the game not in legislation but in a changing relation of the cricketer to the life around him. He must become an ordinary member of the community who will play cricket for the fun of it, which does not mean that he will not play it seriously. May is Charterhouse and Cambridge, in other words bred in an atmosphere of respect for the traditions of the game. His batting (a true expression of a man's personality—if he can really bat) is modern, but cast in the classical mould. He has played in the West Indies, in Australia and in South Africa. He has captained England successfully in three hard series of Test matches and has so far won two and lost none. He has been trained in the school of Hutton and of Surridge, and played day by day with such remarkable and diverse personalities as Bedser, Laker and Lock. He is still some way from thirty. His opinions, therefore, should not be seen as those of a mere individual but as a representative expression of an experienced member of the younger generation. And, when all is said and done, the future is with them. Despite his own lack of confidence that "such a revolutionary change will be attempted in the near future", his views are imbued with a deep confidence in the future of the game, and public response to it. They are in harmony with contemporary English life and they leave the essentials of the game untouched.

'Will the West Indians in 1957 demonstrate that the game they play, which remains within the tradition of the Golden Age, is able to defeat or at least hold its own with the exponents of the modern style? It is for this reason that devotees and students of the game are viewing the present Tests with more interest and concern than any perhaps that have taken place since the end of the war. But if the West Indians do demonstrate that style and daring can be both creative and effective it will be a demonstration of the idea that great cricketers and their style must be seen in relation to the social environment which produces them. In 1939, as a result of widespread social and political unrest, a commission was sent to the West Indies and made recommendations, whose effect can now be seen in vastly greater opportunities for West Indians in their own country and abroad, including Federation and Dominion status in the near future. The islands have undergone and are undergoing a social rebirth. There is ferment similar to what was taking place in England from 1890 to 1914. It is in that environment that Weekes, Worrell and Walcott grew to maturity. Is it too far-fetched to say that from the cricketing point of view the commission that went out in 1939, in the famous words of Canning, "called a new world into existence to redress the balance of the old?" '

The West Indies team in England that year seemed to have betrayed me. I was not discouraged, being convinced that the game they were playing was unnatural to them. For this there was a reason. Too many of them played league cricket in England and came together only for international games. They did not play with and against one another in the home environment where both on and off the field they could absorb the national spirit. Nevertheless, I retained my faith in them. The three W's were of a different stamp from most of the cricketers I had seen. Kanhai and Sobers, the juniors, were of the same breed, and though technically he was not up to their standard, so was 'Collie' Smith. To avoid misunderstanding I cannot do better than quote E. W. Swanton on the English county cricketer.

'There are no pleasanter people than the run of present-day cricketers, but one cannot spend long summers in their company without realizing that as a body they are inclined to be just a little short of ambition, to see the day's work in terms of a reasonable performance for their county without much thought of anything higher.'[1]

These are the Welfare Staters. And the conditions which produce them do not exist in the West Indies.

Just a few weeks after I had blown my little trumpet one of the most

[1] *Playfair's Annual, 1956.*

authoritative voices in modern sport raised his voice like the baritone entering in the Ninth Symphony. Franz Stampfl, the trainer of Bannister, Chataway, Hewson, Brasher and many others, published in the *Observer* three articles on the future of athletics. When I read them I knew that the battle was won. This is what Stampfl says:

The achievements of athletes in recent years which have so astonished the world are not as great as so many people imagine that they are. None of them is anywhere near the ultimate limits. By far the most important part of a great performance is played by the mind. Once the athlete is convinced that the prevailing standards are not high, and that improving upon them is a not very difficult task, he will crack them. Long hours of training are not in the least necessary. The Bannisters, the Chataways, the Brashers and the Hewsons produced their record-breaking performances on an average of from forty-five minutes to an hour and a half of training per day. All of them were at the same time either doing full jobs or studying and taking exams. The record-breaker of the future will be a man of intelligence with an imaginative approach. The greatest performances will be produced by 'the poet, the artist, the philosopher'.

Roger Bannister was asked the question that has puzzled so many people: How is it that it took so long to break the four-minute mile and yet once it was broken so many seem able to do it, even three a day? The four minutes, he replied, was a mental barrier, accepted by athletes and public alike. This mental barrier had to be broken. Once it was broken, it became easier and easier to break. The barriers to the regeneration of cricket technique are mental, as are the barriers to the regeneration of its moral values. This is not an inspiring perspective. It promises nothing, advocates nothing, except to make the first-class cricketer once more an ordinary citizen. It has, however, some not inconsiderable negative virtues. It will squash finally the illusion that contemporary cricketers had discovered some high science which their forefathers never knew. It will teach patience. And it will abolish for ever the counsels of despair such as adding a fourth stump, and lessening the length of the bowling crease, which comes from no less a person than Sir Leonard Hutton. Professionalism, non-professionalism, will not produce the poetic, artistic and philosophical qualities which will make the great athlete and the great cricketer of the future. The M.C.C. can appoint as many committees as it may please, and these will present their well-balanced reports. They do no harm. They do no good. It will take more than committees to remove the fetishes which clog the brains of our leading cricketers today.

I use the term 'fetishism'. The dyed-in-the-wool fetishists are not the coaches instructing the young—they preach only what their betters practise. The fetishists are the great batsmen of the day. During 1957 I had long conversations with two of them. One refused absolutely to consider my idea that Laker should have been hit through and over the off-side fieldsmen, both for runs and for the psychological effect on him and his captain. Wrong, he said, that is hitting against the break. With the other I discussed lifting the fast bowler straight back overhead. To do that, he said, you have to make up your mind in advance that as soon as the ball is well pitched up you are going to let him have it. He indicated quite clearly that while that was possible, it was not business. They were representative men, the best of their time, none better. They think as their fellows do and cannot think otherwise. They are as firmly fixed within these ideas as were the batsmen before W.G. created the new technique; batsmen (and great batsmen) must have thought in much the same conservative way (and batting had sunk into a deadening routine) before Trumper and Ranjitsinhji did the impossible and made it common-place. Change, beneficient change, will come as it came then. All this not hitting against the break is no more than keeping the margin of error as large as possible. New technique consists in lessening such margins, not in maintaining or expanding them. Some young Romantic will extend the boundaries of cricket technique with a classical perfection. He will hit against the break so hard and so often that the poor bowlers will wish he would go back to hitting with it. He will drive overhead and push through any number of short-legs, as W.G. used to do, so that a whole race of bowlers will go underground for fifteen years as they did once, and once more emerge with new tricks. Some of the new tricks, it is already clear, will be old, such as pace, sheer pace, pace as new as the pace at which Kuk ran three miles in the Australian Olympics. Our Romantic will do these things or other things—what he will—and the big battalions will follow in his train. We shall extol his eyesight, his wristwork, his footwork, his audacity, to which some nationalist fanatics will add his ancestry and his climate. He may come from Pudsey or South Sydney, Nawanagar or Bridgetown. But wherever he comes from, and whatever he does, he will be doing what W.G. did—so reshaping the medium that it can give new satisfactions to new people.

# PART SEVEN

# VOX POPULI

———

## 18

## *The Proof of the Pudding*

ONCE in a blue moon, i.e. once in a lifetime, a writer is handed on a plate a gift from heaven. I was handed mine in 1958. I had just completed a draft of this book up to the end of the previous chapter when I returned to the West Indies in April 1958, after twenty-six years of absence. I intended to stay three months, I stayed four years. I became the editor of a political paper, the *Nation*, official organ of the People's National Movement of Trinidad, and the secretary of the West Indian Federal Labour Party. Both these parties governed, the one Trinidad, the other the Federation of the West Indies. These were temporary assignments, as I made clear from the start.

Immediately I was immersed up to the eyes in 'The Case for West Indian Self-Government'; and a little later, in the most furious cricket campaign I have ever known, to break the discrimination of sixty years and have a black man, in this case Frank Worrell, appointed captain of a West Indies team. I saw the beginning, the middle, but I am not at all sure that I have seen the end of violent intervention of a West Indian crowd into the actual play of a Test match. The intimate connection between cricket and West Indian social and political life was established so that all except the wilfully perverse could see. It seemed as if I were just taking up again what I had occupied myself with in the months before I left in 1932, except that what was then idea and aspiration was now out in the open and public property.

On January 30th, 1960, there crowded into the Queen's Park Oval at Port of Spain over 30,000 people, this out of a total population of some 800,000. They had come to see a cricket match and I for one loved them for it. They have been slandered, vilified and at best grievously misunderstood. I can't say that I understand them, I wouldn't make such a claim, but at least I have always paid attention to them and their reactions to politics as well as to cricket. I have something to say on their behalf.

Particularly that day they had come to sun themselves in West Indies batting, 22 for none on the previous evening. Alas, the West Indies batsmen collapsed and were 98 for eight! At that stage Singh was given run out. The crowd exploded in anger, bottles began to fly; soon they flew so thickly that the game could not be continued. The Governor; the Premier, Dr. Eric Williams; Learie Constantine, apologized to M.C.C. in England and to the M.C.C. team. The majority placed the blame on a few hooligans. Some few hinted at political tensions. Others talked vaguely about betting. There is not a little truth here and a little truth there which can all add up to something. There is not a glimmer of truth in all this. And if anything annoyed the Trinidad public it was to be lectured about the umpire being the sole judge. They continue to say that they know this and in fact on innumerable occasions have shown that they do.

First, to get out of the way what was not the cause of the explosion. In Melbourne in 1903 there took place a demonstration famous in cricket history. Its cause has never been in doubt. Australia had begun their second innings against England 292 behind. Trumper and Hill made a stand for the fourth wicket and by brilliant and courageous batting were putting Australia back in the game. Playing such cricket as from all accounts no one on the ground had ever seen before, not even from him, Trumper hit Braund for three fours in an over and forced the last ball past mid-off. The batsmen ran three, took another for a bad throw and tried for a fifth. Hill was given run out and both pavilion members and the crowd around the ropes protested so violently and so long that the protests re-echo in the pages of the history books to this day.

There is no problem here. The Australians had been losing, they had seen a chance of winning and winning by play grand and gallant. Hill as a popular idol was second only to Trumper. Hill went back to the wicket to continue batting, which showed that he thought he was in. This was enough to unloose the pent-up emotions.

*Nothing of the kind has ever taken place in the West Indies.*

When the bottle-throwing in Trinidad began the score was 98 for eight, nearly 300 behind. Not a soul on the ground believed that Ramadhin could make twenty. They would have cheered Singh as a hero if he had made ten. The fate of the match was not at stake.

It was not too different in British Guiana in 1954. England had made 435. From seven for 139 the score had been taken to 238 when a run-out precipitated the disturbance. Ram and Val were the remaining batsmen. All witnesses agree that the decision had been given, the batsman given out had reached the pavilion, the incoming batsman came in and took guard. It was only then that the bottle-throwing began.

In Jamaica in 1953 the umpire was threatened when Holt was given lbw at 94. Stollmeyer was threatened when he refused to ask the England team to follow on. None of these faintly resembles the situation in Melbourne in 1903. Again: none of these was a political demonstration against an imperialist Britain. The 1953–4 M.C.C. team was actively disliked. This was not due merely to unsportsmanlike behaviour by individuals. There is evidence to show that the team had given the impression that it was not merely playing cricket but was out to establish the prestige of Britain and, by that, of the local whites. On account of the bad reputation of the 1953–4 M.C.C. team many feared for the 1959 team. Such fears proved needless. Before long the 1959 team was so popular that when May in Jamaica committed the blunder of refusing Kanhai a runner, although the match was at stake, nobody bothered very much. If the crowd was given to losing its temper when a game was being lost there could have been an awful row then. There were a few boos, that was all. May is a certain type and when genuine it still commands respect in the West Indies. He had forced a point and played on in Barbados to give Barbados the chance of a win. Robins spoke his mind freely about any question that was asked him and altogether created a feeling that he was meeting the local people as a man who felt at home. He was an outstanding success. Cowdrey is genial in appearance, almost bucolic and yet shrewd. Trueman, who had had a bad time on the previous tour, bowled so well and clowned with such success that the past was forgotten. It must be quite clear that such politics as there were in the outburst, and it was drenched in politics, did not in any way involve either Britain or the M.C.C. My belief is that consideration for the M.C.C. moderated it both at the time and afterwards.

What then caused the 1960 and other outbursts? It was the conviction that here, as usual, local anti-nationalist people were doing their best to help the Englishmen defeat and disgrace the local players. That is the temper which caused these explosions and as long as that temper remains it will find a way to express itself. This particular political attitude is not declining. It is increasing, and will increase until a new social and political regime is firmly established and is accepted by all.

The history of this in the West Indies is as old as the West Indies itself. No imperialist expatriates can rule an alien population alone. The British therefore incorporated the local whites into their ranks. Later, as the pressure from the people grew, the light-skinned were given privileges. Universal suffrage and the nationalist passions and gains of the last fifteen years have driven many of the former privileged classes to side openly with the British, with Americans, with all or any who for one reason or another find themselves in conflict with or hostile to the nationalist movement. There is the seat of disturbance. It is particularly true of Trinidad. Against Britain as such there is surprisingly little hostility. And despite the passions aroused over the desire for the return of Chaguaramas,[1] where there is an American naval base, and recurrent spasms of anger at racial persecution in the United States, America and Americans are not unpopular.

But those suspected of anti-nationalism are usually rich whites and their retainers. Local politicians, editors, officials, policemen, selectors, umpires, are under scrutiny whenever they have to act on behalf of or on the side of what the people consider a nationalist cause. People feel that in the past some have served the foreigners against the local people and that many of them are still doing it. The nearer the people get to independence, the greater is the suspicion that the enemies of independence and nationalism are scheming against them. You will find this conflict running through every aspect of life in Trinidad, where political development has been late and is all the more explosive. This type of suspicion is embedded deep in the minds of the majority of the people. In the chapter on Wilton St. Hill I have shown how deeply my friends and I (no hooligans) were affected by the failure of the selectors to include him in the 1923 team and I believe I have dealt fairly with the case. We did not throw bottles, but we would have understood the feelings of those who had.

[1] That agitation is for the time being deadened—C.L.R.J.

Now for some details closer to the event.

It is still confidently affirmed that in 1947-8 Jamaica refused to play against England at all if George Headley, a black man, was not made the captain as he had every right to be.[1] There were all sorts of manœuvres and in the end Headley played in only one game. You cannot bluff a public about a captaincy, and the scandal was discussed in every island.

Nineteen-fifty brought another scandal. Many Jamaicans thought Headley should have been in the team to England and should have captained the side. Headley was offered the captaincy of the Jamaica side in the trial games. There was a complicated row over status and finances. (I have in my possession a detailed account of the whole affair written by Headley himself and I have told him that in my opinion he acted unwisely.) George didn't play in the trials, he didn't go to England. But the people did not forget. George played league cricket in England and scored so heavily that the Jamaican public felt that it would be unjust for him not to re-enter big cricket. They raised £1,000 by public subscription to bring him home so that he would be sure to play in the trials. When public feeling is running that high anything can happen. Obviously the public, or certain sections of it, distrusted the officialdom. From there the transition to the explosion over Holt is easy to understand. Holt, like Headley, is a black man, his father was the W.G. of Jamaica. If the batsman given out at 94 had been Headley the explosion would have been even easier to understand. But it is a dangerous blindness which does not see that this is not a question of ignorant or malicious disagreement with an umpire's decision.

It is an historical commonplace that social explosions take place when most of the fundamental causes of dissatisfaction have been removed and only a few remain. This is the result of a feeling of power. In West Indies cricket today selection is honest and straightforward and sometimes brilliant. Anyone, whatever his colour, can become captain of an island team. That is all the more reason why it is the captaincy of the West Indies side on which attention centres.

Clyde Walcott cannot by any stretch of fact or imagination be called a cricket Bolshevik, a term applied to Worrell in the past. Yet Clyde in his *Island Cricketers* had made several pointed references.

[1] From my knowledge of him, and I am fortified by Constantine's opinion, Headley is a master strategist and tactician.

'Before the Australians arrived the West Indies Board did something which at first seemed strange in announcing the names of captain and vice-captain for our tour of New Zealand which was to take place almost a year later. The names were Denis Atkinson and Bruce Pairaudeau. Only after this announcement had sunk in—and had caused a good deal of controversy—did the Board announce that Jeff Stollmeyer and Denis Atkinson would be captain and vice-captain respectively for the Australian series about to start. Although it was hard to see why the announcement of the officials for New Zealand had to be made so far in advance, the apparent discrepancy in selection was more easily explained.

'West Indies had no delusions, nor false politeness, about the strength of New Zealand cricket, and they had decided to send a young side, omitting all but a few of our established Test players. The choice of Atkinson as captain and—to gain experience—as vice-captain against Australia was in line with this policy. The public were not slow to ask why the "three W's" had been left out of the reckoning, particularly after Frank Worrell had been vice-captain against M.C.C. during the 1953–4 series. The public feeling seemed to be that the West Indies Board did not relish the prospect of having a coloured captain, but I do not think this was, in fact, the case. Much more likely, it seemed to me, was that West Indies were following the old-fashioned precedent of standing out against the professional captain: a precedent which, despite Len Hutton's reign as captain, still has its roots deeply laid in England. . . .

'Shortly before the First Test Jeff Stollmeyer hurt a finger in practice, so had to withdraw from the side. Automatically his vice-captain, Denis Atkinson, succeeded him, but the Press and the public took this as an excellent opportunity to renew their plea that Worrell should be given the captaincy. They rightly made the point that he was the more experienced player and captain, but they overlooked the fact that the thing had been decided in the selection room some time before and was unlikely to be changed now.

'Atkinson's experience was, in fact, very slight. Until his selection to captain the side to visit New Zealand he had not normally led his colony, Barbados. But after the announcement John Goddard, the usual Barbados captain, handed over to Atkinson, presumably to help the younger man gain experience. And so, lacking experience and the full confidence of West Indies cricket followers, Denis had a difficult task which was not eased when he had the misfortune to lose the toss.'

Have cricket enthusiasts in any country had to endure a state of affairs as is expressed in *Wisden* for 1956?

'Injuries to Stollmeyer could not have helped the West Indies. Stollmeyer, who captained the side against England in the previous season, hurt a finger while practising before the First Test and the inexperienced Atkinson took over the leadership. Stollmeyer returned to the captaincy for the next two Tests, but damaged a collarbone while fielding in the third, so that Atkinson was again appointed for the fourth and final representative game.'

When you turn to the First Test you see on the West Indies side E. D. Weekes, C. L. Walcott and F. M. Worrell being led by 'the inexperienced' Atkinson. After fifty years of it, to this day I still am unable to understand how people can do these things.

The exclusion of black men from the captaincy becomes all the more pointed when the Prime Minister of the West Indies and Chief Ministers all over the islands are black men. Clyde himself may never speak to me again for writing what I shall now write. I can only plead that the cause must stand higher than the man.

Walcott should have played for the West Indies in Australia in 1960–1. All critics agree that his sixty-odd on a turning wicket in the last Test against Pakistan in 1958 was batting at the peak. I had a good look at him in England, both at the nets and in matches. I saw him bat in a practice game in British Guiana in 1958. For defence and power in putting away the length ball this is one of the greatest of all batsmen. Only Bradman can be mentioned in the same breath for commanding hooking of fast bowlers. His physique is still one of the most powerful in cricket. I begged him to come back, in person, through friends, by overseas telephone. He finally played in one or two matches against the Englishmen, but at the height of his powers Clyde had put big cricket behind him. Why? I would say a general feeling that he was tired of intrigues and manœuvres which were not based on cricket ability.

One evening in British Guiana we were talking about captaincy. Suddenly Clyde, who is always circumspect in his speech, blurted out: 'You know who will be captain in England in 1963? You see that Barbados boy, Bynoe, who went to India? He only has to make fifty in one innings and he will be the captain.'

Bynoe is white.

Walcott was not claiming the captaincy for himself or for anybody in particular. I repeat: he is not that kind of person at all. His chief complaint, as I have gathered it over the years, is: if you are the captain, then captain, carry out your ideas; don't come bothering me about them.

An individual easily gets over the fact that he is disappointed in his desire to be captain. It is the constant, vigilant, bold and shameless manipulation of players to exclude black captains that has so demoralized West Indian teams and exasperated the people—a people, it is to be remembered, in the full tide of the transition from colonialism to independence.

I knew all this. I now heard it and saw it at first hand. The discrimination against black men was now an international scandal. After the 1953–4 tour Trevor Bailey had written about it guardedly in his book on cricket. Now Keith Miller, in his *Cricket from the Grandstand*, had put the issue with a refreshing if brutal frankness. He had written:

'. . . Another problem in West Indies cricket is that the captain has usually been chosen from among the European stock. Just think of the most famous West Indies cricketers . . . Learie Constantine, George Headley, Frank Worrell, Everton Weekes, Clyde Walcott . . . all are coloured, but none has led his country. Yet Worrell was often skipper of Commonwealth tours in India, and he did a fine job.'

Miller has also written:

'Politics interfere with cricket more in the West Indies than in most places. There is a terrific bias in each of the various islands in favour of their own players. . . .'

From what I saw in the West Indies that was no longer true.

I was editor of a newspaper. I was primed for action and made up my mind to clean up this captaincy mess once and for all. When the M.C.C. tour drew near I gave notice in the *Nation* that I proposed to wage an all-out campaign for Worrell to replace Alexander as captain. My argument was simply this: there was not the slightest shadow of justification for Alexander to be captain of a side in which Frank Worrell was playing.

Worrell had been offered the captaincy after the 1957 season in England, but owing to his studies at Manchester University he had had to refuse. That offer didn't matter very much to some of us who were watching. Worrell as captain at home or in India was bad enough, but that could be swallowed by the manipulators. What was at stake was the captaincy in Australia and still more in England. Their whole point was to continue to send to populations of white people, black or brown men under a white captain. The more brilliantly the black men played, the more it would emphasize to millions of English people: 'Yes, they are fine players, but, funny, isn't it, they cannot be responsible for themselves—they must always have a white man to lead them.'

The populace in the West Indies are not fools. They knew what was going on and, if not altogether sure of all the implications, they were quite sure that these, whatever they might be, were directed against them. I was told of an expatriate who arrived in Trinidad to take up an important post which the people thought should be filled by a local candidate. Such a storm arose that the expatriate had to be sent away. In 1959 British Guiana was thrown into turmoil and strikes over a similar issue and the Governor had to retreat. In cricket these sentiments are at their most acute because everyone can see and can judge.

What do they know of cricket who only cricket know? West Indians crowding to Tests bring with them the whole past history and future hopes of the islands. English people, for example, have a conception of themselves breathed from birth. Drake and mighty Nelson, Shakespeare, Waterloo, the Charge of the Light Brigade, the few who did so much for so many, the success of parliamentary democracy, those and such as those constitute a national tradition. Underdeveloped countries have to go back centuries to rebuild one. We of the West Indies have none at all, none that we know of. To such people the three W's, Ram and Val wrecking English batting, help to fill a huge gap in their consciousness and in their needs. In one of the sheds on the Port of Spain wharf is a painted sign: 365 Garfield Sobers. If the old Maple-Shannon-Queen's Park type of rivalry was now insignificant, a nationalist jealousy had taken its place.

All this was as clear to me as day. I tried to warn the authorities that there was danger in the air. Many of them, I am sure of this, were unable even to understand what I was saying. Our argument centred around the case of Gilchrist.

Gilchrist had been sent home from India and had been censured by the Board. The terms of its censure had been so couched as to imply that Gilchrist was banned for ever from Test cricket. Members of the Board denied this and there is no reason to disbelieve the denial. In any case, the denial was never officially made.

Gilchrist was not merely another West Indian cricketer. He was one of the plebs and to them a hero—he was their boy. They would not judge him by ordinary standards. Let me try to illustrate by a remote example.

Some years ago Mr. Azikiwe, then Premier of Eastern Nigeria, was accused of improper transactions in relation to a bank he had founded in Nigeria. We need not go into the charges. An official enquiry found that they were justified, but made it quite clear that Mr. Azikiwe had in its opinion been guilty only of political impropriety, he had not personally profited in any way. Mr. Azikiwe resigned, ran for election and was re-elected. Nigerians have told me of popular reaction. 'We had no bank here. All the money used to go to England. Zik made a bank for us. *If even Zik took a little for himself, that is O.K. with us.*'

In dealing with a nationalist agitation you have to reckon with such sentiments or you go badly astray.

I was very much interested in Gilchrist. Following the West Indies team around in 1957, I saw Gilchrist against Kent at Canterbury. I got the impression that he resented not being given the new ball by Walcott, acting captain, in the second innings, and didn't care who knew. If it was so I strongly disapproved.

In the next match against an England XI at Hastings we saw Gilchrist driven for five fours in an over by Cowdrey. Later I learnt the reason.

Frank Worrell was the captain and he had told Gilchrist that this was a festival game and in festival games you didn't bowl bumpers. Gilchrist, determined to oblige, preferred to bowl half-volleys and be driven for four after four rather than run the risk of appearing to disobey Frank. Gilchrist worships Frank Worrell (and among West Indian Test players, past and present, is not alone in so doing). They lived about twenty miles apart in England, and when Gilchrist wanted to buy a shirt he drove over to consult Frank.

On a visit to Jamaica I sought out people who knew Gilchrist. I was sent to his employer and patron. He told me how he had first met Gilchrist in a rural area, how he had brought him to Kingston, given him a job, sponsored him. He most certainly did not think Gilchrist a paragon of virtue, but 'Gilchrist,' he said, 'will do anything I tell him to do and would never do anything which he thought would offend me.' I made all this public.

The Board could not understand Gilchrist. The Board could not or would not understand what was the attitude of the public to Gilchrist. They were misled by pontificating articles in the biassed Press, preaching that the game was greater than the player and similar irrelevancies. What I soon discovered was that very few people paid the slightest attention to the extremely grave charges which, it was freely rumoured, had been made and substantiated against Gilchrist. Not only the ordinary man in the street but middle-class people were indifferent: a surprising number of people said: 'What is all this about "It isn't cricket"? Who are they to talk? They have been cheating about the captaincy for years.' Most people thought that there was a clash between black plebeian Gilchrist and the light-skinned Cambridge graduate Alexander.

I called up Gerry Gomez and told him what I thought should be done. The Board had taken a firm stand and would have been very wrong not to do so. Now, however, it should go further. Gilchrist was a young man of obscure origin suddenly hurled into the world Press as the fastest of living bowlers. He had made grave mistakes, but it was to be presumed that with time he would mature. I suggested that the Board get in touch with Frank Worrell and ask him to talk to Gilchrist (I had in mind also that some English friend of West Indian cricket should go with Frank, preferably E. W. Swanton, who alone had written about Gilchrist with a touch of sympathy.)

The Board simply could not understand its responsibility for Gilchrist. It thought it could just excommunicate him and adopt the pharisaical attitude that we were no longer responsible for what he did. They are terribly—and may well be catastrophically—wrong. Gilchrist, we were reliably informed, was bowling bumpers and beamers at league batsmen, an altogether reprehensible and, what was more, dangerous business. He was a West Indian Test cricketer. Unless the Board discovered a way of scrubbing him white he would be considered one of us, whatever decrees the Board might issue. I was convinced that the Board should use Frank Worrell to bring Gilchrist back into the fold. The West Indian populace would be vastly pleased and grateful, and this surely would be the most powerful of influences to make Gilchrist conform to accepted standards.

Gilchrist should be helped to write a substantial apology, both to the Board and to individuals. This would be published, and, with Frank to sponsor him, he could be brought back. If Gilchrist proved obdurate then this too would be published and public unrest would be pacified. Gerry's reply was that West Indian cricketers had gained a great reputation for sportsmanship everywhere and no one should be allowed to spoil it. I simply could not accept that West Indians' reputation at cricket could be spoiled by anything one individual could do, especially if the Board was known to have acted in a firm and yet paternal manner.

The cricket reputation of the West Indies could be spoilt in many ways. I wrote in the *Nation* asking the Board to reconsider: in vain. The Board received another clear warning. Some of Gilchrist's plebeian admirers in Trinidad printed posters calling upon the public to boycott the Trinidad Tests if Gilchrist did not play. One of their leaders came to me and asked me: what next? I told him to take it easy. Even before the situation had become acute Frank Worrell had been broadcasting from England to the West Indies giving discreet but clear hints to the Board that some attempt should be made to bring Gilchrist back. The Board continued to emphasize what Gilchrist had done.

This was not the first time that I had had doubts of the inability of the Board to understand the age in which it was living. First there had been the readiness of McLean and Waite, the South Africans, to go to the West Indies with E. W. Swanton's team. From the start I took the position that if at all possible they should have been welcomed. *They were ready to break the barrier.* We should have been ready to accept. I wrote to the West Indies to that effect. I understood finally that the Board was afraid that there might be incidents either from the public or a section of the Press. I think I know the West Indian crowd better than they do. All that was needed was that responsible political figures should have been asked to give their approval publicly, and West Indians would have welcomed them. It would have been different if one of the visitors had been a fast bowler given to bumpers. Instead, one hook off his face by McLean would have made him a favourite of the crowd.

Later there was another rather sharp dispute over the proposal of the 'cricket Bolshevik' Worrell to take a team of coloured West Indians to play against Africans in South Africa. Canon Collins and others protested against this as accepting apartheid. Constantine was with them. I took an opposite view. The team, I thought, should go. Apartheid sought the isolation of the Africans not only from whites but from free blacks. The tour would have had world-wide publicity. The African cricketers and the African crowds would have made contact with world-famous cricketers who had played in England and in Australia. There might have been incidents? So much the better. A pitiless light would have been thrown on the irrationality and stupidity of apartheid. African cricketers would have benefited, and, it was to be hoped, one or two African cricketers might have emerged and become widely known as naturals for an All South African team. From the beginning I was certain that, whatever the South African Government might say, it did not want this tour. Racialists do not ever want the eyes of the world on their crimes. Constantine and I differed openly on this issue in the *Nation*. The public discussion was wide and acute. It is the sort of problem that the ordinary West Indian pays close attention to. I would say that at the beginning he was against. But I found that he listened attentively to my arguments. He knew me as a life-long opponent of racialism and an established supporter of African nationalism. He knew that whatever opinions I might express *I was on his side*. All this was stirring in the people just before the M.C.C. tour. The conduct of West Indian crowds, like everything else West Indian, is open for judgment. But those who judge should remember that there are no more devoted lovers of the game anywhere. That prejudices me in their favour. And secondly, before you judge, find out what they are thinking and why.

I firmly believe that if the Board had taken the steps I suggested, whatever had been Gilchrist's response, there would have been no outburst in Trinidad. The people would have felt that the Board was on their side, was with them and the whole temper would have been different. If Gilchrist had shown himself obstinate I would certainly have upheld the Board and strongly condemned him. Things being as they were, I was pretty certain that there was an even chance of a violent explosion in the coming series, though I and others expected it in Jamaica over Gilchrist, and this also I made clear in the paper. But with crowds you never can tell exactly what will set off an underlying tension. In this case it was the umpiring, nor was this strange.

Trinidad intercolonial cricketers have a slogan about local umpiring. 'They do not do such things in England and in Barbados.' It is a tradition that Trinidad umpires are severe with Trinidad players. Let me give an example.

In 1946 in Port of Spain, Trinidad, the home team faced a total of 671 in the fourth innings with plenty of time left for play. Trestrail, who made 151, and Ganteaume, who made 85, put up over 200 runs for the first wicket, when Ganteaume was given run out by a Trinidad umpire, a very close decision. The umpire, V. Guillen, is an old intercolonial cricketer, a friend of mine for many years, with whom I have played and talked a lot of cricket. I sat and listened to him and Andy Ganteaume discuss the decision in the most amicable manner. Whether Ganteaume was out or not did not and does not interest me in the slightest. What I was interested in was popular opinion that in England or Barbados a local umpire would not have given a local player out at such a time in a decision which was admittedly a matter of inches.

I remain convinced of my own views because I at any rate was paying close attention and I have not yet met or heard of anybody who was.[1]

In the matches against the Englishmen three decisions had caused comment. The boy Davis, batting well, had been given run out, a decision which displeased the crowd. An English batsman had been given out but remained at the crease, presumably unaware of the decision. When the bowler appealed again the umpire changed his mind and gave the batsman not out. This he was perfectly entitled to do. In that situation it was an additional stick of dynamite. The islands are small—during big cricket people talk fanatically about nothing else. Every street corner is a seething cauldron of cricket experiences, cricket memories, fears, suspicions, hopes, aspirations. On that very January 30th Hunte had been given out, and for a long time even those manipulating the scoreboard had been unable to say how he was out, whether lbw or caught by Trueman on the leg-side. The crowd had watched the collapse of the West Indian batting, that same batting which had made 563 in the Barbados Test. When Ramadhin hit a boundary or two and showed that he was not going to give in the crowd woke up. This had nothing whatever to do with winning or losing the match. They sensed the opportunity for some fun and rejoicing and took it gladly. If after their excitement Singh had been bowled for nought they would have laughed uproariously as at a good joke against themselves. It was the abrupt

---

[1] Three or four years ago I could have had a lot to say about English crowds at cricket, and twenty-five years ago I was quite familiar with Lancashire League crowds. But you have to keep in close touch.

termination of their quite facetious gaiety which brought decades of dissatisfaction to a head. There is no question in my mind or in the minds of many that Singh was out. The three decisions I have mentioned gave far more ground, as decisions, for popular protest. But no one can tell how and when these outbursts will take place. Revolutions, someone has said, come like a thief in the night. The apparent causes are nearly always trivial and to the superficial eye unjustified.

The theory of a few hooligans is not only dangerous but without sense. I know of no instance where a few hooligans have disrupted a major public function, unless they knew or sensed that public opinion was either on their side or at least neutral. I have made systematic enquiries both at the time and since and a secret poll would to this day show a majority for the view: 'Wrong, yes, but the people had to do something.' A recurrent defiance was the following: 'The bottles should have been thrown into the pavilion.' Not a word was ever said against the English players.

Who doubts the validity of the above has to reckon with what now followed. I had been waiting to get a sight of Alexander as captain and before the Test was over I launched an attack against his captaincy: Alexander must go. I based it on Worrell's superior experience and status and Alexander's errors of judgment. I refused to make it a question of race, though I made it clear that if the rejection of Worrell was continued I would reluctantly have to raise the racial issue. To have raised it would have switched the discussion away from cricket and involved all sorts of other issues. The anti-nationalists, with their usual brazenness, would have countered with 'Race introduced into sport'. And in any case everybody in the West Indies understood what I was leaving out even better than what I was actually writing.

The effect was beyond all expectation. The *Nation* was an official organ and a highly political paper. (Some even queried whether such a paper should express an opinion on cricket captaincy at all.) They were wrong. This was politics and very serious politics. The 'Alexander Must Go' issue was sold out by the day following publication. People who had read or heard of the article rushed around looking for copies to buy. The man in the street expressed deep feelings. 'Thank God for the *Nation*.' 'Someone to speak for us at last.' He was not speaking about the explosion. The *Nation* had been as uncompromising as any in condemning it.

Week after week I carried on unsparingly, putting everything that I had into it. Here, for the sake of the records, is one example of many.[1]

*'Frank Worrell is at the peak of his reputation not only as a cricketer but as a master of the game. Respect for him has never been higher in all his long and brilliant career. . . .*

'His bearing on the field, all grace and dignity, evoked general admiration [in England in 1957]. In every sphere, and others beside myself know this, the opinion was that he should have been the captain. . . .

'In India, owing to his many tours with Commonwealth sides, during one of which he took over the captaincy with great success, he is remembered as one of the greatest cricketers of the age. . . .

'But, more important than this: AUSTRALIA WANTS HIM AS CAPTAIN.

'This is the authentic fact. When Australian critics talk of Trumper, Kippax and the few half-dozen batsmen who have batted as if they were born to it they include Worrell. As a man he made a tremendous impression in Australia. Thousands will come out on every ground to see an old friend leading the West Indies. In fact, I am able to say that if Worrell were captain and Constantine or George Headley manager or co-manager, the coming tour would be one of the greatest ever.'

It was hard on Alexander. He was not a good captain and in any case he was keeping wicket, which is no place for a captain. But it was hard on me also. Alexander is a fine soccer player, he kept wicket magnificently, he is a good defensive bat and is a hard fighter. I put my scruples aside and I think that for the first, and I hope the last, time in reporting cricket I was not fair. But I was determined to rub in the faces of everybody that Frank Worrell, the last of the three W's, was being discriminated against. Charles Bray of the *Daily Herald*, no mean campaigner himself, told me that he wondered how I was able to keep it up. I would have been able to keep it up for fifty weeks, for there was fifty years' knowledge of discrimination behind it and corresponding anger. When I confessed I was angry, even sympathizers balked at this. According to the code, anger should not intrude into cricket. I understood them well, I had been as foolish in my time. According to the colonial version of the code, you were to show yourself a 'true sport' by not making a fuss about the most barefaced discrimination because it wasn't cricket.

[1] The *Nation*, March 4th, 1960.

Not me any longer. To that I had said, was saying, my final good-bye[1]; and no one knew better than I how much dangerous trouble was ahead if that sort of thing continued. Worrell was finally appointed and then, strange but not unusual, there was universal jubilation. All classes approved. It is often so. Even those who had been led astray to give silent support to their extremists seemed genuinely relieved that the whole mess was over and they could participate with their fellow men in the general rejoicing. H. B. G. Austin was the natural captain of the West Indies as long as he chose to play. You took that for granted. But I don't believe that any cricket appointment in the West Indies was ever so universally and warmly approved as that of Frank Worrell as captain of our team to Australia. I have kept the politics out of it, but great cheers rang from the audience as the Premier, Dr. Eric Williams, in his address to the Fourth National Convention of his party, said:

'. . . If C. L. R. James took it upon his individual self to wage a campaign for Worrell as captain of the West Indies, and in so doing to give expression not only to the needs of the game but also to the sentiments of the people, we know as well as he that it is the *Nation* and the P.N.M. to whom the people will give the praise.'

Those words were the literal truth. The 'Case for West Indian Self-Government' and 'It isn't cricket' had come together at last and together had won a signal victory.

I didn't like the look of things after the bottle-throwing, I didn't like it at all. So on February 12th, 1960, I summed up the whole, all the past, the present and hopes for the future, in an open letter to the Queen's Park Club. Here it is:

'The Queen's Park Cricket Club

'Gentlemen:

'You are exercising a public reponsibility, the importance of which seems to have exceeded your comprehension. It is for this reason that I

---

[1] Certain critics, not only West Indian, deplored the tone of my advocacy and doubted if the high-minded Worrell would approve of it. If any of these delicate souls had shown me models of advocating one of the three W's as a West Indies captain I might have benefited from their instruction. Unfortunately, none of them offered any model, reproved not selectors but me. Hence my untutored vulgarity.

address you this letter. The letter has to be an open letter because the matters it deals with are now wide open, not only to the public in this territory and in the West Indies but to the whole world.

'You are in charge of the organization and management of cricket tours at home and abroad. Recent events should have shown you that, among us today, this is one of the most responsible tasks that is being performed by a non-governmental body. What has happened to Carnival should teach us all a great deal. The people of Trinidad and Tobago are devoted to their Carnival. It is possible that they would be better employed studying Shakespeare, listening to classical music or taking physical culture in order to improve the health of the community. They don't. They play Carnival, spend time and money on it. That is what they want to do. With the jump that all our affairs are taking, Carnival expanded until the old organizers had to be cast aside.

'It is equally clear, to a degree of which I had no conception, that cricket has made mighty strides among our people. International cricket matters to them. They are passionately interested in it. That from a small island like this you can get well over 30,000 people to see a Test match, much the same number that you get at Lord's or the Oval in a London of ten million people, that is a circumstance which, as far as I know, is unprecedented in its scope and implications. It confers tremendous credit upon the game of cricket and upon the people of Trinidad and Tobago. It also confers great credit upon you as the local representatives of the West Indian Board of Control. I am not only aware of this, I am anxious to point it out.

'In this letter I shall have to say some hard and unpleasant things. For this reason I wish to make my own position in regard to you as a club and as organizers of international cricket quite clear from the start. There have long been murmurings, and now they are very strong, that the management of international cricket which has grown to such remarkable proportions should no longer be in the hands of what is a private club. Such a responsibility, runs the argument, should be held by a democratically elected body representing the cricket clubs and associations of the country; the Football Association is run that way and very efficiently and satisfactorily run. It would doubtless surprise you to know that, though not an opponent of that view, I am not at present an advocate of it. We in the West Indies have very little historical background to which we are able to look. It is over sixty years that the Queen's Park Club has been organizing international tours. It has helped more than any other organization to build the game of cricket here. It has produced some great players and still produces them. The Queen's Park Oval is a magnificent cricket ground, one of the most beautiful in the world. There are even some with experience abroad who give it pride of place.

'Looking over the booklet produced by the Club to celebrate its Diamond Jubilee, I saw the following in the message from the Governor, Sir Edward Beetham.

' "In this year in which the Queen's Park Cricket Club celebrates the Diamond Jubilee of its occupancy of the Oval, the club can look back on a proud record of achievement.

' "In its sixty years of occupancy the club has taken the lead in promoting and financing intercolonial and international cricket tournaments, and the Oval has become a focal point of first-class cricket in Trinidad and the West Indies. The club's unremitting initiative for more than half a century in relation to first-class cricket, and the encouragement which it has given to other forms of sport, represents a signal service to sport generally in the Caribbean. It also represents a public service to the sport-loving people of Trinidad and Tobago who, through the club, have been enabled to see the world's leading cricketers in action at the Oval. That the club has been recognized as the Cricket Authority for Trinidad is fitting tribute to the service it has rendered to West Indies cricket for so many years."

'That I think is a just statement of a fine record.

'There is also the example of M.C.C. Here is a private club which runs big cricket on a truly international scale. No theory of democracy can overcome the fact that Australia, South Africa, the West Indies, New Zealand, India and Pakistan, cricketers the world over, give their ungrudging allegiance to M.C.C. Furthermore, as a general rule, I am always in favour of public affairs being carried on by organizations of citizens who are not in any way connected with the government (except to get some money out of them every now and then). The inherent strength of the older countries owes much to the fact that they have had time and opportunities to develop such bodies. Some of them are very old and very reactionary. Nevertheless some can be transformed, as Oxford and Cambridge have been transformed so that today 80 per cent of the students are not the sons of the aristocracy and the wealthy but are winners of scholarships. If things can be so developed that the Queen's Park Club continues to manage or to exercise an assured position in the organization and management of international cricket in the West Indies and in Trinidad and Tobago, I see nothing against that and I see much to be said for it. But that requires a vivid and active sense of public obligation on your part. Unfortunately at the present time what you are heading for is a clamour to the Government that the projected stadium be begun immediately, and that the Board of Control in Trinidad be represented by a body elected from top to bottom.

'That is what you are heading for. It is possible that this is inevitable. Meanwhile, however, we are faced with an immediate and present situation. I had hoped that things would stay more or less as they are until the tour is over; we do not want any unnecessary agitation while our visitors are in the West Indies. But the public mind is unsettled and as a responsible public body you have to take that into consideration and you have to act.

'The *Nation* has suggested that a public enquiry be instituted into the events that took place on January 30th. Nothing else will ever be able to give an authoritative account of what happened and why and what to do to prevent it happening again. It is possible that the Government may in the end institute such an enquiry: it can well come within the province of the Ministry of Home Affairs, or the Ministry of Education and Culture, or the Police. The West Indies Board of Control may order an enquiry. The incident took place on your ground. A public enquiry can very well be instituted by you. The Queen's Park Club not only has every right to appoint a commission of enquiry. It is its duty to do so. But let me give you a warning. Such a commission of enquiry should not be appointed to whitewash the club. Its business should be to give the public the confidence that what is being done is in the public interest. It would not be at all difficult to select a body of men and women, not necessarily all members of the club, whose very names would inspire confidence.

'Why is this so necessary? It is necessary because although public sentiment, as far as I have been able to discover, realizes that what took place was wrong, nevertheless, too many continue to think that the people were justified. What is still more alarming, many people who have never thrown and would never throw a bottle remain obdurate in their opinion that what was done, however wrong, was necessary, being the only way in which attention could be drawn to grave grievances.

'A commission of enquiry would have to bear in mind the following:

'1. The Oval on Saturday, January 30th, was over-sold. There were too many people in the ground.

'2. Too many people have to stand. No one should be asked to stand at a Test when he may enter the ground at half past nine, have to stay there till five o'clock, and do this for six days.

'3. Charges for refreshments such as are bought by the ordinary folk are too high, and it is believed that the reason for this is the high price of concessions.

'4. The public is profoundly irritated by its conviction that the captaincy of the West Indies team for years has been manipulated in such a manner as deliberately to exclude black men.

'5. The public is convinced that the Board has mismanaged the Gilchrist affair and that Gilchrist should be playing in the West Indies side.

'6. The public is not satisfied that the umpires appointed in Trinidad carry out their duty with the impartiality that they should. They have felt this for years.

'7. There is a widespread rumour that the bottle-throwing was not begun by the crowd but was a retaliation for a bottle thrown at it.

'8. Finally there is the conviction now deep-seated that the Queen's Park Club represents the old regime in Trinidad and that it is indifferent and even hostile to what the masses of the people think.

'Gentlemen, I ask you to believe me when I say that the above is a mild statement of public sentiment. Merely to list them is not to accept them. To take No. 1, the overcrowding. When Secretary Botha Tench says that he would gladly have given back all the money if what happened could have been avoided I quite believe him. I have stood outside Lord's for hours only to be shut out in the end, and along with others used all our powers of persuasion to try to get ourselves in. (Finally I had to pay £5 to a scoundrel who had bought some tickets for just such an emergency.)

'I do not bring prejudice to any of the charges. In the campaign I am carrying on against Alexander instead of Worrell as captain I shall exhaust every argument before I touch the racial aspect of it. Public sentiments, however, are as I have stated them. You are a body exercising a public function. You cannot be indifferent to what the public thinks. This cannot be answered by saying: hooligans. If to have the kind of doubts and suspicions that the people have is to be a hooligan, then I have been a hooligan for fifty years and my brother and sister hooligans include some of the most highly placed and responsible people in the country.

'If the Queen's Park Club is indifferent or shows indifference to these public sentiments then it is totally unfit to control or manage big cricket in the island any longer. The only way that it can show that it is not indifferent and that it recognizes the responsibility that it holds is to take steps along the lines that I have outlined here. Whenever there are disturbances anywhere the British Government does not hesitate to appoint a commission of enquiry consisting for the most part of trusted public figures who at any rate make the facts known and draw their own independent conclusions.

'The Queen's Park Club, like the M.C.C., is a private club. Obviously members of the club and their families enjoy certain advantages in regard to seats at important events, etc. As with the M.C.C., there are continued complaints and criticisms of the exclusiveness and privileges enjoyed by members of such a club. M.C.C. has taken pains to see to it that all cricketers of a certain standing and number of years of service to the game should become members. For the rest the membership of a private club which is exercising a public function is always likely to cause dissatisfaction. I pay little attention to it because if the feelings and needs of the general public are taken into consideration the public will not be particularly concerned as to the privileges exercised by a few individuals. The public does not think in those terms.

'If, gentlemen, you are unable to understand, or if you understand but for one reason or another you refuse to take action along the lines I have indicated, then events will take their course. I shall tell you some of them.

'1. There is certain to arise a clamour which in the end will be irresistible for the stadium as a means of removing your club entirely, except on the same basis as other clubs, from the management and organization of international tours.

'2. The *Nation* printed the other day some extracts from the book of Clyde Walcott on cricket. No one should mistake the moderation of the tone and the obvious desire not to give offence and thereby believe that the three W's do not bitterly feel the injustice and humiliation to which they have been subjected by the attitude of the Board towards them and the captaincy of the West Indies. This is not lost on the younger players. And before very long we shall see some of our finest cricketers abandoning League cricket and taking up county cricket as Marshall has done and Ramadhin tried to do. They will have a beautiful ground to play on if they are batsmen, they will play cricket to their hearts' content, and after some years they will be granted a benefit which may well give them eight or ten thousand pounds about the time when their powers are beginning to wane. That is not clear on the horizon today. It will be clearer tomorrow. Who will blame them for thus letting West Indies cricket see after itself? You who could have done so much for them have not only done very little. You stand accused of having deliberately contrived to deprive some of them of honours which in any other country under the sun would have been theirs.

'This which I shall now say is the most important of all. I have heard repeatedly that the bottles should have been thrown not on to the ground but into the pavilion. I state freely for all to know that in the middle of my work and sometimes awakening suddenly in the middle of the night I have some terrible moments thinking of how easily this might have happened and the awful consequence for all of us which would have ensued.

'I repeat: when the disturbances broke out in 1937 in the West Indies the British Government did not say: hooligans. It sent to find out what had happened and why and to seek recommendations to cure the ills. You, gentlemen, should not feel yourselves above doing that. It will be a sign of strength, not of weakness. It will make for peace and not for a continued cold war. I talked to Denis Atkinson in England in Hastings in 1957 and he told me that he was a member of the old club of H. B. G. Austin and the Challenor brothers and I told him I was glad to hear that: I hoped the time would never come when a member of that club, the originator of the great tradition of Barbados batting, would not represent the West Indies. Here as everywhere else I am primarily concerned with the building of a truly national community, incorporating all of the past that is still viable.

'Among you is the head of a West Indian family that for three generations has distinguished itself in religion, education, commerce, sport, politics and social work. Two world-famous cricketers are now active in your councils and were yesterday active on the field. They know a great deal more about cricket than I do. I want to assure them, first that I know much more about crowds than they do, and, secondly, that they do not exceed me in love for the game, respect for its traditions and a desire that these should flourish in the West Indies to a degree inferior to no other part of the world. If this letter, which draws to their attention and to the attention of their fellow members the true state of affairs in Trinidad and Tobago and what to do about it, if this letter meets with no response, then here, as elsewhere, the general prospect for harmonious development and adjustment is bleak indeed. It would have been very simple for the *Nation* to have gathered up enough of the mass of information floating around and launched a ferocious and sustained attack against the Queen's Park Club. Vast sections of the public would have greeted it with deep satisfaction. But if the problem is urgent it is not urgent in the way that the removal of Alexander as captain is urgent. On that we are giving no quarter at all. But on this far larger question we have preferred a more friendly and more cautious approach. If, however, there has to be a fight to cure our society of a dangerous abscess which has now burst, then fight there will be. Foremost in the desire for a peaceful solution, the *Nation* likewise, if nothing else suffices, will lead the attack: it will be strategic, comprehensive and final.

'Yours, gentlemen,
'I assure you, very sincerely,
'C. L. R. James'

Once more the general public read with deep satisfaction. It saw in print what it wanted expressed. I believe that, in Trinidad at least, a great deal of tension, dating back many years, has been eased. The selection committee made a brilliant selection for Australia. Gerry Gomez was appointed manager, a good choice. Gerry is popular at home among all classes and in Australia, knowledgeable and tough. The *Nation*'s approval was freely expressed and generously approved. Despite the public request of Frank Worrell, the new captain, the Board refused to reinstate Gilchrist. I thought it was a mistake, but I let it pass. I have said that explosions can occur again. They most certainly can, but only if an atavistic idiocy persists in outmoded and discredited foolishness.

I must say that after it was all over my regard for cricket and my interest in it were greater than ever before. During all this time the

*Nation* was vigorously supporting the Premier in political campaigns against the Colonial Office and the State Department, campaigns in which it was made clear that in pursuit of what he considered legitimate and inalienable rights the Premier was ready to take Trinidad and Tobago out of the Federation and out of the Commonwealth if need be. He was confident of the support of the people. All that is now over. Yet considered opinion is that the campaign for Worrell was the most popular and the most effective of all the *Nation* campaigns. The people simply saw it as a part of the whole movement. There might be arguments, and considerations to be taken into account in regard to the other issues— this one they understood and accepted completely. All art, science, philosophy, are modes of apprehending the world, history and society. As one of these, cricket in the West Indies at least could hold its own. A professor of political science publicly bewailed that a man of my known political interests should believe that cricket had ethical and social values. I had no wish to answer. I was just sorry for the guy.

It is easy to misunderstand and overdraw conclusions from the above campaign, sharp as it was. West Indian society isn't easy for outsiders to understand. Our Maple-Shannon-Queen's Park rivalries, keen as they were, never, or very rarely, exceeded the bounds. So it is today, despite the apparently irreconcilable antagonisms. The secretary of Queen's Park, Botha Tench, is an old and favourite pupil (I had refereed or umpired countless matches in which he and Victor Stollmeyer, boys in short trousers, played). He complained to me that I had certain facts wrong. I offered him the paper to correct them, but he didn't accept the offer. Yet when we spoke about it I hadn't seen him since I had come home and our greetings were warm and cordial.

The two cricketers referred to in the open letter are, of course, Gerry Gomez and Jeffrey Stollmeyer. Soon after I came home I tried to find outstanding sportsmen who were popular with all classes and could play a mediating social role in the acute political tensions. Two names were given to me: Gerry Gomez and Lindsay Grant. When Gerry was appointed manager for Australia I wrote in the *Nation* quite plainly what are his opportunities and responsibilities in the building of a national community. He did not take it amiss.

The other cricketer is Jeffrey Stollmeyer. Looking for someone to write capably for the paper about a visiting English soccer team his name was mentioned to me. (He and Gerry starred in intercolonial soccer as well as in international cricket.) I called him up and asked him to write. He said he was very sorry but it was just about the time the matches were played that he had to deal with his workers. I regretted this. I had found his judgment on West Indian players to be as sound and more balanced than all I had heard with the exception of Andy Ganteaume's. He would have been quite willing to write and surprised me by not merely giving me condolences about my father's death but spoke about him in a way that showed he had some idea of my father's work and personality. Cyril Merry must have talked to him. Jeffrey and Gerry are, of course, and have been for many years, the embodiment of Queen's Park. Michael Gibbes, the assistant secretary of the Queen's Park Club and an able journalist, wrote regularly on cricket for the *Nation*.

The other person referred to, Lindsay Grant, is head of the Grant family and the Grant business firm, brother of two West Indian captains, umpire in Tests and a Queen's Park stalwart. When there was a financial problem about my staying in the West Indies Lindsay subscribed substantially, though he knows my political views. Premier Williams wanted Jack Grant to come home and be the Chief Officer in the Education Department. But Jack will not leave his missionary work in Africa. One day an African in transit who had been President of the African National Congress of South Africa paid me a visit. I asked him if by any chance he knew Jack. Most surprisingly, he said yes: once when attending a conference of the Congress he had stayed incognito at Jack's house. I called Lindsay and they had a long conversation. Whenever I want information which Lindsay may have I call him or drop in at the office and am always welcome. We both won exhibitions the same year and came up the school side by side.

The most pointed reference of all in the open letter is to the organization of football. The secretary of the West Indian Football Association is my brother Eric. He had managed two teams to England, had brought one to the West Indies and was bringing another. He had been the secretary of the Government committee in charge of the projected stadium. About the cricket controversies he was noncommittal, but everyone knew that the Football Associations which he was responsible for were run on strictly democratic lines, all clubs and all classes represented, and were supported by the entire community. The football organization interested me enormously, owing to the perfect integration of all elements in the community. That it is so is no accident, and nationalist politics are not confined to speeches and laws. My brother has made it that way and kept it that way, though he will recoil with horror at the mere thought of being called a politician. He has had his troubles, and speaks of the unswerving support he has had, among others, from Courtenay Rooks, a white man who was at school with me, and from George Rochford, at one time head of Gordon, Grant & Co., perhaps the biggest firm in the island. The most curious fact to the stranger who would read my open letter is that some of the staunchest supporters of the Football Association and members of its committees have been and are active members of Queen's Park. In fact it is precisely because of the above that I could write so freely. Under different circumstances the open letter would have been tantamount to a declaration of war. Staunch Queen's Park members told me, 'A little harsh in places but not so bad.'

So there we are, all tangled up together, the old barriers breaking down and the new ones not yet established, a time of transition, always and inescapably turbulent. In the inevitable integration into a national community, one of the most urgent needs, sport, and particularly cricket, has played and will play a great role. There is no one in the West Indies who will not subscribe to the aphorism: what do they know of cricket who only cricket know? But what is most strange is that what I have written here and in the early chapters on Maple-Shannon-Queen's Park has been known to everyone in the West Indies for the last fifty years. Yet it had been allowed to fester under the surface, a source of corruption and hypocrisy. From now on that is over.

# 19

## Alma Mater: Lares and Penates

I N A L L this turmoil what of the old school and the old school-tie?
Miraculous transposition of roles! The old school-tie was flourishing,
the old school was not. There was an Old Boys' Association, there was
an Old Boys' Dinner, there were annual matches with other Old Boys.
All the paraphernalia of the old school-tie, all new to me. But the school
itself? Thomas Arnold and Thomas Hughes, Oxford and Cambridge,
were strangers. W.G. alone held his place.

The course of events was easy to follow. More and more of the
masters were local men, West Indians. Some had taken their degrees
externally from London University. The stamp of a united body of
Oxford and Cambridge men had gone, and nothing had yet taken its
place. There was national personnel but no national personality. How
could there be! When I arrived in April 1958 the nationalist movement
was barely two years old, and was immersed in politics. A nationalist
ideology was taking shape, but that is necessarily of slow growth. Time
and work will be needed for it to acquire form, to give a structural and
instructive frame to teachers, far less to pupils. Disturbed at the vacuum,
and seeking stability on shifting sands, some local people are building a
new home for the two Thomases, private school, site remote, boarding
houses, English-trained staff, the latest and most up-to-date version of 1900.

It is the democratic current which goes from strength to strength.
Where in my time there were four free exhibitions, there are now 400.

Where there were less than half a dozen accredited secondary schools there will soon be a score situated all over the island. As for private secondary schools, unassisted by Government, their pupils grow by the hundreds every year. The taxi-driver, the cook, the housemaid, are giving their children at least three or even two years of 'college education'. The elementary-school teachers are among the most active nationalists in the country. Some crystallization of national ethics, mode and code of behaviour will emerge; it always has, it always will.

The games rivalry between the schools continues. More people than ever see Q.R.C. *v.* St. Mary's. When one side defeated the other, to my astonishment the victors and their supporters paraded the streets to the accompaniment of steel band and calypso. Whereupon another argument was given to those who contend that the dead do not rise again—if they did Mr. Burslem, my old master, would have met that sacrilegious and pagan bacchanal (he was strong on vituperation) in cap and gown, bamboo rod in hand and old Carter, the porter, like Sancho Panza in attendance, with a fresh supply of corrective. If the two Thomases are to survive in the West Indies they will do so only by donning slacks and hot shirts. The calypso and the jump-up received the accolade at Lord's in 1950 and in the *Wisden* of 1951. All that, however, is another story.

With my family I was on more familiar ground, perhaps more enduring. When I returned my father was already eighty but active in intellect, his memory unimpaired to the last. He and my sister told me much and filled in gaps about the matter contained in the first three chapters of this book. I do not feel inclined to go into all that here: it will not be disciplined within the original framework which I have stretched enough already. He did tell me, however, that Cudjoe was such a favourite because of his abnormal skill in flicking off a bail when a ball passed close to the wicket, thus making the umpire think that the batsman was bowled. Poor Cudjoe. Misled by his betters.

My Aunt Judith, I learnt, became the matriarch of her neighbourhood. Fathers and children, husbands and wives, sweethearts and lovers, all brought their troubles to her. Judith sought and often achieved reconciliation and peace. Her character as I had known it never changed but stood out among those around her like a lighthouse.

I walked behind my father's hearse with my sister. My mother had been paralysed for thirteen years. My sister had tended her without complaint. She had smoothed my father's last years. When his coffin was about to be lifted from the house she shed two or three quick tears. During the service she sat while one hymn was being sung. That was all. It was Judith all over again.

In the turmoil around me my family fascinated me as never before. On that spot from which I looked through the window at Matthew Bondman and Arthur Jones succeeding generations of the James family have lived in direct descent for over 150 years. That in the West Indies is a long time. We were established before our Norman conquest, i.e. the abolition of slavery. We are of the West Indies West Indian. From an ancient citizen of ninety-three years of age, I learnt that my grandfather, he of the Sunday-morning frock-coat, high collar and silver-headed cane, used to teach in Sunday school. Some members of the family must have helped to build the Church of the Good Shepherd where I memorized the chapters and verses of the lessons so as to look them up in the Bible, where the last rites were said for my father. When he was married in 1900 my great grandmother presented him with a mahogany table and a wardrobe which had been given to her at her wedding 120 years ago. They are still in use.

The continuity is strong.

We have travelled, but only the outlines of character are changed. I have changed little. I know that more than ever now. Another aunt, Eva, is back from the United States where she spent many years. She is of a quick and volatile temperament, always has been. But in her own way she is as firm as Judith. She denounces West Indian food, the stews and the gravies and the sauces. She eats an American diet of broils, roasts and fresh vegetables lightly cooked. 'That's why these West Indian women are so fat,' she declares. 'It's the kind of food they eat.' She is an active and slender seventy-two. Despite her Americanism, her ideas of what is proper bear the Victorian stamp, and she responds to deviations with rapidity and eloquence.

I watch my brother and his three children. In very different ways they all are Jameses: sometimes hidden but always present is the Puritan sense of discipline.

My son, who is an American citizen, visited me in the West Indies. His mother is of a race different from mine, and the family awaited him eagerly. Each member scrutinized him carefully and then declared with approval and perhaps relief, 'Yes, he is a James.'

I see what they mean. But is he a James as I know the Jameses? I can't say, and as far as I am aware I am not particularly anxious that he should be. He has to live his life, not mine. He is, in the family tradition, a scholarship winner and goes to an excellent school in New York. 'It isn't cricket' doesn't mean a thing to him. Why should it? But the son of our house, an American citizen, is a mighty cricket enthusiast, and before he was in his teens, I could trust him to go to a Test match and bring back a report in which I had more confidence than much that appeared in the Press. Both he and my son are readers and will read this book, and if there is a proposal to sell a game I hope this book will help them not merely to say, 'No,' which I expect from them, but to convince the others that 'it isn't cricket' to sell a game at baseball or basketball or whatever the game may be. This hail and farewell to the ancestral creed may be of some use to them after all and in any case it can do them no harm.

# Epilogue and Apotheosis

WHEN it became clear that Frank Worrell and his team in Australia had added a new dimension to cricket history I was not only expected but urged to conclude this book with a diapason. To do that would have been to ruin it ever afterward for me and for my countrymen, its value as a personal record of a journey through cricket country. For I was taken by surprise as much as anybody else. In 1957 I had expected much, but by 1961, after the dust and heat of the Worrell campaign, all I found myself hoping for was that we would give a good account of ourselves, and that we would shed much ancient baggage to lighten ourselves for a long climb. I looked forward (with glee) to that bowler of old-fashioned pace, Hall, carrying all before him, by which I meant wickets, not humans. For years I have believed, and have indeed written, that Sobers was the greatest of living batsmen. But who could have foreseen that Alexander, relieved of the cares of captaincy, would head the batting average of both sides, that an unknown, Lance Gibbs, would at one stroke place himself in the rare tradition of devastating slow bowlers, that Kanhai would hit Test bowlers in Australia as if they were league bowlers in Scotland? What I did not reckon on was the part played by the West Indies captain Frank Worrell. That it is I who should have to make that particular confession is comic, even ironical. But I expanded my knowledge of cricket and, as always with cricket, of life in general. Furthermore, I have not seen what I learnt

248

in print anywhere. So out of this nettle of humility—I had nearly written humiliation—I pluck this flower of discovery and scatter the petals as far and as wide as I can.

After the team returned home I talked more than once with Frank Worrell. I thought I knew him. I didn't. He made exceptionally quick and decisive appreciations of his players. But his first judgment, without exception, was always 'X was [or was not] a good team man'. Even in evaluating members of the 1950 West Indian team in England and the 1951 team in Australia this consideration was always his first. I thought that from my schooldays I knew all there was to be known about this. Yet from him it was new and strange. I have never heard it applied with such urgency and consistency before. It was this, I slowly learnt, which had made cricket history.

As everybody knows, the tour began badly. But, said Worrell, he lectured a few only of his men on taking courses to bring their general knowledge of the appurtenances of life up to the standard expected from so prominent a personage as a Test cricketer; on cricket he lectured nobody.

'If something was wrong I told them what was right and left it to them.'

These words will always ring in my ears. They are something new, not only in West Indies cricket but in West Indies life. West Indians can often tell you what is wrong and some even what will make it right, but they don't leave it to you. Worrell did. It is the ultimate expression of a most finished personality, who knows his business, theory and practice, and knows modern men.

Worrell is one of the few who after a few hours of talk have left me as tired as if I had been put through a wringer. His responses to difficult questions were so unhesitating, so precise, and so took the subject on to unsuspected but relevant areas, that I felt it was I who was undergoing examination. No cricketer, and I have talked to many, ever shook me up in a similar manner: I have seen the same in his articles in the *Observer* on the England-Australia Test series of 1961. Not many journalists will say, in passing, that Lord's ought to be ploughed up and levelled. It is a rare quality. I have met only three such persons, two men and one woman. One of the men is Leon Trotsky, the other a Hungarian refugee in London between the two wars—he was not twenty years old. The woman is Amy Garvey, first wife and collaborator of the celebrated

Negro agitator Marcus Garvey. She is a West Indian. Curiously enough, a fourth person who at brief moments has made me feel that he would make a similar impress upon me if we spoke alone at length, is yet another West Indian, Professor Arthur Lewis, the distinguished economist and Principal of the University College of the West Indies. This is not a register or appraisal of capacity in general. If it were I would have to make a different list (and write another book). What I am dealing with here is a unique capacity to concentrate all the forces available and needed for the matter in hand, usually conversation, but, I suspect, applicable in other fields. Certainly it was so in the case of Worrell. The West Indies team in Australia, on the field and off, was playing above what it knew of itself. If anything went wrong it knew that it would be instantly told, in unhesitating and precise language, how to repair it, and that the captain's certainty and confidence extended to his belief that what he wanted would be done. He did not instil into but drew out of his players. What they discovered in themselves must have been a revelation to few more than to the players themselves. When the time came to say good-bye some of the toughest players could only shake the captain's hand and look away, not trusting themselves to speak. We have gone far beyond a game. This is the only way I can convey the full force of 'If something was wrong I told them what was right and left it to them'.

But Worrell not only said what should be done. Over and over again he did it himself in the very way he wanted things done. Here is A. G. Moyes on what happened in the Third Test:

'Worrell's was a lovely innings. He seemed all the time to know exactly where he wanted to hit the ball and appeared able always to guide it through the gaps in the field. Technically, he was the finest player in the West Indies side and in this innings he simply could not be faulted. If ever a man deserved a century it was Worrell that day, for he entered the arena when three had fallen for 22, and right from the start he batted with a superb mastery that reduced Davidson in a couple of overs to mediocrity.'

This is not 'playing brighter cricket for the sake of spectators who pay', that absurd nostrum for improving cricket. Nor was it the un-buttoning that Peter May thought it was. No, it was simply the return to the batting of the Golden Age; the safest way to prevent being dominated by good bowling is to go after it and yourself do the dominating. The masters of a much more deadly business than cricket lay it down that it is better to give than to take attack.

In the last innings of the Fourth Test, when every run counted, Worrell took over from his regular bowlers and bowled 17 overs for 27 runs and 3 wickets. In the last innings of the last Test he bowled 31 overs for 43 runs and 3 wickets. Hall, Sobers, Gibbs, Valentine, were far better bowlers than the Frank Worrell of 1961. But he knew what was wrong, what was needed to put it right, and went and did it.

Similarly revealing were the full-length motion pictures of the five Tests. The first innings of Sobers at Brisbane was the most beautiful batting I have ever seen. Never was such ease and certainty of stroke, such early seeing of the ball and such late, leisured play, such command by a batsman not only of the bowling but of himself. He seemed to be expressing a personal vision. I had thought of him as having too much bowling to do, but after that innings I knew that such batting can come only at moments, and until they come the unfortunate artist has the disruptive task of adjusting himself to what he can do in relation to what he knows is possible. This is a sphere beyond the unfailing self-mastery of a Bradman or a Hutton. I seem to have met descriptions of play like it in one or two innings, not by Grace, not by Trumper, not by Frank Woolley, but by A. C. MacLaren.

Yet my greatest moment was the speech-making after the last Test. Sir Donald Bradman was remarkably reminiscent of a chairman at a party celebration meeting. Only in the intervals of the return to habitual self while he was being applauded did you catch a glimpse of the relentless scorer of centuries and the watchful, tireless captain. Benaud was fluent, with carefully chosen phrases, full of affection and respect for Frank Worrell and the West Indians (and not forgetting his own team); definitely a man of feeling, not ashamed or wary of it, but a man seeing the whole of his world and steadily. But Frank Worrell, speaking last, was crowned with the olive. Beauty is indeed in the eye of the beholder. I saw all the West Indian ease, humour and easy adaptation to environment. It was after our conversations and I could see his precise and uncompromising evaluations, those it seems are now second nature. But they were draped with that diplomatic graciousness which has apparently so impressed the Australian Prime Minister. If I say he won the prize it is because the crowd gave it to him. They laughed and cheered him continuously. He expanded my conception of West Indian personality. Nor was I alone. I caught a glimpse of what brought a quarter of a million inhabitants of Melbourne into the streets to tell the West Indian cricketers good-bye, a gesture spontaneous and in cricket without precedent, one people speaking to another. Clearing their way with bat and ball, West Indians at that moment had made a public entry into the comity of nations. Thomas Arnold, Thomas Hughes and the Old Master himself would have recognized Frank Worrell as their boy.

# Index

# Index

254

# ABOUT THE AUTHORS

C. L. R. JAMES, historian, novelist, cultural and political critic and activist, was born in Tunapuna, near Port of Spain, Trinidad, in 1901. The son of a schoolteacher, he attended the island's major government secondary school where, in the twenties, he became a teacher himself. During those years he also played club cricket and began writing fiction.

James went to England in 1932 to help his friend and cricketing opponent, Learie Constantine, with his autobiography, and published in that year his first political book, *The Life of Captain Cipriani*, a pioneering argument on behalf of West Indian self-government. He also became cricket correspondent for the *Manchester Guardian* and, later, the *Glasgow Herald*. Now one of the last surviving founders of the African nationalist movement, James edited, during the thirties in London, the journal of the International African Service Bureau, the Pan-African organization whose leaders included Jomo Kenyatta.

James came to America on a lecture tour in 1938 and stayed fifteen years. He was the first man to argue for an autonomous, Socialist black movement, independent of white-majority parties; while in the States, he took part in wartime sharecroppers' strikes and was active in the Socialist Workers' Party. He was interned on Ellis Island in 1952 (where he wrote *Mariners, Renegades and Castaways*, a study of Melville) and was expelled the following year, returning to England.

In 1958, James returned for four years to Trinidad to take part in the preparations for colonial emancipation he'd advocated for a quarter century. Since 1962 he has lived in England, with a brief return to the West Indies to cover a cricketing test series in 1965.

C. L. R. James's many works include his famous study of the Haitian revolution, *The Black Jacobins* (1938); *Minty Alley* (1936), a novel; the play *Toussaint L'Ouverture*, in which he and Paul Robeson performed in London in 1936; *Modern Politics* (1960) and *Party Politics in the West Indies* (1961); *Beyond a Boundary* (1963); *Nkrumah and the Ghana Revolution* (1977); and three volumes of selected writings, *The Future in the Present, Spheres of Existence*, and *At the Rendezvous of Victory*. He continues to write prolifically, contributing to such journals as *Radical America, Freedomways, New Society*, and *New Left Review*.

C. L. R. James is currently living in London and is at work on his autobiography.


ROBERT LIPSYTE was born in New York City. He was a sports reporter and columnist for the *New York Times* for fifteen years and is currently sports columnist for Charles Kuralt's "Sunday Morning" on CBS television. His books include *Nigger* (the autobiography of Dick Gregory), *SportsWorld: An American Dreamland*, and numerous highly acclaimed works for young adults.